Chancel
St. John's Ch.
Sag. City
1869

# HYMNS,

## ANCIENT AND MODERN,

FOR USE IN THE

## Services of the Church.

"Young men and maidens, old men and children, praise the Name of the LORD."

NEW YORK:
POTT & AMERY,
COOPER UNION, FOURTH AVENUE.
1869.

# HYMNS.

## 1.

### Morning.

"I myself will awake right early."

1. AWAKE, my soul, and with the sun
Thy daily stage of duty run;
Shake off dull sloth, and early rise
To pay thy morning sacrifice.

2. Redeem thy mis-spent time that's past,
And live this day as if thy last;
Improve thy talent with due care,
For the great day thyself prepare.

3. Let all thy converse be sincere,
Thy conscience as the noon-day clear;
Think how all-seeing God thy ways
And all thy secret thoughts surveys.

4. By influence of the Light divine
Let thy own light in good works shine
Reflect all heaven's propitious rays
In ardent love and cheerful praise.

## PART II.

1. WAKE and lift up thyself, my heart,
And with the angels bear thy part,
Who all night long unwearied sing
Glory to the Eternal King.

2. I wake, I wake, ye heavenly choir,
May your devotion me inspire,
That I like you my age may spend,
Like you may on my God attend.

3. May I like you in God delight,
Have all day long my God in sight,
Perform like you my Maker's will,
O may I never more do ill.

4. Had I your wings to heaven I'd fly,
But God shall that defect supply,
And my soul, winged with warm desire,
Shall all day long to heaven aspire.

## PART III.

1. GLORY to Thee Who safe hast kept
And hast refreshed me while I slept;
Grant, Lord, when I from death shall wake,
I may of endless light partake.

2. I would not wake, nor rise again,
E'en heaven itself I would disdain,
Wert Thou not there to be enjoyed,
And I in hymns to be employed.

3. Heaven is, dear LORD, where'er Thou art,
O never then from me depart;
For to my soul 'tis hell to be
But for one moment without Thee.

4. LORD, I my vows to Thee renew,
Scatter my sins as morning dew;
Guard my first springs of thought and will,
And with Thyself my spirit fill.

5. Direct, control, suggest this day
All I design, or do, or say;
That all my powers with all their might
In Thy sole glory may unite.

*Doxology to be sung at the end of each Part.*

Praise GOD, from whom all blessings flow;
Praise Him, all creatures here below;
Praise Him above, angelic host;
Praise FATHER, SON, and HOLY GHOST. Amen.

## 2.

"His compassions fail not: they are new every morning."

1. NEW every morning is the love
Our wakening and uprising prove;
Through sleep and darkness safely brought,
Restored to life, and power, and thought.

2. New mercies, each returning day,
Hover around us while we pray;
New perils past, new sins forgiven,
New thoughts of GOD, new hopes of heaven.

3. If on our daily course our mind
Be set to hallow all we find,
New treasures still, of countless price,
God will provide for sacrifice.

4. The trivial round, the common task,
Will furnish all we need to ask,
Room to deny ourselves, a road
To bring us daily nearer God.

5. Only, O Lord, in Thy dear love
Fit us for perfect rest above;
And help us, this and every day,
To live more nearly as we pray. Amen.

## 3.

*"He that followeth Me shall not walk in darkness, but shall have the light of life."*

1. O JESU, Lord of light and grace,
Thou brightness of the Father's Face,
Thou fountain of eternal light,
Whose beams disperse the shades of night.

2. Come Holy Sun of heavenly love,
Come in Thy radiance from above,
And to our inward hearts convey
The Holy Spirit's cloudless ray.

3. So we the Father's help will claim,
And sing the Father's glorious Name,
And His Almighty grace implore
That we may stand, to fall no more.

4. May He our actions deign to bless,
And loose the bonds of wickedness;
From sudden falls our feet defend,
And guide us safely to the end.

5. May faith, deep rooted in the soul,
Subdue our flesh, our minds control:
May guile depart, and discord cease,
And all within be joy and peace.

6. O hallowed thus be every day;
Let meekness be our morning ray,
Our faith like noontide splendour glow,
Our souls the twilight never know.

7. All praise to GOD the FATHER be;
All praise, Eternal SON, to Thee;
Whom, with the SPIRIT, we adore
For ever and for evermore. Amen.

## 4.

"Early in the morning will I direct my prayer unto Thee, and will look up."

1. NOW that the daylight fills the sky
We lift our hearts to GOD on high,
That He, in all we do or say,
Would keep us free from harm to-day.

2. May He restrain our tongues from strife,
And shield from anger's din our life;
And guard with watchful care our eyes
From earth's absorbing vanities.

3. O may our inmost hearts be pure,
From thoughts of folly kept secure,
And pride of sinful flesh subdued
Through sparing use of daily food.

4. So we, when this day's work is o'er,
And shades of night return once more,
Our path of trial safely trod,
Shall give the glory to our God.

5. All praise to God the Father be;
All praise, Eternal Son, to Thee;
Whom, with the Spirit, we adore
For ever and for evermore. Amen.

## 5.

"Unto you that fear My Name shall the Sun of Righteousness arise."

1. CHRIST, Whose glory fills the skies,
Christ, the true, the only Light,
Sun of Righteousness, arise,
Triumph o'er the shades of night;
Dayspring from on high be near,
Daystar in my heart appear.

2. Dark and cheerless is the morn
Unaccompanied by Thee;
Joyless is the day's return
Till Thy mercy's beams I see,
Till they inward light impart,
Glad my eyes, and warm my heart.

3. Visit then this soul of mine;
   Pierce the gloom of sin and grief;
Fill me, Radiancy Divine;
   Scatter all my unbelief;
More and more Thyself display,
Shining to the perfect day. Amen.

## 6.

"I have set God always before me; for He is on my right hand, therefore I shall not fall."

1. FORTH in Thy name, O Lord, I go,
   My daily labour to pursue;
Thee, only Thee, resolved to know
In all I think, or speak, or do.

2. The task Thy wisdom hath assigned
O let me cheerfully fulfil;
In all my works Thy presence find,
And prove Thy good and perfect will.

3. Thee may I set at my right hand,
Whose eyes my inmost substance see;
And labour on at Thy command,
And offer all my works to Thee.

4. Give me to bear Thy easy yoke,
And every moment watch and pray;
And still to things eternal look,
And hasten to Thy glorious day.

5. Fain would I still for Thee employ
Whate'er Thy bounteous grace hath given,
And run my course with even joy,
And closely walk with Thee to Heaven.

6. To FATHER, SON, and HOLY GHOST,
The GOD Whom heaven and earth adore,
From men and from the angel-host
Be praise and glory evermore. Amen.

## 7.

## The Third Hour.

"It is but the third hour of the day."

1. COME, HOLY GHOST, Who ever One
Art with the FATHER and the SON;
Come, HOLY GHOST, our souls possess
With Thy full flood of holiness.

2. In word and deed, by heart and tongue,
With all our powers, Thy praise be sung;
May love enwrap our mortal frame,
And others catch the living flame.

3. Almighty FATHER, hear our cry
Through JESUS CHRIST our LORD most High,
Who, with the HOLY GHOST and Thee,
Doth live and reign eternally. Amen.

## 8.

## The Sixth Hour.

"At noonday will I pray."

1. O GOD of truth, O LORD of might,
Who orderest time and change aright,
Brightening the morn with golden gleams,
Kindling the noonday's fiery beams;

2. Quench Thou in us the flames of strife,
From passion's heat preserve our life,
Our bodies keep from perils free,
And give our souls true peace in Thee.

3. Almighty FATHER, hear our cry
Through JESUS CHRIST our LORD most High,
Who, with the HOLY GHOST and Thee,
Doth live and reign eternally. Amen.

## 9.

## The Ninth Hour.

"The hour of prayer being the ninth hour."

1. O GOD, of all the Strength and Power,
Who dost unmoved each passing hour
Through all its changes guide the day,
From early morn to evening's ray;

2. Brighten life's eventide with light
That ne'er shall set in gloom of night;
Till we a holy death attain
And everlasting glory gain.

3. Almighty Father, hear our cry
Through Jesus Christ our Lord most High,
Who, with the Holy Ghost and Thee,
Doth live and reign eternally. Amen.

# 10.

## Evening.

"He shall defend thee under His wings."

1. GLORY to Thee, my God, this night
For all the blessings of the light;
Keep me, O keep me, King of kings,
Under Thine own Almighty wings.

2. Forgive me, Lord, for Thy dear Son,
The ill that I this day have done,
That with the world, myself, and Thee,
I, ere I sleep, at peace may be.

3. Teach me to live, that I may dread
The grave as little as my bed;
Teach me to die, that so I may
Rise glorious at the awful Day.

4. O may my soul on Thee repose,
And may sweet sleep mine eyelids close,
Sleep that shall me more vigorous make
To serve my God when I awake.

5. When in the night I sleepless lie,
My soul with heavenly thoughts supply;
Let no ill dreams disturb my rest,
No powers of darkness me molest.

6. Praise God, from Whom all blessings flow;
Praise Him, all creatures here below;
Praise Him above, angelic host;
Praise Father, Son, and Holy Ghost.
Amen.

## 11.

"Abide with us."

1. SUN of my soul, Thou Saviour dear,
It is not night if Thou be near;
O may no earth-born cloud arise
To hide Thee from Thy servant's eyes.

2. When the soft dews of kindly sleep
My wearied eyelids gently steep,
Be my last thought how sweet to rest
For ever on my Saviour's breast.

3. Abide with me from morn till eve,
For without Thee I cannot live;
Abide with me when night is nigh,
For without Thee I dare not die.

4. If some poor wandering child of Thine
Have spurned to-day the voice divine,
Now, Lord, the gracious work begin;
Let him no more lie down in sin.

5. Watch by the sick; enrich the poor
With blessings from Thy boundless store;
Be every mourner's sleep to-night,
Like infant's slumbers, pure and light.

6. Come near and bless us when we wake,
Ere through the world our way we take;
Till in the ocean of Thy love
We lose ourselves in Heaven above.
Amen.

## 12.

"O look Thou upon me and be merciful unto me."

1. AS now the sun's declining rays
At eventide descend;
So life's brief day is sinking down
To its appointed end.

2. LORD, on the Cross Thine Arms were stretched
To draw Thy people nigh;
O grant us then that Cross to love,
And in those Arms to die.

3. All glory to the FATHER be,
All glory to the SON,
All glory, HOLY GHOST, to Thee,
While endless ages run. Amen.

## 13.

"Thou shalt not be afraid for any terror by night."

1. BEFORE the ending of the day,
Creator of the world, we pray
That Thou with wonted love wouldst keep
Thy watch around us while we sleep.

2. O let no evil dreams be near,
Nor phantoms of the night appear;
Our ghostly enemy restrain,
Lest aught of sin our bodies stain.

3. Almighty FATHER, hear our cry,
Through JESUS CHRIST our LORD most High,
Who, with the HOLY GHOST and Thee,
Doth live and reign eternally. Amen.

## 14.

"Abide with us; for it is toward evening, and the day is far spent."

1. ABIDE with me; fast falls the eventide;
The darkness deepens; LORD, with me abide;
When other helpers fail, and comforts flee,
Help of the helpless, O abide with me.

2. Swift to its close ebbs out life's little day;
Earth's joys grow dim, its glories pass away;
Change and decay in all around I see;
O Thou Who changest not, abide with me.

3. I need Thy presence every passing hour;
What but Thy grace can foil the tempter's power?
Who like Thyself my guide and stay can be?
Through cloud and sunshine, LORD, abide with me.

4. I fear no foe with Thee at hand to bless;
Ills have no weight, and tears no bitterness;
Where is death's sting, where, grave, thy victory?
I triumph still, if Thou abide with me.

5. Hold Thou Thy Cross before my closing eyes;
Shine through the gloom, and point me to the skies;
Heaven's morning breaks, and earth's vain shadows flee;
In life, in death, O LORD, abide with me. Amen.

## 15.

"Let the lifting up of my hands be an evening sacrifice."

1. THE sun is sinking fast,
The daylight dies;
Let love awake, and pay
Her evening sacrifice.

2. As CHRIST upon the Cross
His Head inclined,
And to His FATHER's hands
His parting soul resigned;

3. So now herself my soul
Would wholly give
Into His sacred charge,
In Whom all spirits live;

4. So now beneath His eye
Would calmly rest,
Without a wish or thought
Abiding in the breast;

5. Save that His Will be done,
Whate'er betide;
Dead to herself, and dead
In Him to all beside.

6. Thus would I live: yet now
Not I, but He
In all His power and love
Henceforth alive in me.

7. One Sacred Trinity!
One Lord Divine!
May I be ever His,
And He for ever mine. Amen.

## 16.

"I will lay me down in peace and take my rest."

1. THROUGH the day Thy love has spared us,
Now we lay us down to rest;
Through the silent watches guard us,
Let no foe our peace molest;
Jesu, Thou our Guardian be;
Sweet it is to trust in Thee.

2. Pilgrims here on earth, and strangers
Dwelling in the midst of foes,
Us and ours preserve from dangers,
In Thine Arms may we repose,
And, when life's sad day is past,
Rest with Thee in heaven at last. Amen.

## 17.

"The Lord is my Light."

1. SWEET Saviour, bless us ere we go;
Thy word into our minds instil;
And make our lukewarm hearts to glow
With lowly love and fervent will.
Through life's long day and death's dark night,
O gentle Jesus, be our Light.

2. The day is gone, its hours have run,
   And Thou hast taken count of all,
The scanty triumphs grace hath won,
   The broken vow, the frequent fall.
Through life's long day and death's dark night,
O gentle Jesus, be our Light.

3. Grant us, dear Lord, from evil ways
   True absolution and release;
And bless us, more than in past days,
   With purity and inward peace.
Through life's long day and death's dark night,
O gentle Jesus, be our Light.

4. Do more than pardon; give us joy,
   Sweet fear, and sober liberty,
And simple hearts without alloy
   That only long to be like Thee.
Through life's long day and death's dark night,
O gentle Jesus, be our Light.

5. Labour is sweet, for Thou hast toiled;
   And care is light, for Thou hast cared;
Ah! never let our works be soiled
   With strife, or by deceit ensnared.
Through life's long day and death's dark night,
O gentle Jesus, be our Light.

6. For all we love, the poor, the sad,
   The sinful, unto Thee we call;
O let Thy mercy make us glad:
   Thou art our Jesus, and our All.
Through life's long day and death's dark night,
O gentle Jesus, be our Light. Amen.

## 18.

"He shall give His angels charge over thee."

1. GOD, Who madest earth and heaven,
   Darkness and light;
Who the day for toil hast given,
   For rest the night;
May Thine angel-guards defend us,
Slumber sweet Thy mercy send us,
Holy dreams and hopes attend us,
   This livelong night.

2. Guard us waking, guard us sleeping,
   And, when we die,
May we in Thy mighty keeping
   All peaceful lie:
When the last dread call shall wake us,
Do not Thou our God forsake us,
But to reign in glory take us
   With Thee on high. Amen.

## 19.

"Now unto the King Eternal, Immortal, Invisible, the Only Wise God, be honour and glory for ever and ever."

1. O TRINITY, most Blessèd Light,
   O Unity of Princely Might,
As now the fiery sun departs
Shed Thou Thy beams within our hearts.

2. To Thee our morning song of praise,
To Thee our evening prayer we raise;
Thee may our heart and voice adore
For ever and for evermore. Amen.

# 20.

## Sunday.

EARLY MORNING.

"In Thy Light shall we see light."

1. MORN of morns, and day of days!
Beauteous were thy new-born rays:
Brighter yet from death's dark prison
CHRIST, the Light of lights, is risen.

2. He commanded, and His word
Death and the dread chaos heard:
O shall we, more deaf than they,
In the chains of darkness stay?

3. Nature yet in shadow lies,
Let the sons of light arise
And prevent the morning rays
With sweet canticles of praise.

4. While the dead world sleeps around,
Let the sacred temples sound
Law, and prophet, and blest psalm
Lit with holy light so calm.

5. Unto hearts in slumber weak
Let the heavenly trumpet speak;
And a newer walk express
Their new life to righteousness.

6. Hear us, LORD, and with us be,
O Thou Fount of charity,
Thou Who dost the SPIRIT give
Bidding the dead letter live.

7. Glory to the FATHER, SON,
And to Thee, O HOLY ONE,
By Whose quickening Breath divine
Our dull spirits burn and shine. Amen.

## 21.

### MORNING.

"And GOD said, Let there be light: and there was light. And the evening and the morning were the first day."

1. ON this day, the first of days,
GOD the FATHER'S Name we praise;
Who, creation's Fount and Spring,
Did the world from darkness bring.

2. On this day th' Eternal SON
Over death His triumph won;
On this day the SPIRIT came
With His gifts of living flame.

3. Oh! that fervent love to-day
May in every heart have sway,
Teaching us to praise aright
GOD the Source of life and light.

4. FATHER, Who didst fashion me
Image of Thyself to be,
Fill me with Thy love divine,
Let my every thought be Thine.

5. HOLY JESUS, may I be
Dead and buried here with Thee;
And, by love inflamed, arise
Unto Thee a sacrifice.

6. Thou Who dost all gifts impart,
Shine, Sweet Spirit, in my heart;
Best of gifts Thyself bestow;
Make me burn Thy love to know.

7. God, the Blessèd Three in One,
Dwell within my heart alone;
Thou dost give Thyself to me,
May I give myself to Thee. Amen.

## 22.

"This is the day which the Lord hath made."

1. AGAIN the Lord's own day is here,
The day to Christian people dear,
As, week by week, it bids them tell
How Jesus rose from death and hell.

2. For by His flock their Lord declared
His resurrection should be shared;
And they who trust in Him to save
In Him are risen from the grave.

3. We, one and all, of Him possest
Are with exceeding treasures blest;
For all He did, and all He bare,
He gives us as our own to share.

4. Eternal glory, rest on high,
A blessèd immortality,
True peace and gladness, and a throne,
Are all His gifts, and all our own.

And therefore unto Thee we sing,
O Lord of Peace, Eternal King;
Thy love we praise, Thy Name adore,
Both on this day and evermore. Amen.

## 23.

EVENING.

"There shall be no night there."

1. GREAT God, Who, hid from mortal sight,
Dost dwell in unapproachèd light,
Before Whose presence angels bow
With faces veiled, in homage low;

2. Awhile in darkness we remain,
And round us yet are sin and pain;
But soon the everlasting day
Shall chase our shades of night away.

3. For Thou hast promised, gracious Lord,
A day of gladness and reward;
A day but faintly imaged here
By brightest sun at noontide clear.

4. Too long, alas! it still delays;
It lingers yet, that day of days;
Our mortal strife and toil must cease
Before we win its heavenly peace.

5. Then, from its fleshly bonds set free,
The soul shall fly, O God, to Thee;
To see Thee, love Thee, and adore,
Her blissful task for evermore.

6. Great TRINITY, our hearts prepare,
The fulness of Thy joy to share;
Life's transient light may we improve,
And gain eternal light above. Amen.

## 24.

EVENING.

"The day is Thine, the night also is Thine."

1. BLEST Creator of the light,
Making day with radiance bright,
Thou didst o'er the forming earth
Give the golden light its birth.

2. Shade of eve with morning ray
Took from Thee the name of Day;
Now again the shades are nigh,
Listen to our humble cry.

3. May we ne'er by guilt depressed
Lose the way to endless rest;
Nor with idle thoughts and vain
Bind our souls to earth again.

4. Rather may we heavenward rise
Where eternal treasure lies;
Purified by grace within,
Hating every deed of sin.

5. HOLY FATHER, hear our cry
Through Thy SON, our LORD most High,
Whom our thankful hearts adore
With the SPIRIT evermore. Amen.

# 25.

## Monday.

"And God made the firmament, and divided the waters which were under the firmament from the waters which were above the firmament. And the evening and the morning were the second day."

1. COME, let us praise the Name of God,
   Who on the second day
Spread out the firmament above,
   His glory to display.

2. Slow floating on the blue expanse
   The watery clouds we view,
Whence fruitful showers at His command
   The thirsty soil bedew.

3. How fair an image of the Grace
   His mercy doth impart,
Like morning dew or gentle rain,
   To gladden every heart.

4. And when the faithful soul drinks in
   Those showers with blessings rife,
A well of water springeth up
   To everlasting life.

5. O happy saints, on whom are poured
   Such treasures from above;
Lord, may they ne'er forgetful be,
   But render love for love.

6. To God, Who freely loved us first,
   All might, all glory, be;
To Father, Son, and Holy Ghost,
   Through all eternity. Amen.

# 26.

## Tuesday.

"And God said, Let the waters be gathered together into one place, and let the dry land appear; and it was so.... And the evening and the morning were the third day."

1. THOU spak'st the word, and into one
   The floods together flowed;
The dry land, freed from watery veil,
   Its verdant pastures showed.

2. O Father, Who this earth assigned
   Our place of toil to be,
Bind all within its one wide bound
   In one true charity.

3. A brotherhood of exiles here
   We seek a home above,
Where Thou wilt gather in Thine Own
   Who live in holy love.

4. Unloving souls, with deeds of ill
   And words of angry strife,
Shall never, Lord, Thy glory see
   Nor win the heavenly life.

5. Lo, earth itself from day to day
   Their burthen scarce sustains,
And yearns, in travail, to be free
   From dark corruption's chains.

6. Yea, we too groan within ourselves,
   And that adoption wait
For which the Holy Spirit's seal
   Did us predestinate.

7. Eternal glory be ascribed
   To God, the One in Three,
By Whom is poured into our hearts
   The grace of charity. Amen.

# 27.

## Wednesday.

'And God said, Let there be lights in the firmament of heaven: and it was so. And the evening and the morning were the fourth day."

1. NEW wonders of Thy mighty Hand,
   Lord, we to-day admire,
Writ on the firmament above
   In glittering orbs of fire.

2. The sun is ruler of the day,
   The silver moon of night,
The starry hosts adorn the sky
   In ordered ranks of light.

3. But e'en that glorious sun must set,
   And knows his going down;
That silver moon must wax and wane;
   The stars their courses own.

4. Still in an everchanging round
   The daylight comes and goes;
But Thou art evermore the same,
   No change Thy mercy knows.

5. Why waver then our troubled hearts?
   Thine is a Father's care:
And they, eternal life who seek,
   Eternal life shall share.

6. All praise, all glory be ascribed
   To God, the One in Three,
Who bids us cast our care on Him,
   To Him for comfort flee. Amen.

## 28.

### Thursday.

"And God said, Let the waters bring forth abundantly the moving creature that hath life, and fowl that may fly above the earth....And the evening and the morning were the fifth day."

1. THE fish in wave and bird on wing
   God made the waters bear;
Both for our mortal body's food
   His mercy doth prepare.

2. But other food, of richer cost,
   The immortal spirit needs;
By faith it lives on every Word
   That from His Mouth proceeds.

3. Faith springing from the Blood of Christ
   Has flowed o'er every land;
And sinners through the vanquished world
   Bow down to its command.

4. Its light the joy of heaven reveals
   To hearts made pure within;
And bids us seek by worthy deeds
   Eternal crowns to win.

5. By faith the saints of old were strong
The lion's wrath to tame;
By faith they spurned the tyrant's threats,
And scorned the raging flame.

6. LORD, grant that we the path may tread
Whereon its light doth shine;
And gather, as we onward go,
The fruits of love divine.

7. O praise the FATHER; praise the SON,
From Whose most precious Blood
Springs all our faith; and praise to HIM
Who with Them Both is GOD. Amen.

## 29.

### Friday.

"And GOD said, Let us make man in Our Image. And the evening and the morning were the sixth day."

1. TO-DAY, O LORD, a holier work
Thy secret counsels frame,
A ruler for Thy new-made world,
A herald of Thy Name.

2. Thou formest man: Thy Spirit breathes
Life into dust of earth:
Man, in Thine own true image made,
Receives from Thee his birth.

3. And henceforth he dominion has
O'er all in earth and sea;
Yet mindful whence his being came
Must humbly walk with Thee.

4. Alas! his wilful heart rebels
   Against Thy gentle sway;
 Proud dust of earth would fain be like
   The God Whom all obey.

5. O griefs, O sorrows numberless,
   Which hence the world o'erspread;
 Jesu! Thy mercy succoured us,
   Or every hope had fled.

6. O praise the Father, and the Son
   Who saved us by His death,
 And Holy Ghost who quickens us
   With His life-giving breath. Amen.

## 30.

### Saturday.

"And on the seventh day God ended His work which He had made."

1. SIX days of labour now are past;
   Thou restest, Holy God;
 And with approving Eye hast seen
   That all is very good.

2. Blest is the seventh morn of light,
   Hallowed for rest divine;
 Yet, Lord, a new creation needs
   That mighty power of Thine.

3. Ten thousand voices praise Thy Name
   In earth and sea and sky;
 But fallen man by sin has marred
   The blissful harmony.

4. Come, Lord, create his heart anew;
His heart of stone remove:
Then hymns of praise again shall rise,
The fruits of holy love.

5. Oh! for the songs that Thou wilt bless,
Where heart and voice agree;
Oh! for the prayers that plead aright
With Thy dread Majesty.

6. All praise to God, the Three in One,
Who high in glory reigns;
Who by His Word hath all things made,
And by His Word sustains. Amen.

# 31.

## Advent.

"Which cometh forth as a Bridegroom out of His chamber."

1. CREATOR of the starry height,
Thy people's everlasting Light,
Jesu, Redeemer of us all,
Hear Thou Thy servants when they call.

2. Thou, sorrowing at the helpless cry
Of all creation doomed to die,
Didst save our lost and guilty race
By healing gifts of heavenly grace.

3. When earth was near its evening hour,
Thou didst, in love's redeeming power,
Like bridegroom from his chamber, come
Forth from a Virgin-mother's womb.

4. At Thy great Name, exalted now,
All knees in lowly homage bow;
All things in heaven and earth adore,
And own Thee King for evermore.

5. To Thee, O Holy One, we pray,
Our Judge in that tremendous day,
Ward off, while yet we dwell below,
The weapons of our crafty foe.

6. To God the Father, God the Son,
And God the Spirit, Three in One,
Praise, honour, might, and glory be,
From age to age eternally. Amen.

## 32.

"His Name is called the Word of God."

1. O HEAVENLY Word, Eternal Light,
Begotten of the Father's Might,
Who, in these latter days, art born
For succour to a world forlorn;

2. Our hearts enlighten from above,
And kindle with Thine own true love;
That we, who hear Thy call to-day,
May cast earth's vanities away.

3. And when as Judge Thou drawest nigh,
The secrets of all hearts to try;
When sinners meet their awful doom,
And saints attain their heavenly home;

4. O let us not, for evil past,
Be driven from Thy Face at last;
But with the blessèd evermore
Behold and love Thee and adore.

5. To God the Father, God the Son,
And God the Spirit, Three in One,
Praise, honour, might, and glory be,
From age to age eternally. Amen.

## 33.

"Now it is high time to awake out of sleep."

1. HARK! a thrilling voice is sounding:
"Christ is nigh," it seems to say;
"Cast away the dreams of darkness,
O ye children of the day!"

2. Wakened by the solemn warning,
Let the earth-bound soul arise;
Christ, her Sun, all ill dispelling,
Shines upon the morning skies.

3. Lo! the Lamb, so long expected,
Comes with pardon down from heaven;
Let us haste, with tears of sorrow,
One and all to be forgiven;

4. That when next He comes with glory,
And the world is wrapped in fear,
With His mercy He may shield us,
And with words of love draw near.

5. Honour, glory, might, and blessing
To the FATHER and the SON,
With the Everlasting SPIRIT,
While eternal ages run. Amen.

## 34.

"Tell ye the daughter of Sion, Behold thy King cometh unto thee."

1. THE Advent of our King
Our prayers must now employ,
And we must hymns of welcome sing
In strains of holy joy.

2. The Everlasting SON
Incarnate deigns to be;
Himself a servant's form puts on,
To set His servants free.

3. Daughter of Sion, rise
To meet thy lowly King;
Nor let thy faithless heart despise
The peace He comes to bring.

4. As Judge, on clouds of light,
He soon will come again,
And His true members all unite
With Him in heaven to reign.

5. Before the dawning day
Let sin's dark deeds be gone,
The old man all be put away,
The new man all put on.

6. All glory to the SON,
Who comes to set us free,
With FATHER, SPIRIT, ever One,
Through all eternity. Amen.

## 35.

"The voice of one crying in the wilderness, Prepare ye the way of the LORD, make His paths straight."

1. ON Jordan's bank the Baptist's cry
Announces that the LORD is nigh;
Awake, and hearken, for He brings
Glad tidings of the King of kings.

2. Then cleansed be every breast from sin;
Make straight the way for GOD within;
Prepare we in our hearts a home,
Where such a mighty Guest may come.

3. For Thou art our Salvation, LORD,
Our Refuge, and our great Reward;
Without Thy grace we waste away,
Like flowers that wither and decay.

4. To heal the sick stretch out Thine Hand,
And bid the fallen sinner stand;
Shine forth, and let Thy light restore
Earth's own true loveliness once more.

5. All praise, Eternal SON, to Thee
Whose Advent doth Thy people free;
Whom with the FATHER we adore
And HOLY GHOST for evermore. Amen.

## 36.

"The Redeemer shall come to Zion."

1. O COME, O come, Emmanuel,
And ransom captive Israel;
That mourns in lonely exile here,
Until the Son of God appear.
Rejoice! Rejoice! Emmanuel
Shall come to thee, O Israel!

2. O come, Thou Rod of Jesse, free
Thine own from Satan's tyranny;
From depths of hell Thy people save,
And give them victory o'er the grave.
Rejoice! Rejoice! Emmanuel
Shall come to thee, O Israel!

3. O come, Thou Day-Spring, come and cheer
Our spirits by Thine Advent here;
Disperse the gloomy clouds of night,
And death's dark shadows put to flight.
Rejoice! Rejoice! Emmanuel
Shall come to thee, O Israel!

4. O come, Thou Key of David, come
And open wide our heavenly home;
Make safe the way that leads on high,
And close the path to misery.
Rejoice! Rejoice! Emmanuel
Shall come to thee, O Israel!

5. O come, O come, Thou Lord of Might!
Who to Thy tribes, on Sinai's height,
In ancient times didst give the law,
In cloud, and majesty, and awe.
Rejoice! Rejoice! Emmanuel
Shall come to thee, O Israel! Amen.

## 37.

"The Lord Himself shall descend from heaven with a shout, with the voice of the archangel, and with the trump of God."

1. GREAT God, what do I see and hear?
The end of things created:
The Judge of all men doth appear
On clouds of glory seated:
The trumpet sounds, the graves restore
The dead which they contained before;
Prepare, my soul, to meet Him.

2. The dead in Christ are first to rise
At that last trumpet's sounding;
Caught up to meet Him in the skies,
With joy their Lord surrounding:
No gloomy fears their souls dismay;
His presence sheds eternal day
On those prepared to meet Him.

3. The ungodly, filled with guilty fears,
Behold His wrath prevailing;
In woe they rise, but all their tears
And sighs are unavailing:
The day of grace is past and gone;
Trembling they stand before His throne,
All unprepared to meet Him.

4. Great Judge, to Thee our prayers we pour,
In deep abasement bending;
O shield us through that last dread hour,
Thy wondrous love extending:
May we, in this our trial day,
With faithful hearts Thy word obey,
And thus prepare to meet Thee. Amen.

## 38.

"The day of the Lord will come as a thief in the night."

1. THAT day of wrath, that dreadful day,
When heaven and earth shall pass away,
What power shall be the sinner's stay?
How shall he meet that dreadful day?

2. When shrivelling, like a parchèd scroll,
The flaming heavens together roll;
When louder yet, and yet more dread,
Swells the high trump that wakes the dead;

3. Oh! on that day, that wrathful day,
When man to judgment wakes from clay,
Be Thou, O Christ, the sinner's stay
Though heaven and earth shall pass away. Amen.

## 39

"Behold He cometh with clouds; and every eye shall see Him, and they also which pierced Him."

1. LO! He comes in clouds descending,
Once for favoured sinners slain;
Thousand thousand saints attending
Swell the triumph of His train:
Alleluia!
Christ appears on earth again.

2. Every eye shall now behold Him
Robed in dreadful majesty;
They who set at naught and sold Him,
Pierced and nailed Him to the tree,
Deeply wailing,
Shall the true Messiah see.

3. Those dear tokens of His Passion
Still His dazzling Body bears;
Cause of endless exultation
To His ransomed worshippers;
With what rapture
Gaze we on those glorious scars.

4. Yea, Amen, let all adore Thee,
High on Thine eternal throne;
Saviour, take the power and glory;
Claim the kingdoms for Thine own:
O come quickly!
Alleluia! Amen.

## 40.

"He hath sent Me to bind up the broken-hearted, to proclaim liberty to the captives."

1. HARK the glad sound! the Saviour comes,
The Saviour promised long:
Let every heart prepare a throne,
And every voice a song.

2. He comes, the prisoners to release
In Satan's bondage held;
The gates of brass before Him burst,
The iron fetters yield.

3. He comes, the broken hearts to bind,
   The bleeding souls to cure,
 And with the treasures of His grace
   To bless the humble poor.

4. Our glad hosannas, Prince of Peace,
   Thine Advent shall proclaim;
 And heaven's eternal arches ring
   With Thy belovèd Name. Amen.

## 41.

### EVENING.

"I sleep, but my heart waketh."

1. WHEN shades of night around us close,
   And weary limbs in sleep repose,
 The faithful soul awake may be,
 And longing sigh, O LORD, to Thee.

2. Thou true Desire of nations hear;
 Thou WORD OF GOD, Thou SAVIOUR dear;
 In pity heed our humble cries,
 And bid at length the fallen rise.

3. O come, REDEEMER, come and free
 Thine own from guilt and misery;
 The gates of heaven again unfold,
 Which Adam's sin had closed of old.

4. All praise, Eternal SON, to Thee
 Whose Advent doth Thy people free;
 Whom with the FATHER we adore
 And HOLY GHOST for evermore. Amen.

*The hymn,* Day of wrath, O Day of mourning, *may also be used at this Season.*

# 42.

## Christmas.

"Let us now go even unto Bethlehem."

1. O COME, all ye faithful,
Joyful and triumphant;
O come ye, O come ye, to Bethlehem;
Come and behold Him
Born, the King of Angels:
O come, let us adore Him,
O come, let us adore Him,
O come, let us adore Him, CHRIST the LORD.

2. GOD of GOD,
LIGHT of LIGHT,
Lo! He abhors not the Virgin's womb;
Very GOD,
Begotten, not created;
O come, let us adore Him, &c.

3. Sing, choirs of angels,
Sing in exultation,
Sing, all ye citizens of heaven above,
Glory to GOD
In the highest;
O come, let us adore Him, &c.

4. Yea, LORD, we greet Thee,
Born this happy morning;
JESU, to Thee be glory given;
WORD of the FATHER,
Now in flesh appearing;
O come, let us adore Him,
O come, let us adore Him,
O come, let us adore Him, CHRIST the LORD. Amen.

# 43.

"Glory to God in the highest, and on earth peace, goodwill toward men."

1. HARK! the herald-angels sing
Glory to the new-born King,
Peace on earth, and mercy mild,
God and sinners reconciled.
Joyful, all ye nations, rise,
Join the triumph of the skies;
With the angelic host proclaim
Christ is born in Bethlehem.
Hark! the herald-angels sing
Glory to the new-born King.

2. Christ, by highest heaven adored,
Christ, the Everlasting Lord,
Late in time behold Him come,
Offspring of a Virgin's womb.
Veiled in flesh the Godhead see!
Hail, the Incarnate Deity!
Pleased as Man with man to dwell,
Jesus, our Emmanuel.
Hark! the herald-angels sing
Glory to the new-born King.

3. Hail, the heaven-born Prince of Peace!
Hail, the Sun of Righteousness!
Light and life to all He brings,
Risen with healing in His wings.
Mild He lays His glory by,
Born that man no more may die,

Born to raise the sons of earth,
Born to give them second birth.
Hark! the herald-angels sing
Glory to the new-born KING.
Amen.

## 44.

"Unto you is born this day in the city of David a SAVIOUR which is CHRIST the LORD."

1. WHILE shepherds watched their flocks [by night,
All seated on the ground,
The angel of the LORD came down,
And glory shone around.

2. "Fear not," said he; for mighty dread
Had seized their troubled mind;
"Glad tidings of great joy I bring
To you and all mankind.

3. "To you, in David's town, this day
Is born of David's line
A SAVIOUR, Who is CHRIST the LORD;
And this shall be the sign:

4. "The heavenly Babe you there shall find
To human view displayed,
All meanly wrapped in swathing bands,
And in a manger laid."

5. Thus spake the seraph; and forthwith
Appeared a shining throng
Of angels praising GOD, who thus
Addressed their joyful song:

6. "All glory be to God on high,
And in the earth be peace;
Good-will henceforth from heaven to men
Begin and never cease." Amen.

## 45.

"The Word was made flesh."

1. O CHRIST, Redeemer of our race,
Thou Brightness of the Father's Face,
Of Him and with Him ever One,
Ere times and seasons had begun;

2. Thou that art very Light of Light,
Unfailing Hope in sin's dark night,
Hear Thou the prayers Thy people pray,
The wide world o'er, this blessèd day.

3. Remember, Lord of life and grace,
How once, to save a ruined race,
Thou didst our very flesh assume
In Mary's undefilèd womb.

4. To-day, as year by year its light
Sheds o'er the world a radiance bright,
One precious truth is echoed on,
"'Tis Thou hast saved us, Thou alone,"

5. Thou from the Father's throne didst come
To call His banished children home;
And heaven, and earth, and sea, and shore
His love Who sent Thee here adore.

6, And gladsome too are we to-day
Whose guilt Thy Blood has washed away;
Redeemed the new-made song we sing;
It is the birthday of our KING.

7. O LORD, the Virgin-born, to Thee
Eternal praise and glory be;
Whom with the FATHER we adore
And HOLY GHOST for evermore. Amen.

## 46.

"GOD was manifest in the flesh."

1. OF the FATHER'S Love begotten
Ere the worlds began to be,
He is Alpha and Omega,
He the source, the ending He,
Of the things that are, that have been,
And that future years shall see,
Evermore and evermore!

*2. At His word the worlds were framèd;
He commanded; it was done:
Heaven and earth and depths of ocean
In their threefold order one;
All that grows beneath the shining
Of the moon and burning sun,
Evermore and evermore!

*3. He is found in human fashion,
Death and sorrow here to know,

* These verses may be omitted, if the hymn be thought too long.

That the race of Adam's children,
Doomed by Law to endless woe,
May not henceforth die and perish
In the dreadful gulf below,
Evermore and evermore!

4. O that Birth for ever blessèd,
When the Virgin, full of grace,
By the HOLY GHOST conceiving,
Bare the SAVIOUR of our race;
And the Babe, the world's REDEEMER,
First revealed His sacred Face,
Evermore and evermore!

5. This is He Whom seers in old time
Chanted of with one accord;
Whom the voices of the Prophets
Promised in their faithful word;
Now He shines, the long-expected:
Let creation praise its Lord:
Evermore and evermore!

6. O ye heights of heaven adore Him!
Angel-hosts His praises sing!
All dominions bow before Him
And extol our God and King!
Let no tongue on earth be silent,
Every voice in concert ring,
Evermore and evermore!

*7. Righteous Judge of souls departed,
Righteous King of them that live,
On the FATHER'S throne exalted

* These verses may be omitted, if the hymn be thought too long.

None in might with Thee may strive;
Who at last in vengeance coming
Sinners from Thy Face shalt drive,
Evermore and evermore!

8. Thee let old men, Thee let young men,
Thee let boys in chorus sing;
Matrons, virgins, little maidens
With glad voices answering;
Let their guileless songs re-echo,
And the heart its praises bring,
Evermore and evermore!

9. CHRIST! to Thee, with GOD the FATHER,
And, O HOLY GHOST, to Thee!
Hymn, and chant, and high thanksgiving,
And unwearied praises be,
Honour, glory, and dominion,
And eternal victory,
Evermore and evermore! Amen.

## 47.

"Behold I bring you glad tidings of great joy."

1. CHRISTIANS, awake, salute the happy morn,
Whereon the SAVIOUR of mankind was born;
Rise to adore the mystery of love,
Which hosts of angels chanted from above;
With them the joyful tidings first begun
Of GOD INCARNATE and the Virgin's SON.

2. Then to the watchful shepherds it was told,
Who heard the angelic herald's voice: "Behold,
I bring good tidings of a SAVIOUR's birth
To you and all the nations upon earth:
'This day hath GOD fulfilled His promised word,
This day is born a SAVIOUR, CHRIST the LORD.'"

3. He spake; and straightway the celestial choir
In hymns of joy, unknown before, conspire:
The praises of redeeming love they sang,
And heaven's whole orb with alleluias rang:
GOD's highest glory was their anthem still,
Peace upon earth, and unto men good-will.

4. To Bethlehem straight th' enlightened shepherds ran,
To see the wonders GOD had wrought for man:
Then to their flocks, still praising GOD, return,
And their glad hearts with holy rapture burn:
To all the joyful tidings they proclaim,
The first apostles of the SAVIOUR's Name.

5. Oh! may we keep and ponder in our mind
GOD's wondrous love in saving lost mankind;
Trace we the Babe, Who hath retrieved our loss,
From the poor manger to the bitter cross;
Tread in His steps, assisted by His grace,
Till man's first heavenly state again takes place.

6. Then may we hope, the angelic hosts among,
To join, redeemed, a glad triumphant throng:
He that was born upon this joyful day
Around us all His glory shall display;
Saved by His love, incessant we shall sing
Eternal praise to heaven's Almighty King. Amen.

# 48.

"He is our Peace."

1. GOD from on high hath heard,
Let sighs and sorrows cease;
Lo! from the opening heaven descends
To man the promised Peace.

2. Hark through the silent night
Angelic voices swell;
Their joyful songs proclaim that "GOD
Is born on earth to dwell."

3. See how the shepherd-band
Speed on with eager feet;
Come to the hallowed cave with them
The Holy Babe to greet.

4. But oh! what sight appears
Within that lowly door:
A manger, stall, and swaddling clothes,
A Child and Mother poor.

5. Art Thou the CHRIST? the SON?
The FATHER's Image bright?
And see we Him Whose arm upholds
Earth and the starry height?

6. Yea, faith can pierce the cloud
Which veils Thy glory now;
We hail Thee GOD, before Whose Throne
The angels prostrate bow.

7. A silent Teacher, Lord,
Thou bid'st us not refuse
To bear what flesh would have us shun,
To shun what flesh would choose.

8. Our swelling pride to cure
With that pure love of Thine,
O be Thou born within our hearts,
Most holy Child Divine. Amen.

## 49

EVENING.

"The Lord is our defence; the Holy One of Israel is our King."

1. O SAVIOUR of the world forlorn,
This day to save us Thou wast born;
Protect us through the coming night,
And ever save us by Thy might.

2. Now, Lord, be Thou in mercy nigh,
And spare Thy servants when they cry;
Our sins blot out, our prayers receive,
Thy light throughout our darkness give.

3. O let not sleep the soul oppress,
Nor secret foe the heart possess;
Our flesh keep chaste, that it may be
A holy temple unto Thee.

4. To Thee, Who makest souls anew,
Our hearts in prayer would humbly sue,
That pure and free from inward stain
We from our beds may rise again.

5. All praise to God the Father be;
All praise, Eternal Son, to Thee;
Whom, with the Spirit, we adore
For ever and for evermore. Amen.

## 50.

### St. Stephen's Day.

"Be thou faithful unto death, and I will give thee a crown of life."

(*The word "Stephen" means a crown.*)

1. FIRST of Martyrs, thou whose name
Doth thy golden crown proclaim,
Not of flowers that fade away
Weave we this thy crown to-day.

2. Bright the stones, which bruise thee, gleam,
Sprinkled with thy life-blood's stream;
Stars around thy sainted head
Never could such radiance shed.

3. Every wound upon thy brow
Sparkles with unearthly glow;
Like an angel's is thy face
Beaming with celestial grace.

4. Oh! how blessèd first to be
Slain for Him Who bled for thee;
First like Him in dying hour
Witness to Almighty power;

5. First to follow where He trod
Through the deep Red Sea of blood;
First; but in thy footsteps press
Saints and martyrs numberless.

6. Glory to the FATHER be,
Glory, VIRGIN-BORN, to Thee,
Glory to the HOLY GHOST,
Praised by men and heavenly host. Amen.

## 51.

## St. John the Evangelist's Day.

"That which we have looked upon and our hands have handled of the WORD of Life, declare we unto you."

1. THE life, which GOD'S Incarnate WORD
Lived here below with men,
Three blest Evangelists record
With heaven-inspirèd pen;

2. John soars on high, beyond the three,
To GOD the Father's throne;
And shews in what deep mystery
The WORD with GOD is One.

3. Upon the SAVIOUR'S loving breast
Invited to recline,
'Twas thence he drew, in moments blest,
Rich stores of truth divine.

4. There too with that angelic love
Did he his bosom fill,
Which, once enkindled from above,
Breathes in his pages still.

5. JESU, the Virgin's Holy SON,
We praise Thee and adore,
Who art with GOD the FATHER One
And SPIRIT evermore. Amen.

## 52.

"The disciple whom Jesus loved."

1. WORD Supreme, before creation
   Born of God eternally,
Who didst will for our salvation
   To be born on earth, and die;
Well Thy saints have kept their station,
   Watching till Thine hour drew nigh.

2. Now 'tis come, and faith espies Thee;
   Like an eaglet in the morn,
One in steadfast worship eyes Thee,
   Thy beloved, Thy latest born;
In Thy glory he descries Thee
   Reigning from the tree of scorn.

3. He upon Thy bosom lying
   Thy true tokens learned by heart;
And Thy dearest pledge in dying,
   Lord, Thou didst to him impart;
Shew'dst him how, all grace supplying,
   Blood and water from Thee start.

4. He first, hoping and believing,
   Did beside the grave adore;
Latest he, the warfare leaving,
   Landed on th' eternal shore;
And his witness we receiving
   Own Thee Lord for evermore.

5. Much he asked in loving wonder,
On Thy bosom leaning, LORD;
In that secret place of thunder
Answer kind didst Thou accord,
Wisdom for Thy Church to ponder
Till the day of dread award.

6. Lo! heaven's doors lift up, revealing
How Thy judgments earthward move;
Scrolls unfolded, trumpets pealing,
Wine cups from the wrath above;
Yet o'er all a soft voice stealing—
"Little children, trust and love!"

7. Thee, the almighty King eternal,
FATHER of th' eternal WORD,
Thee, the FATHER's WORD supernal,
Thee, of Both, the BREATH adored,
Heaven and earth and realms infernal
Own, One glorious GOD and LORD. Amen.

## 53.

## The Innocents' Day.

"These are they which follow the Lamb whithersoever He goeth."

1. A HYMN for Martyrs sweetly sing;
For Innocents your praises bring;
Of whom in tears was earth bereaved,
Whom heaven with songs of joy received:
Whose angels see the FATHER's Face
World without end, and hymn His grace,
And, while they praise their glorious King,
A hymn for Martyrs sweetly sing.

2. A voice from Ramah was there sent,
A voice of weeping and lament,
While Rachel mourned her children sore
Whom for the tyrant's sword she bore.
Triumphal is their glory now
Whom earthly sufferings could not bow;
For whom, by cruel torments rent,
A voice from Ramah was there sent.

3. Fear not, O little flock and blest,
The lion that your life oppressed:
To heavenly pastures ever new
The heavenly Shepherd leadeth you,
Who dwelling now on Sion's hill
The Lamb's own footsteps follow still,
By tyrant there no more distressed:
Fear not, O little flock and blest.

4. And every tear is wiped away
By your dear FATHER's hands for aye:
Death hath no power to hurt you more;
Your own is life's eternal shore.
And all who, good seed bearing, weep,
In everlasting joy shall reap;
What time they shine in heavenly day,
And every tear is wiped away. Amen.

## 54.

"They are without fault before the throne of GOD."

1. GLORY to Thee, O LORD,
Who, from this world of sin,
By cruel Herod's ruthless sword
Those precious ones didst win.

2. Baptized in their own blood,
Earth's untried perils o'er,
They passed unconsciously the flood,
And safely gained the shore.

3. Glory to Thee for all
The ransomed infant band,
Who since that hour have heard Thy call,
And reached the quiet land.

4. Oh, that our hearts within,
Like theirs, were pure and bright;
Oh, that as free from deeds of sin
We shrank not from Thy sight.

5. LORD, help us every hour
Thy cleansing grace to claim;
In life to glorify Thy power,
In death to praise Thy Name. Amen.

## 55.

### Circumcision.

"And when eight days were accomplished for the circumcising of the Child, His Name was called JESUS."

1. THE ancient law departs
And all its terrors cease;
For JESUS makes with faithful hearts
A covenant of peace.

2. The Light of Light divine,
True Brightness undefiled,
He bears for us the shame of sin,
A Holy Spotless Child,

3. His Infant Body now
   Begins our pain to feel;
Those precious drops of Blood that flow
   For death the victim seal.

4. To-day the Name is Thine
   At which we bend the knee;
They call Thee JESUS, Child Divine!
   Our JESUS deign to be.

5. All praise, Eternal SON,
   For Thy redeeming love,
With FATHER, SPIRIT, ever ONE,
   In glorious might above. Amen.

## 56.

"GOD sent forth His Son, made of a woman, made under the law, to redeem them that were under the law."

1. O BLESSÈD Day, when first was poured
The Blood of our Redeeming Lord!
O Blessèd Day, when first began
His sufferings borne for sinful man!

2. Scarce entered on this life of woe,
His Infant Blood begins to flow;
A foretaste of His death He feels,
An earnest of His love reveals.

3. From heaven descending to fulfil
The bidding of His FATHER's will,
A victim even now He lies
Before the day of sacrifice.

4. For love of us His woes begin;
The Sinless suffers for our sin;
The Law's great Maker for our aid
Obedient to the Law is made.

5. The wound He through the Law endures
Our freedom from that Law secures;
Henceforth a holier law prevails,
The law of love which never fails.

6. LORD, circumcise our hearts, we pray,
And take what is not Thine away;
Write Thine own Name within our hearts,
Thy law upon our inmost parts.

7. O LORD, the Virgin-born, to Thee
Eternal praise and glory be;
Whom with the FATHER we adore
And HOLY GHOST for evermore. Amen.

## 57.

"Let this mind be in you which was also in CHRIST JESUS."

1. THE WORD, with GOD the FATHER One
Before the heavens and earth were made,
Is now the Virgin's new-born Son,
Upon her lowly bosom laid.

2. Already o'er His sinless Head
The streams of wrath begin to flow;
Already on His infant bed
The taste of grief He deigns to know.

3. The lowliest poverty He bears
That we may be with wealth supplied;
He weeps: O precious grief and tears!
Through Him the world is purified.

4. An humble dress, a mean abode,
A life obscure His glory hide:
Proud man, behold thy lowly God,
And let the sight destroy thy pride.

5. Jesu, Who camest from on high
To be the Lamb for sinners slain,
Leave not Thy ransomed flock to die,
Nor let Thy toil be spent in vain. Amen.

*ee also the hymns for New Year's Day, and Nos.* 146 *and* 168.

## 58.

## Epiphany.

"We have seen His star in the east."

1. WHAT star is this, with beams so bright,
More beauteous than the noonday light?
It shines to herald forth the King,
And Gentiles to His cradle bring.

2. See now fulfilled what God decreed,
"From Jacob shall a star proceed;"
And eastern sages with amaze
Upon the wondrous vision gaze.

3. The guiding star above is bright,
Within them shines a clearer light,
Which leads them on with power benign
To seek the Giver of the sign.

4. True love can brook no dull delay;
Nor toil nor dangers stop their way:
Home, kindred, father-land, and all
They leave at their Creator's call.

5. O Jesu! while the star of grace
Allures us now to seek Thy face,
Let not our slothful hearts refuse
The guidance of that light to use.

6. All glory, Jesu, be to Thee
For this Thy glad Epiphany:
Whom with the Father we adore
And Holy Ghost for evermore. Amen.

## 59.

"And thou, Bethlehem, in the land of Juda, are not the least among the princes of Juda; for out of thee shall come a Governor, that shall rule My people Israel."

1. EARTH has many a noble city;
Bethlehem, thou dost all excel:
Out of thee the Lord from heaven
Came to rule His Israel.

2. Fairer than the sun at morning
Was the star that told His birth,
To the world its God announcing
Seen in fleshly form on earth.

3. Eastern sages at His cradle
Make oblations rich and rare;
See them give, in deep devotion,
Gold, and frankincense, and myrrh.

4. Sacred gifts of mystic meaning:
   Incense doth their God disclose,
Gold the King of kings proclaimeth,
   Myrrh His sepulchre foreshows.

5. Jesu, Whom the Gentiles worshipped
   At Thy glad Epiphany,
Unto Thee, with God the Father
   And the Spirit, glory be. Amen.

## 60.

"The Life was manifested and we have seen it."

1. WHY doth that impious Herod fear,
   When told that Christ the King is near?
He takes not earthly realms away,
Who gives the realms that ne'er decay.

2. The Eastern sages saw from far
And followed on His guiding star;
By light their way to Light they trod,
And by their gifts confessed their God.

3. Within the Jordan's sacred flood
The heavenly Lamb in meekness stood,
That He, to Whom no sin was known,
Might cleanse His people from their own.

4. And oh! what miracle divine,
When water reddened into wine;
He spake the word, and forth it flowed
In streams that nature ne'er bestowed.

5. All glory, JESU, be to Thee
For this Thy glad Epiphany:
Whom, with the FATHER, we adore
And HOLY GHOST for evermore. Amen.

## 61.

"The people which sat in darkness saw great light."

1. THE people that in darkness sat
A glorious Light have seen;
The Light has shined on them who long
In shades of death have been.

2. To hail Thee, Sun of Righteousness,
The gathering nations come;
They joy as when the reapers bear
Their harvest treasures home.

3. For Thou their burden dost remove,
And break the tyrant's rod,
As in the day when Midian fell
Before the sword of GOD.

4. For unto us a Child is born,
To us a Son is given,
And on His Shoulder ever rests
All power in earth and heaven.

5. His Name shall be the Prince of Peace,
The Everlasting LORD,
The Wonderful, the Counsellor,
The GOD by all adored.

6. His righteous government and power
   Shall over all extend;
   On judgment and on justice based,
   His reign shall have no end.

7. LORD JESUS, reign in us, we pray,
   And make us Thine alone;
   Who with the FATHER ever art
   And HOLY SPIRIT One. Amen.

## 62.

"And He went down with them, and came to Nazareth, and was subject unto them."

1. THE Heavenly Child in stature grows
   And growing learns to die;
   And still His early training shows
   His coming agony.

2. The SON of GOD His glory hides
   With parents mean and poor;
   And He Who made the heavens abides
   In dwelling-place obscure.

3. Those mighty Hands that rule the sky
   No earthly toil refuse;
   The Maker of the stars on high
   An humble trade pursues.

4. He, Whom the choirs of angels praise
   Bearing each dread decree,
   His earthly parents now obeys
   In deep humility.

5. For this Thy lowliness revealed,
   Jesu, we Thee adore;
   And praise to God the Father yield
   And Spirit evermore. Amen.

## 63.

"God be merciful unto us and bless us; and shew us the light of His countenance."

1. GOD of mercy, God of grace,
   Shew the brightness of Thy Face;
   Shine upon us, Saviour, shine,
   Fill Thy Church with light divine;
   And Thy saving health extend
   Unto earth's remotest end.

2. Let the people praise Thee, Lord
   Let Thy love on all be poured;
   Let the nations shout and sing
   Glory to their Saviour King;
   At Thy Feet their tribute pay,
   And Thy holy Will obey.

3. Let the people praise Thee, Lord;
   Earth shall then her fruits afford;
   God to man His blessing give,
   Man to God devoted live;
   All below, and all above,
   One in joy, and light, and love. Amen.

## 64.

"When they saw the star they rejoiced with exceeding great joy."

1. AS with gladness men of old
Did the guiding star behold;
As with joy they hailed its light,
Leading onward, beaming bright;
So, most gracious LORD, may we
Evermore be led to Thee.

2. As with joyful steps they sped
To that lowly manger-bed;
There to bend the knee before
Him Whom heaven and earth adore;
So may we with willing feet
Ever seek the mercy-seat.

3. As they offered gifts most rare
At that manger rude and bare;
So may we with holy joy,
Pure and free from sin's alloy,
All our costliest treasures bring,
CHRIST! to Thee our heavenly King.

4. Holy JESUS, every day
Keep us in the narrow way;
And, when earthly things are past,
Bring our ransomed souls at last
Where they need no star to guide,
Where no clouds Thy glory hide.

5. In the heavenly country bright
Need they no created light;

Thou its Light, its Joy, its Crown,
Thou its Sun which goes not down;
There for ever may we sing
Alleluias to our King. Amen.

## 65.

"Unto you which believe He is precious."

1. JESU! the very thought is sweet!
In that dear Name all heart-joys meet:
But oh! than honey sweeter far
The glimpses of His presence are.

2. No word is sung more sweet than this,
No sound is heard more full of bliss,
No thought brings sweeter comfort nigh,
Than JESUS SON of GOD most High.

3. JESU, the hope of souls forlorn,
How good to them for sin that mourn!
To them that seek Thee, oh how kind!
But what art Thou to them that find?

4. No tongue of mortal can express,
No pen can write the blessedness,
He only who hath proved it knows
What bliss from love of JESUS flows.

5. O JESU, King of wondrous might!
O Victor, glorious from the fight!
Sweetness that may not be expressed
And altogether loveliest!

6. Abide with us, O Lord, to-day,
Fulfil us with Thy grace, we pray;
And with Thine own true sweetness feed
Our souls from sin and darkness freed.
Amen.

## 66.

All the earth shall be filled with His Majesty."

1. HAIL to the Lord's Anointed,
Great David's greater Son!
Hail, in the time appointed,
His reign on earth begun!
He comes to break oppression,
To set the captive free;
To take away transgression,
And rule in equity.

2. He shall come down like showers
Upon the fruitful earth,
And joy and hope, like flowers,
Spring in His path to birth:
Before Him on the mountains
Shall Peace, the herald, go;
From hill to vale the fountains
Of Righteousness o'erflow.

3. Kings shall bow down before Him,
And gold and incense bring;
All nations shall adore Him,
His praise all people sing;

To Him shall prayer unceasing,
And daily vows ascend;
His kingdom still increasing,
A kingdom without end.

4. O'er every foe victorious,
He on His throne shall rest:
From age to age more glorious,
All-blessing and all-blessed:
The tide of time shall never
His covenant remove;
His Name shall stand for ever,
His changeless Name of Love. Amen.

## 67.

## For the Week before Septuagesima.

"And again they said, Alleluia."

1. ALLELUIA, song of sweetness,
Voice of joy that cannot die;
ALLELUIA is the anthem
Ever dear to choirs on high;
In the house of GOD abiding
Thus they sing eternally.

2. ALLELUIA thou resoundest,
True Jerusalem and free;
ALLELUIA, joyful Mother,
All thy children sing with thee:
But by Babylon's sad waters
Mourning exiles now are we.

3. Alleluia cannot always
Be our song while here below;
Alleluia our transgressions
Make us for awhile forego;
For the solemn time is coming
When our tears for sin must flow.

4. Therefore in our hymns we pray Thee,
Grant us, Blessèd Trinity,
At the last to keep Thine Easter
In our Home beyond the sky:
There to Thee for ever singing
Alleluia joyfully. Amen.

## 68.

### Septuagesima, &c.

"How shall we sing the Lord's song in a strange land?"

1. CREATOR of the world, to Thee
An endless rest of joy belongs;
And heavenly choirs are ever free
To sing on high their festal songs.

2. But we are fallen creatures here,
Where pain and sorrow daily come;
And how can we in exile drear
Sing out, as they, sweet songs of Home?

3. O Father! Who dost promise still
That they who mourn shall blessèd be;
Grant us to weep for deeds of ill
That banish us so long from Thee:

4. But weeping grant us faith to rest
In hope upon Thy loving care;
Till Thou restore us, with the blest,
Their songs of praise in heaven to share.

5. To Father, Son, and Holy Ghost,
The God Whom heaven and earth adore,
From men and from the angel-host
Be praise and glory evermore. Amen.

## 69.

"Behold, I create new heavens and a new earth."

1. O LORD, in perfect bliss above
Thou couldst not need created love;
And yet Thou didst Thy power display,
And earth's foundations firmly lay.

2. Things that were not, at Thy command
In perfect form before Thee stand:
And all to their Creator raise
A wondrous harmony of praise.

3. But even while the world came forth
In all the beauty of its birth,
In Thy deep thought Thou didst behold
Another world of nobler mould.

4. For Thou didst will that Christ should frame
A new creation by His Name;
Its seed the living word of grace
He scatters wide in every place;

5. Its home, when time shall be no more,
In heaven with Thee for evermore;
Accepted in Thy boundless love
To share His throne and joy above.

6. O Father, bless, for they are Thine,
O Son, direct in love divine,
O Holy Ghost, with grace endue
The old creation and the new. Amen.

## 70.

"These all died in faith, not having received the promises, but having seen them afar off, and were persuaded of them, and embraced them, and confessed that they were strangers and pilgrims on the earth."

1. HOW blest were they who walked in love
With Christ, while yet He dwelt above;
A righteous band, sustained by grace,
The fathers of the faithful race.

2. O who can tell as should be told
The praises of those men of old,
Their patient faith, their longing sighs
Of hope uplifted to the skies?

3. Strangers and pilgrims here below
They deemed the world an empty show:
To purer joys their hearts were given,
The better land they sought was Heaven.

4. The soul that truly cleaves to God
Still longs to gain that blest abode:
O Christ, forbid our souls to roam,
And fix them on our own true Home.

5. All praise to God the Father be;
All praise, Eternal Son, to Thee;
Whom, with the Spirit, we adore
For ever and for evermore. Amen.

# 71.

"The invisible things of Him from the creation of the world are clearly seen, being understood by the things that are made."

1. THERE is a book, who runs may read,
Which heavenly truth imparts,
And all the lore its scholars need,
Pure eyes and Christian hearts.

2. The works of God, above, below,
Within us and around,
Are pages in that book to show
How God Himself is found.

3. The glorious sky, embracing all,
Is like the Maker's love,
Wherewith encompassed great and small
In peace and order move.

4. The moon above, the church below,
A wondrous race they run;
But all their radiance, all their glow,
Each borrows of its Sun.

5. The Saviour lends the light and heat
That crown His holy hill;
The saints, like stars, around His seat
Perform their courses still.

6. Thou, Who hast given me eyes to see
And love this sight so fair,
Give me a heart to find out Thee,
And read Thee everywhere. Amen.

## 72.

"Now abideth faith, hope, charity, these three; but the greatest of these is charity."

1. GREAT Mover of all hearts, Whose Hand
Doth all the secret springs command
Of human thought and will,
Thou, since the world was made, dost bless
Thy saints with fruits of holiness,
Their order to fulfil.

2. Faith, hope, and love here weave one chain;
But love alone shall then remain,
When this short day is gone:
O Love, O Truth, O endless Light,
When shall we see Thy Sabbath bright
With all our labours done?

3. We sow 'mid perils here and tears;
There the glad hand the harvest bears,
Which here in grief hath sown:
GREAT THREE IN ONE, the increase give;
These gifts of grace, by which we live,
With heavenly glory crown. Amen.

*The hymns for Sunday and other days of the week may fitly be used at this season.*

# 73.

## Lent.

"Rend your heart and not your garments, and turn unto the LORD your God."

1. ONCE more the solemn season calls
   A holy fast to keep;
And now within the temple walls
   Both priest and people weep.

2. But vain all outward sign of grief,
   And vain the form of prayer,
Unless the heart implore relief,
   And penitence be there.

3. We smite the breast, we weep in vain,
   In vain in ashes mourn,
Unless with penitential pain
   The smitten soul be torn.

4. In sorrow true then let us pray
   To our offended GOD,
From us to turn His wrath away
   And stay the uplifted rod.

5. O GOD, our JUDGE and FATHER, deign
   To spare the bruisèd reed;
We pray for time to turn again,
   For grace to turn indeed.

6. Blest THREE IN ONE, to Thee we bow;
   Vouchsafe us in Thy love
To gather from these fasts below
   Immortal fruit above. Amen.

# 74.

"Now, saith the LORD, turn ye even to Me with all your heart, and with fasting, and with weeping, and with mourning."

1. BY precepts taught of ages past,
Now let us keep again the fast
Which, year by year, in order meet
Of forty days is made complete.

2. The law and seers that were of old
In divers ways this Lent foretold,
Which CHRIST Himself, the LORD and Guide
Of every season, sanctified.

3. More sparing therefore let us make
The words we speak, the food we take,
Deny ourselves in mirth and sleep,
In stricter watch our senses keep.

4. In prayer together let us fall,
And cry for mercy, one and all;
And weep before the Judge, and say,
Oh, turn from us Thy wrath away.

5. Thy grace have we offended sore
By sins, O GOD, which we deplore;
Pour down upon us from above
The riches of Thy pardoning love.

6. Remember, LORD, though frail we be,
That yet Thine handiwork are we;
Nor let the honour of Thy Name
Be by another put to shame.

7. Forgive the sin that we have wrought,
Increase the good that we have sought;
That we at length, our wanderings o'er,
May please Thee here and evermore.

8. Blest Three in One, and One in Three,
Almighty God, we pray to Thee,
That Thou wouldst now vouchsafe to bless
Our fast with fruits of righteousness. Amen.

## 75.

"O deliver us, and be merciful unto our sins, for Thy Name's sake."

1. O MERCIFUL Creator, hear;
To us in pity bow Thine ear:
Accept the tearful prayer we raise
In this our fast of forty days.

2. Each heart is manifest to Thee;
Thou knowest our infirmity:
Repentant now we seek Thy Face;
Impart to us Thy pardoning grace.

3. Our sins are manifold and sore,
But spare Thou them who sin deplore;
And for Thine own Name's sake make whole
The fainting and the weary soul.

4. Grant us to mortify each sense
By means of outward abstinence,
That so from every stain of sin
The soul may keep her fast within.

5. Blest Three in One, and One in Three,
Almighty God, we pray to Thee,
That Thou wouldst now vouchsafe to bless
Our fast with fruits of righteousness. Amen.

## 76.

"Behold, now is the accepted time; behold, now is the day of salvation."

1. LO! now is our accepted day,
The time for purging sins away,
The sins of thought, and deed, and word,
That we have done against the Lord.

2. For He the Merciful and True
Hath spared His people hitherto;
Not willing that the soul should die
Though great its past iniquity.

3. Then let us all with earnest care,
And contrite fast, and tear, and prayer,
And works of mercy and of love,
Entreat for pardon from above;

4. That He may all our sins efface,
Adorn us with the gifts of grace,
And join us to the angel band
For ever in the heavenly land.

5. Blest Three in One and One in Three,
Almighty God, we pray to Thee,
That Thou wouldst now vouchsafe to bless
Our fast with fruits of righteousness. Amen.

# 77.

"In due season we shall reap, if we faint not."

1. O THOU Who dost to man accord
His highest prize, his best reward,
Thou Hope of all our race,
Jesu, to Thee we now draw near,
Our earnest supplications hear,
Who humbly seek Thy Face.

2. With self-accusing voice within,
Our conscience tells of many a sin
In thought and word and deed:
O cleanse that conscience from all stain,
The penitent restore again
From every burthen freed.

3. If Thou reject us, who shall give
Our fainting spirits strength to live?
'Tis Thine alone to spare;
With cleansèd hearts to pray aright
And find acceptance in Thy sight,
Be this our lowly prayer.

4. 'Tis Thou hast blessed this solemn fast;
So may its days by us be passed
In self-control severe,
That, when our Easter morn we hail,
Its mystic feast we may not fail
To keep with conscience clear.

5. O Blessed TRINITY, bestow
Thy pardoning grace on us below,
And shield us evermore;
Until, within Thy courts above,
We see Thy Face, and sing Thy love,
And with Thy saints adore. Amen.

# 78.

"And JESUS was led by the SPIRIT into the wilderness, being forty days tempted of the devil. And in those days He did eat nothing."

1. FORTY days and forty nights
Thou wast fasting in the wild;
Forty days and forty nights
Tempted, and yet undefiled.

2. Sunbeams scorching all the day;
Chilly dew-drops nightly shed;
Prowling beasts about Thy way;
Stones Thy pillow; earth Thy bed.

3. Shall not we Thy sorrows share,
And from earthly joys abstain,
Fasting with unceasing prayer,
Glad with Thee to suffer pain?

4. And if Satan, vexing sore,
Flesh or spirit should assail,
Thou, his Vanquisher before,
Grant we may not faint or fail.

5. So shall we have peace divine;
Holier gladness ours shall be;
Round us, too, shall angels shine,
Such as ministered to Thee.

6. Keep, O keep us, SAVIOUR dear,
Ever constant by Thy side;
That with Thee we may appear
At th' eternal Eastertide. Amen.

## 79.

"A broken and contrite heart, O GOD, Thou wilt not despise."

LORD, when we bend before Thy Throne,
And our confessions pour,
Teach us to feel the sins we own,
And hate what we deplore.

2. Our broken spirit pitying see;
True penitence impart;
Then let a kindling glance from Thee
Beam hope upon the heart.

3. When we disclose our wants in prayer,
May we our wills resign;
And not a thought our bosoms share,
Which is not wholly Thine.

4. May faith each weak petition fill,
And waft it to the skies,
And teach our hearts 'tis goodness still
That grants it or denies.

5. All glory to the FATHER be,
   All glory to the SON,
All glory, HOLY GHOST, to Thee,
   While endless ages run. Amen.

## 80.

"Enter not into judgment with Thy servant, O LORD; for in thy sight shall no man living be justified."

1. O LORD, turn not Thy Face from me,
   Who lie in woeful state,
Lamenting all my sinful life
   Before Thy mercy-gate;

2. A gate that opens wide to those
   That do lament their sin;
Shut not that gate against me, LORD,
   But let me enter in.

3. And call me not to strict account
   How I have sojourned here;
For then my guilty conscience knows
   How vile I shall appear.

4. Mercy, Good LORD, mercy I ask;
   This is my humble prayer;
For mercy, LORD, is all my suit,
   O let Thy mercy spare.

5. To FATHER, SON, and HOLY GHOST,
   The GOD Whom we adore,
Be glory, as it was, is now,
   And shall be evermore. Amen.

## 81.

"Have mercy upon me, O God, after Thy great goodness; according to the multitude of Thy mercies do away mine offences."

1. HAVE mercy, Lord, on me,
   As Thou wert ever kind;
Let me, opprest with loads of guilt,
   Thy wonted mercy find.

2. Wash off my foul offence,
   And cleanse me from my sin;
For I confess my crime, and see
   How great my guilt has been.

3. The joy Thy favour gives
   Let me again obtain;
And Thy free Spirit's firm support
   My fainting soul sustain.

4. To God the Father, Son,
   And Spirit, glory be;
As 'twas, and is, and shall be so
   To all eternity. Amen.

## 82.

"My soul fleeth unto the Lord."

1. LORD, in this Thy mercy's day
   Ere it pass for aye away,
On our knees we fall and pray.

2. Holy Jesu, grant us tears,
Fill us with heart-searching fears
Ere that awful doom appears.

3. Lord, on us Thy Spirit pour
Kneeling lowly at the door
Ere it close for evermore.

4. By Thy night of agony,
By Thy supplicating cry,
By Thy willingness to die,

5. By Thy tears of bitter woe
For Jerusalem below,
Let us not Thy love forego.

6. Grant us 'neath Thy wings a place,
Lest we lose this day of grace
Ere we shall behold Thy face. Amen.

## 83.

EVENING.

"I am the Light of the world."

1. O CHRIST, Who art the Light and Day,
Thy beams chase night's dark shades away;
The very Light of Light Thou art,
Who dost that blessèd Light impart.

2. All-Holy Lord to Thee we bend,
Thy servants through this night defend,
And grant us calm repose in Thee,
A quiet night from perils free.

3. Let not dull sleep the soul oppress,
Nor secret foe the heart possess,
Nor Satan's wiles the flesh allure,
And make us in Thy sight impure.

4. Light slumber let our eyelids take,
The heart to Thee be still awake;
And Thy Right Hand protection be
To those who love and trust in Thee.

5. O Lord, our strong defence, be nigh;
Bid all the powers of darkness fly;
Preserve and watch o'er us for good,
Whom Thou hast purchased with Thy Blood.

6. Remember us, dear Lord, we pray,
Whilst burthened in the flesh we stay;
Thou only canst the soul defend,
Be with us, Saviour, to the end.

7. Blest Three in One and One in Three,
Almighty God, we pray to Thee,
That Thou wouldst now vouchsafe to bless
Our fast with fruits of righteousness. Amen.

*Many of the hymns on the Passion may also be used during this season.*

# 84.

## The Fifth Sunday in Lent.

OTHERWISE CALLED PASSION SUNDAY.

"God forbid that I should glory save in the Cross of our Lord Jesus Christ."

1. THE Royal Banners forward go,
The Cross shines forth in mystic glow;
Where He in flesh, our flesh Who made,
Our sentence bore, our ransom paid.

2. There whilst He hung, His sacred Side
By soldier's spear was opened wide,
To cleanse us in the precious flood
Of Water mingled with His Blood.

3. Fulfilled is now what David told
In true prophetic song of old,
How God the heathen's King should be;
For God is reigning from the tree.

4. O tree of glory, tree most fair,
Ordained those Holy Limbs to bear,
How bright in purple robe it stood,
The purple of a Saviour's Blood!

5. Upon its arms, like balance true,
He weighed the price for sinners due,
The price which none but He could pay,
And spoiled the spoiler of his prey.

6. To Thee, Eternal Three in One,
Let homage meet by all be done:
As by the Cross Thou dost restore,
So rule and guide us evermore. Amen.

## 85.

"God forbid that I should glory save in the Cross of our Lord Jesus Christ."

1. WE sing the praise of Him Who died,
Of Him Who died upon the Cross;
The sinner's hope let men deride,
For this we count the world but loss.

2. Inscribed upon the Cross we see
In shining letters, "GOD is Love;"
He bears our sins upon the tree,
He brings us mercy from above.

3. The Cross! it takes our guilt away;
It holds the fainting spirit up;
It cheers with hope the gloomy day,
And sweetens every bitter cup.

4. It makes the coward spirit brave,
And nerves the feeble arm for fight;
It takes its terror from the grave,
And gilds the bed of death with light.

5. The balm of life, the cure of woe,
The measure and the pledge of love,
The sinner's refuge here below,
The angels' theme in heaven above.

6. To CHRIST, Who won for sinners grace
By bitter grief and anguish sore,
Be praise from all the ransomed race
For ever and for evermore. Amen.

## 86.

## The Sunday next before Easter,

OTHERWISE CALLED PALM SUNDAY.

"Out of the mouth of babes and sucklings Thou hast perfected praise."

1. ALL glory, laud, and honour
To Thee, Redeemer, King!
To Whom the lips of children
Made sweet Hosannas ring.
All glory, &c.

2. Thou art the King of Israel,
 Thou David's Royal Son,
Who in the LORD's Name comest,
 The King and Blessèd One.
 All glory, &c.

3. The company of Angels
 Are praising Thee on high,
And mortal men, and all things
 Created make reply.
 All glory, &c.

4. The people of the Hebrews
 With palms before Thee went,
Our praise and prayer and anthems
 Before Thee we present.
 All glory, &c.

5. To Thee before Thy Passion
 They sang their hymns of praise;
To Thee now high exalted
 Our melody we raise.
 All glory, &c

6. Thou didst accept their praises;
 Accept the prayers we bring,
Who in all good delightest,
 Thou good and gracious King.
 All glory, &c. Amen.

## 87.

"And the multitudes that went before, and that followed, cried saying, Hosanna to the Son of David."

1. RIDE on! ride on in majesty!
 Hark! all the tribes Hosanna cry;
O SAVIOUR meek, pursue Thy road
With palms and scattered garments strowed.

2. Ride on! ride on in majesty!
In lowly pomp ride on to die:
O CHRIST, Thy triumphs now begin
O'er captive death and conquered sin.

3. Ride on! ride on in majesty!
The angel armies of the sky
Look down with sad and wondering eyes
To see the approaching Sacrifice.

4. Ride on! ride on in majesty!
The last and fiercest strife is nigh:
The FATHER on His sapphire Throne
Awaits His own anointed SON.

5. Ride on! ride on in majesty!
In lowly pomp ride on to die;
Bow Thy meek Head to mortal pain,
Then take, O GOD, Thy Power, and reign.
Amen.

## 88.

## Hymns on the Passion.*

"We love Him because He first loved us."

1. MY GOD, I love Thee; not because
I hope for heaven thereby,
Nor yet because who love Thee not
Must burn eternally.

2. Thou, O my JESUS, Thou didst me
Upon the Cross embrace;
For me didst bear the nails, and spear,
And manifold disgrace,

* Many of these hymns may be sung from Septuagesima to Easter, and some of them throughout the year.

3. And griefs and torments numberless,
And sweat of agony;
Yea, death itself; and all for me
Who was Thine enemy.

4. Then why, O blessèd Jesu Christ,
Should I not love Thee well?
Not for the hope of winning heaven,
Nor of escaping hell;

5. Not with the hope of gaining aught,
Not seeking a reward;
But as Thyself hast lovèd me,
O ever-loving Lord.

6. So would I love Thee, dearest Lord,
And in Thy praise will sing;
Solely because Thou art my God,
And my Eternal King. Amen.

## 89.

"And being in an agony, He prayed more earnestly."

1. SION'S Daughter, weep no more,
Though thy troubled heart be sore;
He of Whom the Psalmist sung,
He Who woke the Prophet's tongue,
Christ, the Mediator blest,
Brings thee everlasting rest.

2. In a garden man became
Heir of sin, and death, and shame:
Jesus in a garden wins
Life, and pardon for our sins;
Through His hour of agony
Praying in Gethsemane.

3. There for us He intercedes;
There with God the Father pleads;
Willing there for us to drain
To the dregs the cup of pain,
That in everlasting Day
He may wipe our tears away.

4. Therefore to His Name be given
Glory both in earth and heaven;
To the Father, and the Son,
And the Spirit, Three in One,
Honour, praise, and glory be,
Now and through eternity. Amen.

## 90.

"Thou wast slain, and hast redeemed us to God by Thy Blood."

1. HE, Who once in righteous vengeance
Whelmed the world beneath the flood,
Once again in mercy cleansed it
With His own most precious Blood;
Coming from His throne on high
On the painful Cross to die.

2. O the wisdom of th' Eternal!
   O the depth of love divine!
O the sweetness of that mercy
   Which in Jesus Christ did shine!
We were sinners doomed to die;
Jesus paid the penalty.

3. When before the Judge we tremble,
   Conscious of His broken laws,
May the Blood of His atonement
   Cry aloud, and plead our cause,
Bid our guilty terrors cease,
Be our pardon and our peace.

4. Prince and Author of salvation,
   Lord of majesty supreme,
Jesu, praise to Thee be given
   By the world Thou didst redeem;
Glory to the Father be
And the Spirit One with Thee. Amen.

## 91.

"Looking unto Jesus."

1. O'ERWHELMED in depths of woe
   Upon the tree of scorn
Hangs the Redeemer of mankind,
   With racking anguish torn.

2. See how the nails those Hands
   And Feet so tender rend;
See down His Face, and Neck, and Breast
   His sacred Blood descend.

3. Oh, hear that awful cry
Which pierced His Mother's heart,
As into God the Father's Hands
He bade His soul depart.

4. Earth hears, and trembling quakes
Around that tree of pain;
The rocks are rent; the graves are burst:
The veil is rent in twain.

5. The sun withdraws his light;
The mid-day heavens grow pale;
The moon, the stars, the universe
Their Maker's death bewail.

6. Shall man alone be mute?
Have we no griefs, or fears?
Come, old and young, come, all mankind,
And bathe those Feet in tears.

7. Come, fall before His Cross
Who shed for us His Blood;
Who died, the Victim of pure love,
To make us sons of God.

8. Jesu, all praise to Thee,
Our joy and endless rest;
Be Thou our guide while pilgrims here,
Our crown amid the blest. Amen.

## 92.

"The precious Blood of CHRIST."

1. GLORY be to JESUS,
Who, in bitter pains,
Poured for me the life-blood
From His sacred veins.

2. Grace and life eternal
In that Blood I find;
Blest be His compassion
Infinitely kind.

3. Blest through endless ages
Be the precious stream,
Which from endless torments
Did the world redeem.

4. Abel's blood for vengeance
Pleaded to the skies;
But the Blood of JESUS
For our pardon cries.

5. Oft as it is sprinkled
On our guilty hearts,
Satan in confusion
Terror-struck departs;

6. Oft as earth exulting
Wafts its praise on high,
Angel-hosts rejoicing
Make their glad reply

7. Lift ye then your voices;
   Swell the mighty flood:
Louder still and louder
   Praise the precious Blood. Amen.

## 93.

"Behold the Man."

1. O SINNER, lift the eye of faith,
   To true repentance turning;
Bethink thee of the curse of sin,
   Its awful guilt discerning;
Upon the Crucified One look,
And thou shalt read, as in a book,
   What well is worth thy learning.

2. Look on His Head, that bleeding Head,
   With crown of thorns surrounded;
Look on His sacred Hands and Feet
   Which piercing nails have wounded:
See every Limb with scourges rent:
On Him, the Just, the Innocent,
   What malice hath abounded!

3. 'Tis not alone those Limbs are racked,
   But friends too are forsaking;
And more than all, for thankless man
   That tender Heart is aching;
Oh, fearful was the pain and scorn
By JESUS, Son of Mary, borne,
   Their peace for sinners making.

4. None ever knew such pain before,
   Such infinite affliction;
None ever felt a grief like His
   In that dread crucifixion:
For us He bare those bitter throes,
For us those agonizing woes
   In oft-renewed infliction.

5. O sinner, mark, and ponder well
   Sin's awful condemnation;
Think what a sacrifice it cost
   To purchase thy salvation;
Had Jesus never bled and died,
Then what could thee and all betide
   But uttermost damnation?

6. Lord, give us grace to flee from sin,
   And Satan's wiles ensnaring,
And from those everlasting flames
   For evil ones preparing.
Jesu, we thank Thee, and entreat
To rest for ever at Thy Feet,
   Thy heavenly glory sharing. Amen.

## 94.

"He was wounded for our transgressions."

1. NOW, my soul, thy voice upraising,
   Tell in sweet and mournful strain,
How the Crucified, enduring
   Grief, and wounds, and dying pain,
Freely of His love was offered,
   Sinless was for sinners slain.

2. Scourged with unrelenting fury
   For the sins which we deplore,
By His livid Stripes He heals us,
   Raising us to fall no more;
All our bruises gently soothing,
   Binding up the bleeding sore.

3. See! His Hands and Feet are fastened;
   So He makes His people free:
Not a wound whence Blood is flowing
   But a Fount of Grace shall be;
Yea the very nails which nail Him
   Nail us also to the Tree.

4. Through His Heart the spear is piercing,
   Though His foes have seen Him die;
Blood and Water thence are streaming
   In a tide of mystery,
Water from our guilt to cleanse us,
   Blood to win us crowns on high.

5. JESU, may those precious Fountains
   Drink to thirsting souls afford;
Let them be our Cup and Healing,
   And at length our full Reward;
So a ransomed world shall ever
   Praise Thee, its Redeeming LORD. Amen.

## 95.

"Unto you therefore which believe He is precious."

SWEET the moments, rich in blessing,
   Which before the Cross I spend,
Life, and health, and peace possessing
   From the sinner's dying Friend.

2. Here I rest, for ever viewing
 Mercy poured in streams of Blood;
Precious drops, my soul bedewing,
 Plead and claim my peace with God.

3. Truly blessèd is the station,
 Low before His cross to lie,
Whilst I see divine compassion
 Beaming in His languid Eye.

4. Lord, in ceaseless contemplation
 Fix my thankful heart on Thee,
Till I taste Thy full salvation
 And Thine unveiled glory see. Amen.

## 96.

"The love of Christ constraineth us."

1. In the Lord's atoning grief
Be our rest and sweet relief;
Store we deep in heart's recess
All the shame and bitterness.

2. Thorns, and cross, and nails, and lance,
Wounds, our treasure that enhance,
Vinegar, and gall, and reed,
And the pang His soul that freed

3. May these all our spirits sate,
And with love inebriate;
In our souls plant virtue's root,
And mature its glorious fruit.

4. Crucified! we Thee adore,
Thee with all our hearts implore,
Us with saintly bands unite
In the realms of heavenly light.

5. CHRIST, by coward hands betrayed,
CHRIST, for us a captive made,
CHRIST, upon the bitter tree
Slain for man, be praise to Thee. Amen.

## 97.

"Who loved me and gave Himself for me."

1. O SACRED Head, surrounded
By crown of piercing thorn!
O bleeding Head, so wounded,
Reviled, and put to scorn!
Death's pallid hue comes o'er Thee,
The glow of life decays,
Yet angel-hosts adore Thee,
And tremble as they gaze.

2. I see Thy strength and vigour
All fading in the strife,
And death with cruel rigour
Bereaving Thee of life;
O agony and dying!
O love to sinners free!
JESU, all grace supplying,
O turn Thy Face on me.

3. In this Thy bitter passion,
Good Shepherd, think of me
With Thy most sweet compassion,
Unworthy though I be:
Beneath Thy Cross abiding
For ever would I rest,
In Thy dear love confiding,
And with Thy presence blest. Amen.

## 98.

"Now there stood by the Cross of Jesus His Mother."

1. AT the Cross her station keeping,
Stood the mournful Mother weeping,
Where He hung, the dying Lord;
For her soul of joy bereavèd,
Bowed with anguish, deeply grievèd,
Felt the sharp and piercing sword.

2. Oh, how sad and sore distressèd
Now was she, that Mother blessèd
Of the Sole-begotten One;
Deep the woe of her affliction
When she saw the Crucifixion
Of her ever-glorious Son.

3. Who, on Christ's dear Mother gazing
Pierced by anguish so amazing,
Born of woman, would not weep?
Who, on Christ's dear Mother thinking
Such a cup of sorrow drinking,
Would not share her sorrows deep?

4. For His people's sins chastisèd
She beheld her Son despisèd, [twined;
Scourged, and crowned with thorns en-
Saw Him then from judgment taken,
And in death by all forsaken,
Till His Spirit He resigned.

5. Jesu, may such deep devotion
Stir in me the same emotion,
Fount of love, Redeemer kind,
That my heart, fresh ardour gaining
And a purer love attaining,
May with Thee acceptance find. Amen.

## 99.

"Is it nothing to you, all ye that pass by? Behold, and see if there be any sorrow like unto My sorrow."

1. SEE the destined day arise!
See, a willing Sacrifice,
Jesus, to redeem our loss,
Hangs upon the shameful Cross!

2. Jesu, who but Thou had borne,
Lifted on that tree of scorn,
Every pang and bitter throe,
Finishing Thy life of woe?

3. Who but Thou had dared to drain,
Steeped in gall, the cup of pain;
And with tender body bear
Thorns, and nails, and piercing spear?

4. Thence the cleansing Water flowed
Mingled from Thy Side with Blood;
Sign to all attesting eyes
Of the finished Sacrifice.

5. Holy Jesu, grant us grace
In that Sacrifice to place
All our trust for life renewed,
Pardoned sin, and promised good. Amen.

## 100.

"They crucified Him."

1. O COME and mourn with me awhile;
O come ye to the Saviour's side;
O come, together let us mourn;
Jesus, our Lord, is crucified.

2. Have we no tears to shed for Him,
While soldiers scoff and Jews deride?
Ah! look how patiently He hangs;
Jesus, our Lord, is crucified.

3. How fast His Hands and Feet are nailed;
His Throat with parching thirst is dried;
His failing Eyes are dimmed with Blood;
Jesus, our Lord, is crucified.

4. Seven times He spake, seven words of love;
And all three hours His silence cried
For mercy on the souls of men;
Jesus, our Lord, is crucified.

5. Come, let us stand beneath the Cross;
So may the Blood from out His Side
Fall gently on us drop by drop;
Jesus, our Lord, is crucified.

6. A broken heart, a fount of tears
Ask, and they will not be denied;
Lord Jesus, may we love and weep,
Since Thou for us art crucified. Amen.

## 101.

"What things were gain to me, those I counted loss for Christ."

1. WHEN I survey the wondrous Cross
On which the Prince of Glory died,
My richest gain I count but loss,
And pour contempt on all my pride.

2. Forbid it, Lord, that I should boast
Save in the Cross of Christ my God;
All the vain things that charm me most,
I sacrifice them to His Blood.

3. See, from His Head, His Hands, His Feet,
Sorrow and love flow mingling down;
Did e'er such love and sorrow meet,
Or thorns compose so rich a crown?

4. Were the whole realm of nature mine,
That were an offering far too small;
Love so amazing, so divine,
Demands my life, my soul, my all.

5. To CHRIST, Who won for sinners grace
By bitter grief and anguish sore,
Be praise from all the ransomed race
For ever and for evermore. Amen.

## 102.

"CHRIST also suffered for us, leaving us an example that ye should follow His steps."

1. ANGELS, lament; behold, your GOD
Man's sinful likeness wears;
Behold, upon the accursèd tree
Man's sins the SAVIOUR bears.

2. O CHRIST, with wondering minds we see
What mighty love was Thine:
Did GOD consent to suffer thus,
And, oh, shall man repine?

3. No, SAVIOUR, no! the power of death
Thy Cross hath overcome,
To save us, not from earthly woe
But from th' eternal doom.

4. The flesh may shrink, but we submit,
Whate'er our Cross may be,
So Thou by grace enable us
To bear it after Thee.

5. Thy stripes have healed us, and Thy Blood
Our guilty stains effaced;
Then may Thy Name by sin of ours
Be never more disgraced. Amen.

## 103.

"Remembering mine affliction and my misery, the wormwood and the gall."

1. GO to dark Gethsemane,
Ye that feel the Tempter's power,
Your Redeemer's conflict see,
Watch with Him one bitter hour;
Turn not from His griefs away,
Learn of JESUS CHRIST to pray.

2. Follow to the judgment-hall,
View the Lord of life arraigned,
Oh, the wormwood and the gall!
Oh, the pangs His soul sustained!
Shun not suffering, shame, or loss;
Learn of Him to bear the cross.

3. Calvary's mournful mountain climb;
There, adoring at His Feet,
Mark that miracle of time,
GOD's own sacrifice complete;
"It is finished," hear Him cry;
Learn of JESUS CHRIST to die. Amen.

## 104.

"JESUS, Master, have mercy upon us."

1. SAVIOUR, when in dust to Thee
Low we bow the adoring knee;
When, repentant, to the skies
Scarce we lift our weeping eyes;
Oh, by all Thy pains and woe
Suffered once for man below,
Bending from Thy Throne on high,
Hear our solemn litany.

2. By Thy birth and early years;
By Thy life of want and tears;
By Thy fasting and distress
In the lonely wilderness;
By the dread mysterious hour
Of the subtle tempter's power;
Jesu, look with pitying eye;
Hear our solemn litany.

3. By the sacred grief that wept
O'er the grave where Lazarus slept;
By the gracious tears that flowed
Over Salem's loved abode;
By the mournful word that told
Treachery lurked within Thy fold;
Jesu, look with pitying eye;
Hear our solemn litany.

4. By Thine hour of whelming fear;
By Thine agony, and prayer;
By the purple robe of scorn;
By Thy wounds, Thy crown of thorn;
By Thy cross, Thy pangs, and cries;
By Thy perfect sacrifice;
Jesu, look with pitying eye;
Hear our solemn litany.

5. By Thy deep expiring groan;
By the sealed sepulchral stone;
By Thy triumph o'er the grave;
By Thy power from death to save;
Mighty God, ascended Lord,
To Thy Throne in Heaven restored,
Prince and Saviour, hear our cry;
Hear our solemn litany. Amen.

## 105.

"And when Joseph had taken the Body, he wrapped It in a clean linen cloth, and laid It in his own new tomb, which he had hewn out in the rock. . . . And there was Mary Magdalene and the other Mary, sitting over against the sepulchre."

1. RESTING from His work to-day
In the tomb the SAVIOUR lay;
Still He slept, from Head to Feet
Shrouded in the winding-sheet,
Lying in the rock alone,
Hidden by the sealèd stone.

2. Late at even there was seen
Watching long the Magdalene;
Early, ere the break of day,
Sorrowful she took her way
To the holy garden glade,
Where her buried LORD was laid.

3. So with Thee, till life shall end,
I would solemn vigil spend:
Let me hew Thee, LORD, a shrine
In this rocky heart of mine,
Where in pure embalmèd cell
None but Thou may ever dwell.

4. Myrrh and spices will I bring,
True affection's offering;
Close the door from sight and sound
Of the busy world around;
And in patient watch remain
Till my LORD appear again. Amen.

# 106.

## Easter.

"O death, where is thy sting? O grave, where is thy victory?

1. YE choirs of new Jerusalem,
   Your sweetest notes employ,
The Paschal victory to hymn
   In strains of holy joy.

2. For Judah's Lion bursts His chains,
   Crushing the serpent's head;
And cries aloud through death's domains
   To wake the imprisoned dead.

3. Devouring depths of hell their prey
   At His command restore;
His ransomed hosts pursue their way
   Where JESUS goes before.

4. Triumphant in His glory now
   To Him all power is given;
To Him in one communion bow
   All saints in earth and heaven.

5. While we, His soldiers, praise our King,
   His mercy we implore,
Within His palace bright to bring
   And keep us evermore.

6. All glory to the FATHER be;
   All glory to the SON;
All glory, HOLY GHOST, to Thee,
   While endless ages run.
      Alleluia! Amen.

# 107.

"The LORD is risen indeed."

1. JESUS CHRIST is risen to-day,
Alleluia!
Our triumphant holy day,
Alleluia!
Who did once, upon the Cross,
Alleluia!
Suffer to redeem our loss.
Alleluia!

2. Hymns of praise then let us sing
Alleluia!
Unto CHRIST, our heavenly King,
Alleluia!
Who endured the Cross and Grave,
Alleluia!
Sinners to redeem and save.
Alleluia!

3. But the pain which He endured
Alleluia!
Our salvation hath procured;
Alleluia!
Now above the sky He's King,
Alleluia!
Where the angels ever sing.
Alleluia! Amen.

## 108.

"This is the day which the LORD hath made; we will rejoice and be glad in it."

ALLELUIA! ALLELUIA! ALLELUIA!

1. O SONS and daughters, let us sing!
The King of heaven, the glorious King,
O'er death to-day rose triumphing.
Alleluia!

2. That Sunday morn, at break of day,
The faithful women went their way
To seek the tomb where JESUS lay.
Alleluia!

3 An Angel clad in white they see,
Who sat and spake unto the three,
"Your LORD doth go to Galilee."
Alleluia!

4. That night the Apostles met in fear;
Amidst them came their LORD most dear,
And said "My peace be on all here."
Alleluia!

5. When Didymus the tidings heard,
He doubted if it were the LORD,
Until He came and spake this word:
Alleluia!

6. "My piercèd Side, O Thomas, see;
My Hands, My Feet, I show to thee;
Nor faithless, but believing be."
Alleluia!

7. No longer Thomas then denied;
He saw the Feet, the Hands, the Side;
"Thou art my LORD and GOD," he cried.
Alleluia!

8. How blest are they who have not seen,
And yet whose faith hath constant been;
For they eternal life shall win.
Alleluia!

9. On this most holy day of days,
To GOD your hearts and voices raise
In laud, and jubilee, and praise.
Alleluia! Amen.

## 109.

"The LORD is KING, and hath put on glorious apparel."

1. LIGHT'S glittering morn bedecks the sky,
Heaven thunders forth its victor-cry,
The glad earth shouts her triumph high,
And groaning hell makes wild reply;

2. While He, the King, the mighty King,
Despoiling death of all its sting,
And, trampling down the powers of night,
Brings forth His ransomed saints to light.

3. His tomb of late the threefold guard
Of watch and stone and seal had barred;
But now, in pomp and triumph high,
He comes from death to victory.

4. The pains of hell are loosed at last;
The days of mourning now are past;
An Angel robed in light hath said,
"The LORD is risen from the dead."

## PART II.

1. THE Apostle's hearts were full of pain
For their dear LORD so lately slain,
By rebel servants doomed to die
A death of cruel agony.

2. With gentle voice the Angel gave
The women tidings at the grave;
"Fear not, your Master shall ye see,
He goes before to Galilee."

3. Then, hastening on their eager way
The joyful tidings to convey,
Their LORD they met, their living LORD,
And falling at His Feet adored.

4. Th' Eleven, when they hear, with speed
To Galilee forthwith proceed,
That there once more they may behold
The LORD's dear Face, as He foretold.

## PART III.

1. THAT Easter-tide with joy was bright,
The sun shone out with fairer light,
When, to their longing eyes restored,
The Apostles saw their risen LORD.

2. He bade them see His Hands, His Side,
Where yet the glorious Wounds abide;
O tokens true, which made it plain
Their LORD indeed was risen again.

3. JESU, the King of Gentleness,
Do Thou Thyself our hearts possess,
That we may give Thee all our days
The tribute of our grateful praise.

*The following may be sung at the end of each Part.*

1. O LORD of all, with us abide
In this our joyful Easter-tide;
From every weapon death can wield
Thine own redeemed for ever shield.

2. All praise be Thine, O risen LORD,
From death to endless life restored:
All praise to GOD the FATHER be,
And HOLY GHOST, eternally. Amen.

## 110.

"Worthy is the Lamb that was slain to receive power, and riches, and wisdom, and strength, and honour, and glory, and blessing."

1. CHRIST the LORD is risen to-day;
Christians, haste your vows to pay;
Offer ye your praises meet
At the Paschal Victim's feet.
For the sheep the Lamb hath bled,
Sinless in the sinner's stead;
"CHRIST is risen," to-day we cry;
Now He lives no more to die.

2. CHRIST, the Victim undefiled,
Man to GOD hath reconciled;
Whilst in strange and awful strife
Met together Death and Life.
Christians, on this happy day
Haste with joy your vows to pay;
"CHRIST is risen," to-day we cry;
Now He lives no more to die.

3. CHRIST, Who once for sinners bled,
Now the first-born from the dead,
Throned in endless might and power,
Lives and reigns for evermore.
Hail, eternal Hope on high!
Hail, Thou King of victory!
Hail, Thou Prince of life adored!
Help and save us, gracious LORD. Amen.

## 111.

"CHRIST our Passover is sacrificed for us; therefore let us keep the feast."

1. THE Lamb's high banquet called to share,
Arrayed in garments white and fair,
Our Red Sea past, we fain would sing
To JESUS our triumphant King.

2. Upon the altar of the Cross
His Body hath redeemed our loss;
And, tasting of His crimson Blood,
Our life is hid with Him in GOD.

3. Protected in the Paschal night
From the destroying angel's might,
In triumph went the ransomed free
From Pharaoh's cruel tyranny.

4. Now CHRIST our Passover is slain,
The Lamb of GOD without a stain;
His Flesh, the true unleavened Bread,
Is freely offered in our stead.

5. O all-sufficient Sacrifice!
Beneath Thee hell defeated lies:
Thy captive people are set free,
And crowns of life restored by Thee.

6. We hymn Thee rising from the grave,
From death returning, strong to save;
Thine own Right Hand the tyrant chains,
And Paradise for man regains.

7. All praise be Thine, O risen LORD,
From death to endless life restored:
All praise to GOD the FATHER be,
And HOLY GHOST, eternally. Amen.

## 112.

"Alleluia! for the LORD GOD Omnipotent reigneth."

1. CHRIST the LORD is risen again;
CHRIST hath broken every chain;
Hark! angelic voices cry,
Singing evermore on high,
Alleluia!

2. He Who gave for us His life,
Who for us endured the strife,
Is our Paschal Lamb to-day;
We too sing for joy, and say
Alleluia!

3. He Who bore all pain and loss
Comfortless upon the cross
Lives in glory now on high,
Pleads for us and hears our cry;
Alleluia!

4. He Who slumbered in the grave
Is exalted now to save;
Now through Christendom it rings
That the Lamb is King of kings.
Alleluia!

5. Now He bids us tell abroad
How the lost may be restored,
How the penitent forgiven,
How we too may enter heaven,
Alleluia!

6. Thou, our Paschal Lamb indeed,
CHRIST, Thy ransomed people feed:
Take our sins and guilt away,
Let us sing by night and day
Alleluia! Amen.

# 113.

"Sing ye to the LORD; for He hath triumphed gloriously."

1. AT the Lamb's high feast we sing
Praise to our victorious King,
Who hath washed us in the tide
Flowing from His piercèd Side;
Praise we Him, Whose love divine
Gives His Sacred Blood for wine,
Gives His Body for the feast,
CHRIST the Victim, CHRIST the Priest.

2. Where the Paschal blood is poured,
Death's dark angel sheathes his sword;
Israel's hosts triumphant go
Through the wave that drowns the foe.
Praise we CHRIST, Whose Blood was shed,
Paschal Victim, Paschal Bread;
With sincerity and love
Eat we Manna from above.

3. Mighty Victim from the sky,
Hell's fierce powers beneath Thee lie;
Thou hast conquered in the fight,
Thou hast brought us life and light:
Now no more can death appal,
Now no more the grave enthral;
Thou hast opened paradise,
And in Thee Thy saints shall rise.

4. Easter triumph, Easter joy,
Sin alone can this destroy;
From sin's power do Thou set free
Souls new-born, O LORD, in Thee.
Hymns of glory and of praise,
Risen LORD, to Thee we raise;
Holy FATHER, praise to Thee,
With the SPIRIT, ever be. Amen.

## 114.

"O sing unto the LORD a new song; for He hath done marvellous things."

ALLELUIA! ALLELUIA! ALLELUIA!

1. THE strife is o'er, the battle done;
The triumph of the LORD is won;
O let the song of praise be sung.
Alleluia!

2. The powers of death have done their worst,
And JESUS hath His foes dispersed;
Let shouts of praise and joy outburst.
Alleluia!

3. On that third morn He rose again
In glorious majesty to reign;
O let us swell the joyful strain.
Alleluia!

4. He closed the yawning gates of hell;
The bars from heaven's high portals fell;
Let songs of joy His triumphs tell.
Alleluia!

5. LORD, by the stripes which wounded Thee
From death's dread sting Thy servants free;
That we may live, and sing to Thee
Alleluia! Amen.

## 115.

"Buried with Him in baptism, wherein also ye are risen with Him through the faith of the operation of GOD, Who hath raised Him from the dead."

1. O CHRIST, the heavens' Eternal King,
Creator, unto Thee we sing;
With GOD the FATHER ever One,
Co-equal, co-eternal SON;

2. Thy Hand, when first the world began,
Made in Thine own pure Image man;
And linked to fleshly form of earth
A living soul of heavenly birth.

3. And when the envious, crafty, foe
Had marred Thy noblest work below,
Thou didst our ruined state repair
By deigning flesh Thyself to wear.

4. Once of a Virgin born to save,
And now new-born from death's dark grave,
O CHRIST, Thou bid'st us rise with Thee
From death to immortality.

5. Eternal Shepherd, Thou art wont
To cleanse Thy sheep within the font;
That mystic bath, that grave of sin,
Where ransomed souls new life begin:

6. Divine Redeemer, Thou didst deign
To bear for us the Cross of pain;
And freely pay the precious price
Of all Thy Blood in sacrifice:

7. Jesu, do Thou to every heart
Unceasing Paschal joy impart:
From death of sin and guilty strife
Set free the new-born sons of life.

8. All praise be Thine, O risen Lord,
From death to endless life restored;
All praise to God the Father be,
And Holy Ghost, eternally. Amen.

## 116.

"The First-begotten of the dead."

1. COME see the place where Jesus lay,
And hear angelic watchers say
"He lives, Who once was slain:
Why seek the living 'midst the dead?
Remember how the Saviour said
That He would rise again."

2. O joyful sound! O glorious hour,
When by His own Almighty power
He rose, and left the grave!
Now let our songs His triumph tell,
Who burst the bands of death and hell,
And ever lives to save.

3. The First-begotten of the dead,
For us He rose, our glorious Head,
Immortal life to bring;
What though the saints like Him shall die,
They share their Leader's victory,
And triumph with their King.

4. No more they tremble at the grave,
For Jesus will their spirits save,
And raise their slumbering dust:
O risen Lord, in Thee we live,
To Thee our ransomed souls we give
To Thee our bodies trust. Amen.

# 117.

"I am He that liveth, and was dead; and behold, I am alive for evermore, Amen; and have the keys of hell and of death."

1. JESUS lives! no longer now
Can thy terrors, Death, appal us;
Jesus lives! by this we know
Thou, O Grave, canst not enthral us.
Alleluia!

2. Jesus lives! henceforth is death
But the gate of Life immortal;
This shall calm our trembling breath,
When we pass its gloomy portal.
Alleluia!

3. Jesus lives! for us He died:
   Then, alone to Jesus living,
Pure in heart may we abide,
   Glory to our Saviour giving.
      Alleluia!

4. Jesus lives! our hearts know well
   Naught from us His love shall sever:
Life, nor death, nor powers of hell
   Tear us from His keeping ever.
      Alleluia!

5. Jesus lives! to Him the Throne
   Over all the world is given:
May we go where He is gone,
   Rest and reign with Him in Heaven.
      Alleluia! Amen.

## 118.

### EVENING.

"When thou liest down, thou shalt not be afraid; yea, thou shalt lie down, and thy sleep shall be sweet."

1. JESU, the world's redeeming Lord,
The Father's co-eternal Word,
Of Light invisible true Light,
Thine Israel's keeper day and night;

2. Our great Creator and our Guide,
Who times and seasons dost divide,
Refresh at night with quiet rest
Our limbs by daily toil oppressed.

3. That, while in weary house of clay
A little longer here we stay,
Our flesh in Thee may sweetly sleep,
Our souls with Thee their vigils keep.

4. We pray Thee, while we dwell below,
Preserve us from our ghostly foe;
Nor let his wiles victorious be
O'er them that are redeemed by Thee.

5. O LORD of all, with us abide
In this our joyful Easter-tide;
From every weapon death can wield
Thine own redeemed for ever shield.

6. All praise be Thine, O risen LORD,
From death to endless life restored:
All praise to GOD the FATHER be,
And HOLY GHOST, eternally. Amen.

## 119.

## Rogation Days.

"The eyes of all wait upon Thee, O LORD; and Thou givest them their meat in due season."

1. LORD, in Thy name Thy servants plead,
And Thou hast sworn to hear;
Thine is the harvest, Thine the seed,
The fresh and fading year.

2. Our hope, when autumn winds blew wild,
We trusted, LORD, with Thee:
And still, now spring has on us smiled,
We wait on Thy decree.

3. The ſormer and the latter rain,
   The summer sun and air,
 The green ear, and the golden grain,
   All Thine, are ours by prayer.

4. Thine too by right, and ours by grace,
   The wondrous growth unseen,
 The hopes that soothe, the fears that brace,
   The love that shines serene.

5. So grant the precious things brought forth
   By sun and moon below,
 That Thee in Thy new heaven and earth,
   We never may forego.

6. To Father, Son, and Holy Ghost,
   The God Whom we adore,
 Be glory, as it was, is now,
   And shall be evermore. Amen.

## 120.

"Ask, and it shall be given you."

1. GOD the Father, from Thy throne,
   Hear us, we beseech Thee;
 God the co-eternal Son,
   Hear us, we beseech Thee;
 God, the Spirit, mighty Lord,
   Hear us, we beseech Thee;
 Three in One, by all adored,
   Hear us, we beseech Thee.

2. Jesu! Jesu!
By Thy wondrous Incarnation,
By Thy Birth for our salvation,
We beseech Thee, we beseech Thee,
From every ill defend us,
Thy grace and mercy send us.

3. Jesu! Jesu!
By Thy Fasting and Temptation,
By Thy nights of supplication,
We beseech Thee, we beseech Thee,
From every ill defend us,
Thy grace and mercy send us.

4. Jesu! Jesu!
By Thy works of sweet compassion,
By Thy Cross and bitter Passion,
We beseech Thee, we beseech Thee,
From every ill defend us,
Thy grace and mercy send us.

5. Jesu! Jesu!
By Thy Blood for sinners flowing,
By Thy Death true life bestowing,
We beseech Thee, we beseech Thee,
From every ill defend us,
Thy grace and mercy send us.

6. Jesu! Jesu!
By Thy glorious Resurrection,
Earnest of our own perfection,
We beseech Thee, we beseech Thee,
From every ill defend us,
Thy grace and mercy send us.

7. Jesu ! Jesu !
To the Father's throne ascended,
All Thy pain and sorrows ended,
We beseech Thee, we beseech Thee,
From every ill defend us,
Thy grace and mercy send us.

8. Jesu ! Jesu !
Advocate for sinners pleading,
With the Father interceding,
We beseech Thee, we beseech Thee,
From every ill defend us,
Thy grace and mercy send us. Amen.

*This litany may also be used in any time of special supplication.*

# 121.

## Ascensiontide.

"Lift up your heads, O ye gates, and be ye lift up, ye everlasting doors; and the King of Glory shall come in."

1. HAIL the day that sees Him rise
Alleluia !
To His Throne above the skies;
Alleluia !
Christ, the Lamb for sinners given,
Alleluia !
Enters now the highest heaven.
Alleluia !

2. There for Him high triumph waits;
Alleluia!
Lift your heads, eternal gates;
Alleluia!
He hath conquered death and sin,
Alleluia!
Take the King of Glory in.
Alleluia!

3. Lo, the heaven its LORD receives,
Alleluia!
Yet He loves the earth He leaves;
Alleluia!
Though returning to His throne,
Alleluia!
Still He calls mankind His own.
Alleluia!

4. See, He lifts His Hands above;
Alleluia!
See, He shows the prints of love;
Alleluia!
Hark, His gracious lips bestow
Alleluia!
Blessings on His Church below.
Alleluia!

5. Still for us He intercedes,
Alleluia!
His prevailing death He pleads,
Alleluia!
Near Himself prepares our place,
Alleluia!
He the first-fruits of our race.
Alleluia!

6. Lord, though parted from our sight
Alleluia!
Far above the starry height,
Alleluia!
Grant our hearts may thither rise,
Alleluia!
Seeking Thee above the skies.
Alleluia. Amen.

## 122.

"All power is given unto Me in heaven and in earth."

1. O LORD most High, Eternal King,
By Thee redeemed Thy praise we sing;
The bonds of death are burst by Thee,
And Grace has won the victory.

2. Ascending to the Father's throne
Thou claim'st the kingdom as Thine own;
Thy days of mortal weakness o'er,
All power is Thine for evermore.

3. To Thee the whole creation now
Shall, in its threefold order, bow,
Of things on earth, and things on high,
And things that underneath us lie.

4. In awe and wonder angels see
How changed is man's estate by Thee,
How Flesh makes pure as flesh did stain,
And Thou, true God, in Flesh dost reign.

5. Be Thou our Joy, O mighty Lord,
As Thou wilt be our great Reward;
Let all our glory be in Thee
Both now and through eternity.

6. All praise from every heart and tongue
To Thee, ascended Lord, be sung;
All praise to God the Father be,
And Holy Ghost, eternally. Amen.

## 123.

"By His own Blood He entered in once into the holy place."

1. O SAVIOUR, Who for man hast trod
The winepress of the wrath of God,
Ascend, and claim again on high
Thy glory left for us to die.

2. A radiant cloud is now Thy seat,
And earth lies stretched beneath Thy feet;
Ten thousand thousands round Thee sing,
And share the triumph of their King.

3. The angel-host enraptured waits:
"Lift up your heads, eternal gates!"
O God-and-Man! the Father's Throne
Is now for evermore Thine own.

4. Our great High Priest and Shepherd Thou
Within the veil art entered now,
To offer there Thy precious Blood
Once poured on earth a cleansing flood.

5. And thence the Church, Thy chosen Bride,
With countless gifts of grace supplied,
Through all her members draws from Thee
Her hidden life of sanctity.

6. O CHRIST, our LORD, of Thy dear care,
Thy lowly members heaven-ward bear;
Be ours with Thee to suffer pain,
With Thee for evermore to reign.

7. All praise from every heart and tongue
To Thee, ascended LORD, be sung;
All praise to GOD the FATHER be
And HOLY GHOST eternally. Amen.

## 124.

"Who is gone into heaven."

1. THOU art gone up on high,
To realms beyond the skies;
And round Thy throne unceasingly
The songs of praise arise:
But we are lingering here,
With sin and care oppressed;
LORD, send Thy promised Comforter,
And lead us to our rest.

2. Thou art gone up on high;
But Thou didst first come down,
Through earth's most bitter misery
To pass unto Thy crown;
And girt with griefs and fears
Our onward course must be,
But only let this path of tears
Lead us at last to Thee.

3. Thou art gone up on high;
But Thou shalt come again,
With all the bright ones of the sky
Attendant in Thy train.
Lord, by Thy saving power,
So make us live and die,
That we may stand in that dread hour
At Thy right hand on high. Amen.

## 125.

"Who being the brightness of His glory, and the express Image of His person, and upholding all things by the word of His power, when He had by Himself purged our sins, sat down on the right hand of the Majesty on high."

1. JESU, our hope, our heart's desire,
Redemption's only spring,
Creator of the world art Thou,
Its Saviour and its King.

2. How vast the mercy and the love,
Which laid our sins on Thee,
And led Thee to a cruel death,
To set Thy people free;

3. But now the bonds of death are burst,
The ransom has been paid;
And Thou art on Thy Father's Throne
In glorious robes arrayed.

4. O may Thy mighty love prevail
Our sinful souls to spare;
O may we stand around Thy throne,
And see Thy glory there!

5. Jesu, our only Joy be Thou,
As Thou our Prize wilt be;
In Thee be all our glory now
And through eternity.

6. All praise to Thee Who dost ascend
Triumphantly to heaven;
All praise to God the Father's Name
And Holy Ghost be given. Amen.

## 126.

### Whitsun-Even.

"If I go not away the Comforter will not come unto you; but if I depart I will send Him unto you."

1. RULER of the hosts of light,
Death hath yielded to Thy might;
And Thy Blood hath marked a road
Which will lead us back to God.

2. From Thy dwelling place above,
From Thy Father's Throne of love,
With Thy look of mercy bless
Those without Thee comfortless.

3. Bitter were Thy throes on earth,
Giving to the Church her birth
From the spear-wound opening wide
In Thine own life-giving Side.

4. Now in glory Thou dost reign,
Won by all Thy toil and pain;
Thence the promised Spirit send,
While our prayers to Thee ascend.

5. Jesu, praise to Thee be given,
With the Father high in heaven;
Holy Spirit, praise to Thee
Now and through eternity. Amen.

## 127.

### Whitsuntide.

"The Comforter, Which is the Holy Ghost."

1. COME, Holy Ghost, our souls inspire,
And lighten with celestial fire;
Thou the anointing Spirit art,
Who dost Thy seven-fold gifts impart:
Thy blessèd unction from above
Is comfort, life, and fire of love;
Enable with perpetual light
The dulness of our blinded sight:
Anoint and cheer our soilèd face
With the abundance of Thy grace:
Keep far our foes, give peace at home;
Where Thou art guide no ill can come.
Teach us to know the Father, Son,
And Thee, of Both, to be but One;
That, through the ages all along,
This may be our endless song:
Praise to Thy eternal merit,
Father, Son, and Holy Spirit. Amen.

## 128.

"When Thou lettest thy Breath go forth they shall be made, and Thou shalt renew the face of the earth."

1. COME, Thou HOLY SPIRIT, come;
And from Thine eternal home
  Shed the ray of light divine;
Come, Thou FATHER of the poor,
Come, Thou source of all our store,
  Come, within our bosoms shine.

2. Thou of Comforters the best,
Thou the soul's most welcome Guest,
  Sweet Refreshment here below!
In our labour rest most sweet,
Grateful shadow from the heat,
  Solace in the midst of woe!

3. O most Blessèd Light Divine,
Shine within these hearts of Thine,
  And our inmost being fill:
If Thou take Thy grace away,
Nothing pure in man will stay,
  All our good is turned to ill.

4. Heal our wounds; our strength renew;
On our dryness pour Thy dew;
  Wash the stains of guilt away:
Bend the stubborn heart and will,
Melt the frozen, warm the chill,
  Guide the steps that go astray.

5. On the faithful, who adore
And confess Thee, evermore
In Thy sevenfold gifts descend;
Give them virtue's sure reward,
Give them Thy salvation, LORD,
Give them joys that never end. Amen.

## 129.

"And when the day of Pentecost was fully come, they were all with one accord in one place."

1. ABOVE the starry spheres,
To where He was before,
CHRIST had gone up, the FATHER'S gift
Upon the Church to pour.

2. At length had fully come,
On mystic circle borne
Of seven times seven revolving days,
The Pentecostal morn:

3. When, as the Apostles knelt
At the third hour in prayer,
A sudden rushing sound proclaimed
That GOD Himself was there.

4. Forthwith a tongue of fire
Is seen on every brow;
Each heart receives the FATHER'S light,
The WORD'S enkindling glow;

5. The HOLY GHOST on all
Is mightily outpoured,
Who straight in divers tongues declare
The wonders of the LORD.

6. While strangers of all climes
   Flock round from far and near,
And their own tongue, wherever born,
   All with amazement hear.

7. But Judah, faithless still,
   Denies the Hand Divine;
And, mocking, jeers the saints of CHRIST
   As full of new-made wine.

8. Till Peter, in the midst,
   By Joel's ancient word
Rebukes their unbelief, and wins
   Three thousand to the LORD.

9. The FATHER and the SON
   And SPIRIT we adore;
O may the SPIRIT's gifts be poured
   On us for evermore. Amen.

## 130.

"And suddenly there came a sound from heaven, as of a rushing mighty wind."

1. WHEN GOD of old came down from heaven,
   In power and wrath He came;
Before His feet the clouds were riven,
   Half darkness and half flame:

2. But, when He came the second time,
   He came in power and love;
Softer than gale at morning prime
   Hovered His holy dove.

3. The fires, that rushed on Sinai down
In sudden torrents dread,
Now gently light, a glorious crown,
On every sainted head.

4. And as on Israel's awe-struck ear
The voice exceeding loud,
The trump, that angels quake to hear,
Thrilled from the deep, dark cloud;

5. So, when the SPIRIT of our GOD
Came down His flock to find,
A voice from heaven was heard abroad,
A rushing, mighty wind.

6. It fills the Church of God; It fills
The sinful world around;
Only in stubborn hearts and wills
No place for It is found.

7. Come LORD, come Wisdom, Love, and Power,
Open our ears to hear;
Let us not miss th' accepted hour;
Save, LORD, by love or fear. Amen.

## 131.

"And the same day there were added unto them about three thousand souls."

1. SPIRIT of mercy, truth, and love,
O shed Thine influence from above;
And still from age to age convey
The wonders of this sacred day.

2. In every clime, by every tongue,
Be God's surpassing glory sung:
Let all the listening earth be taught
The wonders by our Saviour wrought.

3. Unfailing Comfort, Heavenly Guide,
Still o'er Thy Holy Church preside;
Still let mankind Thy blessings prove;
Spirit of mercy, truth, and love.

4. O Holy Father, Holy Son,
And Holy Spirit, Three in One;
Thy grace devoutly we implore,
Thy Name be praised for evermore. Amen.

## 132.

### Trinity Sunday.

"And one cried unto another, and said, Holy, Holy, Holy, is the Lord of Hosts."

1. ALL hail, Adorèd Trinity;
All hail, Eternal Unity;
O God the Father, God the Son,
And God the Spirit, ever One.

2. Behold to Thee, this festal day,
We meekly pour our thankful lay;
O let our work accepted be,
That sweetest work of praising Thee.

4. Three Persons praise we evermore,
One only God our hearts adore;
In Thy sure mercy ever kind
May we our true protection find.

O TRINITY! O UNITY!
Be present as we worship Thee;
And with the songs that Angels sing
Unite the hymns of praise we bring. Amen.

## 133.

"From everlasting to everlasting Thou art GOD."

1. BLEST TRINITY, from mortal sight
Veiled in Thine own eternal Light,
We Thee confess, in Thee believe,
To Thee with loving hearts we cleave.

2. O FATHER, Thou most Holy One!
O GOD of GOD, Eternal SON!
O HOLY GHOST, Thou Love Divine!
To join them Both is ever Thine.

3. The FATHER is in GOD the SON,
And with the FATHER He is One:
In Both the SPIRIT doth abide,
And with them Both is glorified.

4. Such as the FATHER, such the SON,
And such the SPIRIT, THREE IN ONE:
The Three one perfect Verity,
The Three one perfect Charity.

5. Eternal FATHER, Thee we praise;
To Thee, O SON, our hymns we raise;
O HOLY GHOST, we Thee adore;
One mighty GOD for evermore. Amen.

## 134.

"O praise God in His holiness."

1. O GOD of life, Whose power benign
Doth o'er the world in mercy shine,
Accept our praise, for we are Thine.

2. O Father, all-creating Lord,
Be Thou by every tongue implored,
Be Thou by every heart adored.

3. O Son of God, for sinners slain,
We bless Thee, Lord, Whose dying pain
For us did endless life regain.

4. O Holy Ghost, Whose guardian care
Doth us for heavenly joys prepare,
May we in Thy communion share.

5. O Holy Blessèd Trinity,
With faith we sinners bow to Thee;
In heaven and earth exalted be. Amen.

## 135.

"They rest not day and night, saying, Holy, Holy, Holy, Lord God Almighty, Which was, and is, and is to come."

1. HOLY, Holy, Holy! Lord God Almighty!
Early in the morning our song shall rise to Thee:
Holy, Holy, Holy, merciful and mighty
God in Three Persons, Blessèd Trinity!

2. Holy, Holy, Holy! all the saints adore Thee,
Casting down their golden crowns around the glassy sea;
Cherubim and Seraphim falling down before Thee,
Which wert, and art, and evermore shalt be.

3. Holy, Holy, Holy! though the darkness hide Thee,
Though the eye of sinful man Thy glory may not see,
Only Thou art Holy: There is none beside Thee
Perfect in power, in love, and purity.

4. Holy, Holy, Holy! LORD GOD ALMIGHTY:
All Thy works shall praise Thy Name, in earth, and sky, and sea:
Holy, Holy, Holy! merciful and mighty;
GOD in THREE PERSONS, Blessèd Trinity!
Amen.

# 136.

## General Hymns.

"O be joyful in the LORD, all ye lands."

1. ALL people that on earth do dwell,
Sing to the LORD with cheerful voice;
Him serve with fear, His praise forth tell,
Come ye before Him and rejoice.

2. The LORD, ye know, is GOD indeed;
Without our aid He did us make:
We are His flock, He doth us feed,
And for His sheep He doth us take.

3. O enter then His gates with praise,
Approach with joy His courts unto;
Praise, laud, and bless His Name always,
For it is seemly so to do.

4. For why? the LORD our GOD is good,
His mercy is for ever sure;
His truth at all times firmly stood,
And shall from age to age endure.

5. To FATHER, SON, and HOLY GHOST,
The GOD Whom heaven and earth adore,
From men and from the angel-host
Be praise and glory evermore. Amen.

## 137.

"Sing unto the LORD, and praise His Name."

1. THREE IN ONE, and ONE IN THREE,
Ruler of the earth and sea,
Hear us, while we lift to Thee
Holy chant and psalm.

2. Light of lights! with morning, shine:
Lift on us Thy Light divine;
And let charity benign
Breathe on us her balm.

3. Light of lights! when falls the even,
Let it close on sin forgiven;
Fold us in the peace of heaven,
Shed a holy calm.

4. THREE IN ONE and ONE IN THREE,
Dimly here we worship Thee;
With the saints hereafter we
Hope to bear the palm. Amen.

## 138.

"Let us therefore come boldly unto the throne of grace, that we may obtain mercy, and find grace to help in time of need."

1 FATHER of heaven, Whose love profound
A ransom for our souls hath found,
Before Thy Throne we sinners bend,
To us Thy pardoning love extend.

2. Almighty SON, Incarnate WORD,
Our PROPHET, PRIEST, REDEEMER, LORD,
Before Thy Throne we sinners bend,
To us Thy saving grace extend.

3. Eternal SPIRIT, by Whose breath
The soul is raised from sin and death,
Before Thy Throne we sinners bend,
To us Thy quickening power extend.

4. Thrice Holy! FATHER, SPIRIT, SON;
Mysterious GODHEAD, THREE in ONE;
Before Thy Throne we sinners bend,
Grace, pardon, life, to all extend. Amen.

## 139.

"If I go not away the Comforter will not come unto you; but if I depart I will send Him unto you."

1. OUR blest Redeemer, ere He breathed
His tender last farewell,
A Guide, a Comforter, bequeathed
With us to dwell.

2. He came sweet influence to impart,
A gracious willing Guest,
While He can find one humble heart
Wherein to rest.

3. And His that gentle voice we hear,
Soft as the breath of even,
That checks each thought, that calms each fear,
And speaks of heaven.

4. And every virtue we possess,
And every conquest won,
And every thought of holiness
Are His alone.

5. SPIRIT of purity and grace,
Our weakness, pitying, see:
O make our hearts Thy dwelling-place,
And worthier Thee.

6. O praise the FATHER; praise the SON;
Blest SPIRIT, praise to Thee;
All praise to GOD, the THREE IN ONE,
The ONE IN THREE. Amen.

## 140.

"LORD, remember me."

1. O THOU, from Whom all goodness flows,
I lift my soul to Thee;
In all my sorrows, conflicts, woes,
Good LORD, remember me.

2. If on my aching burdened heart
My sins lie heavily,
Thy pardon grant, Thy peace impart:
Good LORD, remember me.

3. If trials sore obstruct my way,
And ills I cannot flee,
Then let my strength be as my day:
Good LORD, remember me.

4. If worn with pain, disease, and grief,
This feeble frame should be,
Grant patience, rest, and kind relief:
Good LORD, remember me.

5. And oh, when in the hour of death
I bow to Thy decree,
JESU, receive my parting breath:
Good LORD, remember me. Amen.

## 141.

"Blessed are the pure in heart, for they shall see GOD."

1. BLEST are the pure in heart
For they shall see our GOD;
The secret of the LORD is theirs;
Their soul is CHRIST'S abode.

2. The LORD, Who left the heavens
Our life and peace to bring,
To dwell in lowliness with men,
Their Pattern and their King;

3. He to the lowly soul
Doth still Himself impart;
And for His dwelling and His throne
Chooseth the pure in heart.

4. LORD, we Thy presence seek;
May ours this blessing be;
Give us a pure and lowly heart,
A temple meet for Thee.

5. All glory, LORD, to Thee,
Whom heaven and earth adore;
To FATHER, SON, and HOLY GHOST,
One GOD for evermore. Amen.

## 142.

**"Here have we no continuing city, but we seek one to come."**

1. BRIEF life is here our portion;
Brief sorrow, short-lived care;
The life that knows no ending,
The tearless life, is *there*.

2. O happy retribution!
Short toil, eternal rest:
For mortals and for sinners
A mansion with the blest.

3. And now we fight the battle,
 But then shall wear the crown
Of full and everlasting
 And passionless renown;

4. And now we watch and struggle,
 And now we live in hope,
And Sion in her anguish
 With Babylon must cope;

5. But He Whom now we trust in
 Shall then be seen and known;
And they that know and see Him
 Shall have Him for their own.

6. The morning shall awaken,
 The shadows shall decay,
And each true-hearted servant
 Shall shine as doth the day;

7. There God, our King and Portion,
 In fulness of His Grace,
Shall we behold for ever,
 And worship face to face.

## PART II.

1. FOR thee, O dear, dear Country,
 Mine eyes their vigils keep;
For very love, beholding
 Thy happy name, they weep.

2. The mention of thy glory
 Is unction to the breast,
And medicine in sickness,
 And love, and life, and rest.

3. O one, O only Mansion!
 O Paradise of Joy!
Where tears are ever banished,
 And smiles have no alloy;

4. The Lamb is all thy splendour;
 The Crucified thy praise;
His laud and benediction
 Thy ransomed people raise.

5. With jasper glow thy bulwarks,
 Thy streets with emeralds blaze,
The sardius and the topaz
 Unite in thee their rays;

6. Thine ageless walls are bonded
 With amethyst unpriced;
The saints build up its fabric,
 And the corner-stone is CHRIST.

7. Thou hast no shore, fair ocean!
 Thou hast no time, bright day!
Dear fountain of refreshment
 To pilgrims far away!

8. Upon the Rock of Ages
 They raise thy holy tower;
Thine is the victor's laurel,
 And thine the golden dower.

## PART III.

1. JERUSALEM the golden!
   With milk and honey blest;
Beneath thy contemplation
   Sink heart and voice opprest.

2. I know not, oh! I know not
   What joys await us there;
What radiancy of glory,
   What bliss beyond compare.

3. They stand, those halls of Sion,
   All jubilant with song,
And bright with many an angel,
   And all the martyr throng:

4. The Prince is ever in them,
   The daylight is serene;
The pastures of the blessèd
   Are decked in glorious sheen.

5. There is the throne of David;
   And there, from care released,
The shout of them that triumph,
   The song of them that feast;

6. And they, who with their Leader
   Have conquered in the fight,
For ever and for ever
   Are clad in robes of white.

*The following may be sung at the end of each Part:*

1. O SWEET and blessèd country,
   The Home of GOD's elect!
O sweet and blessèd country
   That eager hearts expect!

2. JESU, in mercy bring us
   To that dear land of rest;
Who art, with GOD the FATHER,
   And SPIRIT, ever blest. Amen.

## 143.

"The love of CHRIST which passeth knowledge."

1. O LOVE, how deep! how broad! how high!
   It fills the heart with ecstacy,
That GOD, the SON of GOD, should take
Our mortal form for mortals' sake.

2. He sent no angel to our race,
Of higher or of lower place,
But wore the robe of human frame
Himself, and to this lost world came.

3. Nor willed He only to appear;
His pleasure was to tarry here;
And GOD-and-Man with man would be
The space of thirty years and three.

4. For us He was baptized, and bore
His holy fast, and hungered sore;
For us temptation sharp He knew;
For us the tempter overthrew.

5. For us He prayed, for us He taught,
For us His daily works He wrought,
By words, and signs, and actions, thus
Still seeking not Himself, but us.

6. For us to wicked men betrayed,
Scourged, mocked, in purple robe arrayed,
He bore the shameful Cross and death;
For us at length gave up His breath.

7. For us He rose from death again,
For us He went on high to reign,
For us He sent His SPIRIT here
To guide, to strengthen, and to cheer.

8. To Him Whose boundless love has won
Salvation for us through His SON,
To GOD the FATHER, glory be,
Both now and through eternity. Amen.

## 144.

"I reckon that the sufferings of this present time are not worthy to be compared with the glory which shall be revealed in us."

1. O WHAT, if we are CHRIST'S,
Is earthly shame or loss?
Bright shall the crown of glory be
When we have borne the Cross.

2. Keen was the trial once,
Bitter the cup of woe,
When martyred saints, baptized in blood,
CHRIST'S sufferings shared below:

3. Bright is their glory now,
Boundless their joy above,
Where on the bosom of their God
They rest in perfect love.

4. Lord, may that grace be ours,
Like them in faith to bear
All that of sorrow, grief, or pain
May be our portion here:

5. Enough if Thou at last
The word of blessing give,
And let us rest beneath Thy feet,
Where saints and angels live.

6. All glory, Lord, to Thee,
Whom heaven and earth adore;
To Father, Son, and Holy Ghost,
One God for evermore. Amen.

## 145.

"All Thy works praise Thee, O Lord."

1. THE strain upraise of joy and praise,
Alleluia!

2. To the glory of their King
Shall the ransomed people sing
Alleluia!

3. And the choirs that dwell on high
Shall re-echo through the sky
Alleluia!

4. They in the rest of Paradise who dwell,
The blessèd ones, with joy the chorus swell,
Alleluia!

5. The planets beaming on their heavenly way,
The shining constellations join, and say
Alleluia!

6. Ye clouds that onward sweep,
Ye winds on pinions light,
Ye thunders, echoing loud and deep,
Ye lightnings, wildly bright,
In sweet consent unite your Alleluia!

7. Ye floods and ocean billows,
Ye storms and winter snow,
Ye days of cloudless beauty,
Hoar frost and summer glow,
Ye groves that wave in spring
And glorious forests, sing Alleluia!

8. First let the birds, with painted plumage gay,
Exalt their great CREATOR's praise, and say
Alleluia!

9. Then let the beasts of earth, with varying strain,
Join in creation's hymn, and cry again
Alleluia!

10. Here let the mountains thunder forth sonorous
Alleluia!

There let the valleys sing in gentler chorus
Alleluia!

11. Thou jubilant abyss of ocean, cry Alleluia
Ye tracts of earth and continents, reply
Alleluia!

12. To GOD, Who all creation made,
The frequent hymn be duly paid: Alleluia!

13. This is the strain, the eternal strain, the LORD
Almighty loves: Alleluia!
This is the song, the heavenly song, that CHRIST
the King approves: Alleluia!

14. Wherefore we sing, both heart and voice awak-
ing, Alleluia!
And children's voices echo, answer making,
Alleluia!

15. Now from all men be out-poured
Alleluia to the LORD;
With Alleluia evermore
The SON and SPIRIT we adore.

16. Praise be done to the THREE IN ONE.
Alleluia! Alleluia! Alleluia! Amen.

## 146.

"Thou shalt call His name JESUS, for He shall save His people from their sins."

1. CONQUERING kings their titles take
From the foes they captive make;
JESUS, by a nobler deed,
From the thousands He hath freed.

2. Yes; none other name is given
Unto mortals under heaven,
Which can make the dead arise,
And exalt them to the skies.

3. That which CHRIST so hardly wrought,
That which He so dearly bought,
That salvation, mortals, say,
Will ye madly cast away?

4. Rather gladly for that Name
Bear the Cross, endure the shame;
Joyfully for Him to die
Is not death, but victory.

5. JESU, Who dost condescend
To be called the sinner's Friend,
Hear us as to Thee we pray,
Glorying in Thy Name to-day.

6. Glory to the FATHER be,
Glory, HOLY SON, to Thee,
Glory to the HOLY GHOST,
From the saints and angel-host. Amen.

## 147.

"I have loved thee with an everlasting love; therefore with loving-kindness have I drawn thee."

1. JESU, Thy mercies are untold
Through each returning day;
Thy love exceeds a thousandfold
Whatever we can say:

2. That love which in Thy Passion drained
For us Thy precious Blood:
That love whereby the saints have gained
The vision of their God.

3. 'Tis Thou hast loved us from the womb,
Pure source of all our bliss,
Our only hope of life to come,
Our happiness in this.

4. Lord, grant us while on earth we stay
Thy love to feel and know;
And when from hence we pass away
To us Thy glory show. Amen.

## 148.

"The communion of the Holy Ghost."

1. O HOLY SPIRIT, Lord of grace
Eternal fount of love,
Inflame, we pray, our inmost hearts
With fire from heaven above.

2. As Thou in bond of love doth join
The Father and the Son,
So fill us all with mutual love,
And knit our hearts in one.

3. All glory to the Father be,
All glory to the Son,
All glory to the Holy Ghost,
While endless ages run. Amen.

## 149.

"Thus saith the high and lofty One that inhabiteth eternity, whose name is Holy: I dwell in the high and holy place, with him also that is of a contrite and humble spirit."

1. MY GOD, how wonderful Thou art,
 Thy majesty how bright,
How beautiful Thy mercy-seat,
 In depths of burning light.

2. How dread are Thine eternal years,
 O everlasting LORD;
By prostrate spirits day and night
 Incessantly adored.

3. How wonderful, how beautiful,
 The sight of Thee must be,
Thine endless wisdom, boundless power,
 And awful purity.

4. O how I fear Thee, Living GOD,
 With deepest, tenderest fears,
And worship Thee with trembling hope,
 And penitential tears.

5. Yet I may love Thee too, O LORD,
 Almighty as Thou art,
For Thou hast stooped to ask of me
 The love of my poor heart.

6. No earthly father loves like Thee,
 No mother, e'er so mild,
Bears and forbears as Thou hast done
 With me Thy sinful child.

7. FATHER of JESUS, love's reward,
   What rapture will it be,
 Prostrate before Thy throne to lie,
   And ever gaze on Thee! Amen.

## 150.

"That rock was CHRIST."

1. ROCK of ages, cleft for me,
 Let me hide myself in Thee;
 Let the Water and the Blood,
 From Thy wounded Side which flowed,
 Be of sin the double cure,
 Save from wrath and make me pure.

2. Nothing in my hand I bring,
 Simply to Thy Cross I cling:
 Could my tears for ever flow,
 Could my zeal no languor know,
 All for sin could not atone,
 Thou must save and Thou alone.

3. While I draw this fleeting breath,
 When mine eyelids close in death,
 When I rise to worlds unknown,
 See Thee on Thy judgment throne,
 Rock of ages, cleft for me,
 Let me hide myself in Thee. Amen.

# 151.

"He ever liveth to make intercession for us."

1. WHERE high the heavenly temple stands,
The house of God not made with hands,
A great High Priest our nature wears,
The Guardian of mankind appears.

2. He, Who for men their surety stood,
And poured on earth His precious Blood,
Pursues in heaven His mighty plan,
The Saviour and the Friend of man.

2. Jesus, Who suffered here below,
Feels sympathy with human woe,
And still remembers, in the skies,
His tears, His prayers, His agonies.

3. In every pang that rends the heart
The Man of sorrows had a part;
Touched with the feeling of our grief,
He to the sufferer sends relief.

4. With boldness, therefore, at the Throne
Let us make all our sorrows known,
And ask the aid of heavenly power
To help us in the evil hour.

5. All praise to God the Father be,
All praise, Eternal Son, to Thee,
Whom, with the Spirit, we adore
For ever and for evermore. Amen.

## 152.

"I, if I be lifted up from the earth, will draw all men unto Me."

1\. JESU, meek and lowly,
SAVIOUR, pure and holy,
On Thy love relying,
Hear me humble crying.

2\. Prince of life and power,
My salvation's Tower,
On the Cross I view Thee
Calling sinners to Thee.

3\. There behold me gazing
At the sight amazing:
Bending low before Thee,
Helpless I adore Thee.

4\. By Thy red wounds streaming,
With Thy life-blood gleaming,
Blood for sinners flowing,
Pardon free bestowing;

5\. By that fount of blessing
Thy dear love expressing,
All my aching sadness
Turn Thou into gladness.

6\. LORD in mercy guide me,
Be Thou e'er beside me;
In Thy ways direct me,
'Neath Thy wings protect me.

Amen.

## 153.

"I will alway give thanks unto the Lord: His praise shall ever be in my mouth."

1. THROUGH all the changing scenes of life,
In trouble and in joy,
The praises of my God shall still
My heart and tongue employ.

2. O magnify the Lord with me,
With me exalt His Name;
When in distress to Him I called,
He to my rescue came.

3. The hosts of God encamp around
The dwellings of the just;
Deliverance He affords to all
Who on His succour trust.

4. O make but trial of His love,
Experience will decide,
How blessed are they, and only they,
Who in His truth confide.

5. Fear Him, ye saints, and ye will then
Have nothing else to fear;
Make you His service your delight,
Your wants shall be His care.

6. To Father, Son, and Holy Ghost,
The God Whom we adore,
Be glory, as it was, is now,
And shall be evermore. Amen.

## 154.

"From everlasting to everlasting Thou art God!"

1. HAVE mercy on us, God most High,
Who lift our hearts to Thee,
Have mercy on us worms of earth,
Most Holy Trinity.

2. Most ancient of all mysteries!
Before Thy Throne we lie;
Have mercy now, most merciful,
Most Holy Trinity.

3. When heaven and earth were yet unmade,
When time was yet unknown,
Thou, in Thy bliss of majesty,
Didst live and love alone.

4. How wonderful creation is,
The work that Thou didst bless;
And oh, what then must Thou be like,
Eternal Loveliness!

5. Most ancient of all mysteries!
Low at Thy Throne we lie;
Have mercy now, most merciful,
Most Holy Trinity. Amen.

## 155.

And He shewed me a pure river of water of Life, clear as crystal, proceeding out of the throne of God and of the Lamb."

1. A LIVING stream, as crystal clear,.
Welling from out the Throne
Of God and of the Lamb on high,
The Lord to man hath shewn.

2. This stream doth water paradise,
   It makes the angels sing:
   One precious drop within the heart
   Is of all joy the spring:

3. Joy past all speech, of glory full,
   But stored where none may know,
   As manna hid in dewy heaven,
   As pearls in ocean low.

4. Eye hath not seen, nor ear hath heard,
   Nor to man's heart hath come
   What for those, loving Thee in truth
   Thou hast in love's own home.

5. But by His Spirit He to us
   The secret doth reveal;
   Faith sees and hears: but O for wings
   To touch, and taste, and feel:

6. Wings like a dove, to waft us on
   High o'er the flood of sin!
   Lord of the Ark, put forth Thine hand
   And take Thy wanderers in.

7. O praise the Father; praise the Son,
   The Lamb for sinners given;
   And Holy Ghost, through Whom alone
   Our hearts are raised to heaven. Amen.

## 156.

"Praise the Lord, O my soul: O Lord my God, Thou art become exceeding glorious; Thou art clothed with majesty and honour."

1. O WORSHIP the King
   All glorious above;
O gratefully sing
   His power and His love;
Our Shield and Defender,
   The Ancient of days,
Pavilioned in splendour,
   And girded with praise.

2. O tell of His might,
   O sing of His grace,
Whose robe is the light,
   Whose canopy space;
His chariots of wrath
   The thunder clouds form,
And dark is His path
   On the wings of the storm.

3. Frail children of dust,
   And feeble as frail,
In Thee do we trust,
   Nor find Thee to fail.
Thy mercies how tender!
   How firm to the end!
Our Maker, Defender,
   Redeemer, and Friend.

4. O measureless Might,
   Ineffable Love:
While angels delight
   To hymn Thee above,
Thy ransomed creation,
   Though feeble their lays,
With true adoration
   Shall sing to Thy praise. Amen.

## 157.

"Thy Name is as ointment poured forth."

1. JESU, the very thought of Thee
   With sweetness fills the breast;
But sweeter far Thy Face to see,
   And in Thy presence rest.

2. No voice can sing, no heart can frame,
   Nor can the memory find
A sweeter sound than JESU's Name,
   The SAVIOUR of mankind.

3. O Hope of every contrite heart,
   O Joy of all the meek,
To those who fall how kind Thou art,
   How good to those who seek!

4. But what to those who find? Ah! this
   Nor tongue nor pen can show;
The love of JESUS, what it is
   None but His loved ones know.

5. Jesu, our only Joy be Thou,
 As Thou our Prize wilt be;
In Thee be all our glory now,
 And through eternity.

## PART II.

1. O JESU, King most wonderful,
 Thou Conqueror renowned,
Thou Sweetness most ineffable,
 In Whom all joys are found!

2. When once Thou visitest the heart,
 Then truth begins to shine,
Then earthly vanities depart,
 Then kindles love divine.

3. O Jesu, Light of all below,
 Thou Fount of living fire,
Surpassing all the joys we know,
 And all we can desire;

4. Jesu, may all confess Thy Name,
 Thy wondrous love adore;
And, seeking Thee, themselves inflame
 To seek Thee more and more.

5. Thee, Jesu, may our voices bless;
 Thee may we love alone;
And ever in our lives express
 The image of Thine Own.

## PART III.

1. O JESU, Thou the Beauty art
   Of angel-worlds above;
Thy Name is music to the heart,
   Inflaming it with love.

2. Celestial sweetness unalloyed!
   Who eat Thee, hunger still;
Who drink of Thee still feel a void,
   Which naught but Thou can fill.

3. O most sweet Jesu, hear the sighs
   Which unto Thee we send;
To Thee our inmost spirit cries,
   To Thee our prayers ascend.

4. Abide with us, and let Thy Light
   Shine, Lord, on every heart;
Dispel the darkness of our night,
   And joy to all impart.

5. Jesu, our Love and Joy, to Thee,
   The virgin's Holy Son,
All might and praise and glory be
   While endless ages run. Amen.

## 158.

"Come unto Me, all ye that labour and are heavy laden, and I will give you rest."

1. ALL ye who seek for sure relief
   In trouble and distress,
Whatever sorrow vex the mind,
   Or guilt the soul oppress:

2. Jesus, Who gave Himself for you,
Upon the Cross to die,
Opens to you His sacred Heart:
Oh, to that Heart draw nigh.

3. Ye hear how kindly He invites;
Ye hear His words so blest;
"All ye that labour, come to Me,
And I will give you rest."

4. O Jesus, Joy of saints on high,
Thou Hope of sinners here,
Attracted by those loving words
To Thee I lift my prayer.

5. Wash Thou my wounds in that dear Blood
Which forth from Thee doth flow;
New grace, new hope inspire; a new
And better heart bestow. Amen.

## 159.

"I go to prepare a place for you."

1. O CHRIST, Who dost prepare a place
For us around Thy throne of grace,
We pray Thee, lift our hearts above,
And draw them with the cords of love.

2. Source of all good, Thou, gracious Lord,
Art our exceeding great reward;
How transient is our present pain!
How boundless our eternal gain!

3. With open face and joyful heart
We then shall see Thee as Thou art;
Our love shall never cease to glow,
Our praise shall never cease to flow.

4. Thy never-failing grace to prove,
A surety of Thine endless love,
Send down Thy Holy Ghost, to be
The raiser of our souls to Thee.

5. O future Judge, Eternal Lord,
Thy name be hallowed and adored;
Whom with the Father we adore
And Holy Ghost for evermore. Amen.

## 160.

"When I laid the foundations of the earth.....when the morning stars sang together, and all the sons of God shouted for joy."

1. SONGS of praise the angels sang,
Heaven with Alleluias rang,
When creation was begun,
When God spake and it was done.

2. Songs of praise awoke the morn
When the Prince of Peace was born;
Songs of praise arose when He
Captive led captivity.

3. Heaven and earth must pass away,
Songs of praise shall crown that day;
God will make new heaven and earth,
Songs of praise shall hail their birth.

4. And will man alone be dumb
Till that glorious kingdom come?
No, the Church delights to raise
Psalms and hymns and songs of praise.

5. Saints below, with heart and voice,
Still in songs of praise rejoice:
Learning here, by faith and love,
Songs of praise to sing above.

6. Hymns of glory, songs of praise,
FATHER, unto Thee we raise,
JESU, glory unto Thee,
With the SPIRIT, ever be. Amen.

## 161.

"O how amiable are Thy dwellings: Thou LORD of Hosts."

1. O GOD of Hosts, the mighty LORD,
How lovely is the place,
Where Thou, enthroned in glory, shew'st
The brightness of Thy face.

2. My longing soul faints with desire
To view Thy blest abode;
My panting heart and flesh cry out
For Thee the living GOD.

3. For in Thy Courts one single day
'Tis better to attend,
Than, LORD, in any place besides
A thousand days to spend.

4. O Lord of Hosts, my King and God,
How highly blest are they,
Who in Thy temple always dwell,
And there Thy praise display!

5. To Father, Son, and Holy Ghost,
The God Whom we adore,
Be glory, as it was, is now,
And shall be evermore. Amen.

## 162.

"Jesus saith unto him, I am the Way, the Truth, and the Life."

1. THOU art the Way; by Thee alone
From sin and death we flee;
And he who would the Father seek
Must seek Him, Lord, by Thee.

2. Thou art the Truth; Thy word alone
True wisdom can impart;
Thou only canst inform the mind,
And purify the heart.

3. Thou art the Life; the rending tomb
Proclaims Thy conquering arm;
And those who put their trust in Thee
Nor death nor hell shall harm.

4. Thou art the Way, the Truth, the Life,
Grant us that Way to know,
That Truth to keep, that Life to win,
Whose joys eternal flow. Amen.

## 163.

"Surely He hath borne our griefs and carried our sorrows."

1. WHEN our heads are bowed with woe,
When our bitter tears o'erflow,
When we mourn the lost, the dear,
Jesu, Son of Mary, hear.

2. Thou our throbbing flesh hast worn,
Thou our mortal griefs hast borne,
Thou hast shed the human tear;
Jesu, Son of Mary, hear.

3. When the solemn death-bell tolls
For our own departing souls;
When our final doom is near,
Jesu, Son of Mary, hear.

4. Thou hast bowed the dying head,
Thou the blood of Life hast shed,
Thou hast filled a mortal bier;
Jesu, Son of Mary, hear.

5. When the heart is sad within
With the thought of all its sin;
When the spirit shrinks with fear,
Jesu, Son of Mary, hear.

6. Thou the shame, the grief, hast known,
Though the sins were not Thine own;
Thou hast deigned their load to bear;
Jesu, Son of Mary, hear. Amen.

## 164.

"LORD, I have loved the habitation of Thy house; and the place where Thine honour dwelleth."

1. WE love the place, O God,
Wherein Thine honour dwells;
The joy of Thine abode
All earthly joy excels.

2. It is the House of prayer,
Wherein Thy servants meet;
And Thou, O LORD, art there
Thy chosen flock to greet.

3. We love the sacred Font;
For there the HOLY DOVE
To pour is ever wont
His blessing from above.

4. We love Thine Altar, LORD;
Oh what on earth so dear?
For there, in faith adored,
We find Thy Presence near.

5. We love the Word of Life,
The Word that tells of peace,
Of comfort in the strife,
And joys that never cease.

6. We love to sing below
For mercies freely given;
But oh! we long to know
The triumph-song of heaven.

7. Lord Jesus, give us grace
On earth to love Thee more,
In heaven to see Thy Face,
And with Thy saints adore. Amen.

## 165.

"If any will come after Me, let him deny himself, and take up his cross and follow Me."

1. TAKE up thy cross, the Saviour said,
If thou would'st My disciple be;
Deny thyself, the world forsake,
And humbly follow after Me.

2. Take up thy cross; let not its weight
Fill thy weak spirit with alarm;
His strength shall bear thy spirit up,
And brace thy heart, and nerve thine arm.

3. Take up thy cross, nor heed the shame;
Nor let thy foolish pride rebel:
Thy Lord for thee the Cross endured,
To save thy soul from death and hell.

4. Take up thy cross then in His strength,
And calmly every danger brave;
'Twill guide thee to a better home,
And lead to victory o'er the grave.

5. Take up thy Cross and follow Christ,
Nor think till death to lay it down;
For only he, who bears the cross,
May hope to wear the glorious crown.

6. To Thee, great LORD, the ONE IN THREE,
All praise for evermore ascend;
O grant us in our home to see
The heavenly life that knows no end.
Amen.

## 166.

"Behold the Lamb of GOD, which taketh away the sins of the world."

1. BEHOLD the LAMB of GOD!
O Thou for sinners slain,
Let it not be in vain
That Thou hast died:
Thee for my SAVIOUR let me take,
My only refuge let me make
Thy piercèd Side.

2. Behold the LAMB of GOD!
Into the sacred flood
Of Thy most precious Blood
My soul I cast:
Wash me and make me clean within,
And keep me pure from every sin,
Till life be past.

3. Behold the LAMB of GOD!
All hail, Incarnate WORD,
Thou everlasting LORD,
SAVIOUR most blest;
Fill us with love that never faints,
Grant us with all Thy blessèd Saints
Eternal rest.

4. Behold the Lamb of God!
Worthy is He alone,
That sitteth on the throne
Of God above:
One with the Ancient of all days,
One with the Comforter in praise,
All Light and Love. Amen.

## 167.

"The things which are seen are temporal; but the things which are not seen are eternal."

1. THE roseate hues of early dawn,
The brightness of the day,
The crimson of the sunset sky,
How fast they fade away!
Oh, for the pearly gates of heaven,
Oh, for the golden floor,
Oh, for the Sun of Righteousness.
That setteth nevermore!

2. The highest hopes we cherish here,
How fast they tire and faint;
How many a spot defiles the robe
That wraps an earthly saint!
Oh, for a heart that never sins,
Oh, for a soul washed white,
Oh, for a voice to praise our King,
Nor weary day nor night.

3. Here faith is ours, and heavenly hope,
  And grace to lead us higher;
But there are perfectness, and peace,
  Beyond our best desire.
Oh, by Thy love, and anguish, Lord,
  And by Thy life laid down,
Grant that we fall not from Thy grace,
  Nor cast away our crown. Amen.

## 168.

"There is none other Name under heaven given among men, whereby we must be saved."

1. TO the Name of our Salvation
  Laud and honour let us pay;
Which for many a generation
  Hid in God's foreknowledge lay,
But with holy exultation
  We may sing aloud to-day.

2. Jesus is the Name we treasure;
  Name beyond what words can tell;
Name of gladness, Name of pleasure,
  Ear and heart delighting well;
Name of sweetness, passing measure,
  Saving us from sin and hell.

3. 'Tis the Name for adoration,
  Name for songs of victory,
Name for holy meditation
  In this vale of misery,
Name for joyful veneration
  By the citizens on high.

4. 'Tis the Name that whoso preacheth
Speaks like music to the ear;
Who in prayer this Name beseecheth
Sweetest comfort findeth near;
Who its perfect wisdom reacheth
Heavenly joy possesseth here.

5. Jesus is the Name exalted
Over every other name;
In this Name, whene'er assaulted,
We can put our foes to shame;
Strength to them who else had halted,
Eyes to blind, and feet to lame.

6. Therefore we in love adoring
This most blessèd Name revere;
Holy Jesu, Thee imploring
So to write it in us here,
That hereafter heavenward soaring
We may sing with angels there. Amen.

## 169.

"Of Whom the whole family in heaven and earth is named."

1. LET saints on earth in concert sing
With those whose work is done;
For all the servants of our King
In heaven and earth are one.

2. One family, we dwell in Him,
   One Church, above, beneath;
Though now divided by the stream,
   The narrow stream of death.

3. One army of the Living God,
   To His command we bow;
Part of the host have crossed the flood,
   And part are crossing now.

4. E'en now to their eternal home
   There pass some spirits blest;
While others to the margin come,
   Waiting their call to rest.

5. Jesu, be Thou our constant Guide;
   Then, when the word is given,
Bid Jordan's narrow stream divide,
   And bring us safe to heaven. Amen.

## 170.

"Thy will be done."

1. MY God, my Father, while I stray,
   Far from my home, in life's rough way,
O teach me from my heart to say
   "Thy will be done."

2. Though dark my path, and sad my lot,
Let me be still and murmur not,
Or breathe the prayer divinely taught,
   "Thy will be done."

3. What though in lonely grief I sigh
For friends beloved no longer nigh,
Submissive would I still reply,
"Thy will be done."

4. If Thou shouldst call me to resign
What most I prize, it ne'er was mine;
I only yield Thee what is Thine;
"Thy will be done."

5. Let but my fainting heart be blest
With Thy sweet Spirit for its guest,
My God, to Thee I leave the rest;
"Thy will be done."

6. Renew my will from day to day,
Blend it with Thine, and take away
All that now makes it hard to say,
"Thy will be done." Amen.

## 171.

"God is Love."

1. O LOVE, Who formedst me to wear
The image of Thy Godhead here;
Who soughtest me with tender care
Thro' all my wanderings wild and drear;
O Love, I give myself to Thee,
Thine ever, only Thine to be.

2. O Love, Who e'er life's earliest dawn
On me Thy choice hast gently laid;
O Love, Who here as Man wast born,
And wholly like to us wast made;
O Love, I give myself to Thee,
Thine ever, only Thine to be.

3. O Love, Who once in time wast slain,
Pierced through and through with bitter woe;
O Love, Who wrestling thus didst gain
That we eternal joy might know;
O Love, I give myself to Thee,
Thine ever, only Thine to be.

4. O Love, Who lovest me for aye,
Who for my soul dost ever plead;
O Love, Who didst my ransom pay,
Whose power sufficeth in my stead;
O Love, I give myself to Thee,
Thine ever, only Thine to be.

5. O Love, Who once shalt bid me rise
From out this dying life of ours;
O Love, Who once o'er yonder skies
Shalt set me in the fadeless bowers;
O Love, I give myself to Thee,
Thine ever, only Thine to be. Amen.

## 172.

"Hosanna in the highest."

1. HOSANNA to the living LORD!
Hosanna to the INCARNATE WORD!
To CHRIST, CREATOR, SAVIOUR, KING,
Let earth, let heaven hosanna sing.
Hosanna in the highest!

2. O SAVIOUR, with protecting care
Abide in this Thy house of prayer,
Where we Thy parting promise claim
Assembled in Thy sacred Name.
Hosanna in the highest!

3. But chiefest, in our cleansèd breast
Bid Thine eternal SPIRIT rest;
And make our secret soul to be
A temple pure, and worthy Thee.
Hosanna in the highest!

4. To GOD the FATHER, GOD the SON,
And GOD the SPIRIT, THREE IN ONE,
Be honour, praise, and glory given
By all on earth and all in heaven.
Hosanna in the highest! Amen.

## 173.

"As many as are led by the SPIRIT of God, they are the sons of God."

1. COME, gracious SPIRIT, heavenly Dove,
With light and comfort from above;
Be Thou our Guardian, Thou our Guide,
O'er every thought and step preside.

2. The light of truth to us display,
And make us know and choose Thy way;
Plant holy fear in every heart,
That we from Thee may ne'er depart.

3. Lead us to CHRIST, the living Way,
Nor let us from His precepts stray;
Lead us to holiness, the road
That we must take to dwell with GOD.

4. Lead us to heaven, that we may share
Fulness of joy for ever there:
Lead us to GOD, our final rest,
To be with Him for ever blest. Amen.

## 174.

"O praise the LORD of heaven; praise Him in the height."

1. PRAISE the LORD! ye heavens, adore Him,
Praise Him, angels, in the height:
* Sun and moon, rejoice before Him,
Praise Him, all ye stars and light:
Praise the LORD! for He hath spoken,
Worlds His mighty voice obeyed;
Laws, which never shall be broken,
For their guidance He hath made.

2. Praise the Lord! for He is glorious;
   Never shall His promise fail;
 God hath made His saints victorious,
   Sin and death shall not prevail.
 Praise the God of our salvation;
   Hosts on high, His power proclaim;
 Heaven and earth, and all creation,
   Laud and magnify His Name! Amen.

## 175.

"Fight the good fight of faith, lay hold on eternal life."

1. OFT in danger, oft in woe,
   Onward, Christians, onward go:
 Bear the toil, maintain the strife,
 Strengthened with the Bread of Life.

2. Let not sorrow dim your eye,
 Soon shall every tear be dry;
 Let not fear your course impede,
 Great your strength, if great your need.

3. Let your drooping hearts be glad;
 March in heavenly armour clad;
 Fight, nor think the battle long,
 Soon shall victory wake your song.

4. Onward then to glory move;
 More than conquerors ye shall prove;
 Though opposed by many a foe,
 Christian soldiers, onward go!

5. Hymns of glory and of praise,
FATHER, unto Thee we raise:
Holy JESUS, praise to Thee,
With the SPIRIT, ever be. Amen.

## 176.

"My soul thirsteth for Thee, my flesh also longeth after Thee; in a barren and dry land where no water is."

1. FAR from my heavenly home,
Far from my FATHER's breast,
Fainting I cry, blest SPIRIT, come,
And speed me to my rest.

2. My spirit homeward turns,
And fain would thither flee;
My heart, O Sion, droops and yearns,
When I remember thee.

3. To thee, to thee I press,
A dark and toilsome road;
When shall I pass the wilderness,
And reach the saints' abode?

4. GOD of my life, be near,
On Thee my hopes I cast,
O guide me through the desert here,
And bring me home at last. Amen.

## 177.

"Thou art a place to hide me in."

1. JESU, grant me this, I pray,
Ever in Thy Heart to stay;
Let me evermore abide
Hidden in Thy wounded Side.

2. If the evil one prepare,
Or the world, a tempting snare,
I am safe when I abide
In Thy Heart and wounded Side.

3. If the flesh, more dangerous still,
Tempt my soul to deeds of ill,
Naught I fear when I abide
In Thy Heart and wounded Side.

4. Death will come one day to me;
JESU, cast me not from Thee:
Dying let me still abide
In Thy Heart and wounded Side. Amen.

## 178.

"Whom have I in heaven but Thee; and there is none upon earth that I desire in comparison of Thee."

1. JESU, my LORD, my GOD, my all,
Hear me, blest SAVIOUR, when I call;
Hear me, and from Thy dwelling-place
Pour down the riches of Thy grace;
JESU, my LORD, I Thee adore,
O make me love Thee more and more.

2. JESU, too late I Thee have sought,
How can I love Thee as I ought?
And how extol Thy matchless fame,
The glorious beauty of Thy name?
JESU, my LORD, I Thee adore,
O make me love Thee more and more.

3. JESU, what didst Thou find in me,
That Thou hast dealt so lovingly?
How great the joy that Thou hast brought,
So far exceeding hope or thought;
JESU, my LORD, I Thee adore,
O make me love Thee more and more.

4. JESU, of Thee shall be my song,
To Thee my heart and soul belong;
All that I have or am is Thine,
And Thou, blest SAVIOUR, Thou art mine.
JESU, my LORD, I Thee adore,
O make me love Thee more and more.
Amen.

## 179.

"A Man shall be as an hiding place from the wind and a covert from the tempest."

1. JESU, Lover of my soul,
Let me to Thy Bosom fly,
While the gathering waters roll,
While the tempest still is high:
Hide me, O my SAVIOUR, hide,
Till the storm of life be past;
Safe into the haven guide,
O receive my soul at last.

2. Other refuge have I none;
Hangs my helpless soul on Thee:
Leave, ah! leave me not alone,
Still support and comfort me.
All my trust on Thee is stayed,
All my help from Thee I bring;
Cover my defenceless head
With the shadow of Thy wing.

3. Plenteous grace with Thee is found,
Grace to cleanse from every sin;
Let the healing streams abound,
Make and keep me pure within:
Thou of Life the Fountain art,
Freely let me take of Thee;
Spring Thou up within my heart,
Rise to all eternity. Amen.

## 180.

"When shall I come to appear before the presence of God?"

1. JERUSALEM, my happy home,
Name ever dear to me,
When shall my labours have an end?
Thy joys when shall I see?

2. When shall these eyes Thy heaven-built walls
And pearly gates behold?
Thy bulwarks, with salvation strong,
And streets of shining gold?

3. Apostles, Martyrs, Prophets, there
Around my SAVIOUR stand;
And all I love in CHRIST below
Will join the glorious band.

4. Jerusalem, my happy home,
When shall I come to thee?
When shall my labours have an end?
Thy joys when shall I see?

5. O CHRIST, do Thou my soul prepare
For that bright home of love;
That I may see Thee and adore,
With all Thy saints above. Amen.

## 181.

"Put on the whole armour of GOD."

1. SOLDIERS of CHRIST, arise,
And put your armour on,
Strong in the strength which GOD supplies
Through His Eternal SON.

2. Strong in the LORD of Hosts,
And in His mighty power;
Who in the strength of JESUS trusts
Is more than conqueror.

3. Stand then in His great might,
With all His strength endued;
And take, to arm you for the fight,
The panoply of GOD.

4. From strength to strength go on,
Wrestle, and fight, and pray;
Tread all the powers of darkness down,
And win the well-fought day:

5. That having all things done,
And all your conflicts past,
Ye may obtain, through CHRIST alone,
A crown of joy at last.

6. JESU, Eternal SON,
We praise Thee and adore,
Who art with GOD the FATHER One
And SPIRIT evermore. Amen.

## 182.

"There remaineth therefore a rest to the people of GOD."

1. THERE is a blessèd Home
Beyond this land of woe,
Where trials never come,
Nor tears of sorrow flow;
Where faith is lost in sight,
And patient hope is crowned,
And everlasting light
Its glory throws around.

2. There is a land of peace,
Good angels know it well;
Glad songs that never cease
Within its portals swell;
Around its glorious Throne
Ten thousand saints adore
CHRIST, with the FATHER One
And SPIRIT, evermore.

3. O joy all joys beyond,
To see the LAMB Who died,
And count each sacred Wound
In Hands, and Feet, and Side;
To give to Him the praise
Of every triumph won,
And sing through endless days
The great things He hath done.

4. Look up ye saints of GOD,
Nor fear to tread below
The path your Saviour trod
Of daily toil and woe;
Wait but a little while
In uncomplaining love,
His own most gracious smile
Shall welcome you above. Amen.

## 183.

"Let this mind be in you, which was also in CHRIST JESUS."

1. LORD, as to Thy dear Cross we flee
And plead to be forgiven,
So let Thy life our pattern be,
And form our souls for heaven.

2. Help us, through good report and ill,
Our daily cross to bear;
Like Thee, to do our FATHER's will,
Our brethren's griefs to share.

3. Let grace our selfishness expel,
Our earthliness refine;
And kindness in our bosoms dwell,
As free and true as Thine.

4. If joy shall at Thy bidding fly,
And grief's dark day come on,
We in our turn would meekly cry,
"FATHER, Thy will be done."

5. Kept peaceful in the midst of strife,
Forgiving and forgiven,
O may we lead the pilgrim's life,
And follow Thee to heaven. Amen.

## 184.

"Blessed are those servants whom the LORD when He cometh shall find watching."

1. YE servants of the LORD,
Each in his office, wait,
Observant of His heavenly word,
And watchful at His gate.

2. Let all your lamps be bright,
And trim the golden flame;
Gird up your loins as in His sight,
For awful is His Name.

3. Watch! 'tis your LORD's command,
And while we speak He's near;
Mark the first signal of His hand,
And ready all appear.

4. O happy servant he,
In such a posture found;
He shall his LORD with rapture see,
And be with honour crowned.

5. CHRIST shall the banquet spread
With His own royal Hand,
And raise that faithful servant's head
Amid his angel-band.

6. All glory, LORD, to Thee,
Whom heaven and earth adore;
To FATHER, SON, and HOLY GHOST,
One GOD for evermore. Amen.

## 185.

"Unto you which believe, He is precious."

1. HOW sweet the Name of JESUS sounds
In a believer's ear!
It soothes his sorrows, heals his wounds,
And drives away his fear.

2. It makes the wounded spirit whole,
And calms the troubled breast;
'Tis manna to the hungry soul,
And to the weary rest.

3. Dear Name! the rock on which I build,
My shield and hiding-place,
My never-failing treasury, filled
With boundless stores of grace.

4. JESUS! my Shepherd, Husband, Friend,
My Prophet, Priest, and King,
My Lord, my Life, my Way, mine End,
Accept the praise I bring.

5. Weak is the effort of my heart,
    And cold my warmest thought;
But when I see Thee as Thou art
    I'll praise Thee as I ought.

6. Till then I would Thy love proclaim
    With every fleeting breath;
And may the music of Thy Name
    Refresh my soul in death. Amen.

## 186.

"Casting all your care upon Him; for He careth for you."

1. O LORD, how happy should we be
If we could cast our care on Thee,
    If we from self could rest;
And feel at heart that One above
In perfect wisdom, perfect love,
    Is working for the best.

2. How far from this our daily life,
How oft disturbed by anxious strife,
    By sudden wild alarms;
Oh, could we but relinquish all
Our earthly props, and simply fall
    On Thine Almighty arms!

3. Could we but kneel and cast our load,
E'en while we pray, upon our GOD,
    Then rise with lightened cheer;
Sure that the FATHER, Who is nigh
To still the famished raven's cry,
    Will hear in that we fear.

4. We cannot trust Him as we should;
So chafes weak nature's restless mood
To cast its peace away;
But birds and flowerets round us preach,
All, all the present evil teach
Sufficient for the day.

5. LORD, make these faithless hearts of ours
Such lessons learn from birds and flowers;
Make them from self to cease,
Leave all things to a FATHER's will
And taste, before Him lying still,
E'en in affliction peace. Amen.

## 187.

"LORD, help me."

1. O HELP us, LORD; each hour of need
Thy heavenly succour give;
Help us in thought, and word, and deed,
Each hour on earth we live.

2. O help us when our spirits bleed
With contrite anguish sore;
And when our hearts are cold and dead,
O help us, LORD, the more.

3. O help us through the prayer of faith
More firmly to believe;
For still the more the servant hath,
The more shall he receive.

4. O help us, Jesu, from on high;
We know no help but Thee;
O help us so to live and die
As Thine in heaven to be. Amen.

## 188.

"Behold, how good and joyful a thing it is, brethren, to dwell together in unity."

1. O LORD, how joyful 'tis to see
The brethren join in love to Thee;
On Thee alone their heart relies,
Their only strength Thy grace supplies.

2. How sweet, within Thy holy place,
With one accord to sing Thy grace,
Besieging Thine attentive ear
With all the force of fervent prayer.

3. O may we love the House of God,
Of peace and joy the blest abode;
O may no angry strife destroy
That sacred peace, that holy joy.

4. The world without may rage, but we
Will only cling more close to Thee,
With hearts to Thee more wholly given,
More weaned from earth, more fixed on heaven.

5. Lord, shower upon us from above
The sacred gift of mutual love;
Each other's wants may we supply,
And reign together in the sky. Amen.

## 189.

"LORD, save us."

1. JESU, meek and gentle,
SON of GOD most high,
Pitying, loving SAVIOUR,
Hear Thy children's cry.

2. Pardon our offences,
Loose our captive chains,
Break down every idol
Which our soul detains.

3. Give us holy freedom,
Fill our hearts with love;
Draw us, HOLY JESUS,
To the realms above.

4. Lead us on our journey,
Be Thyself the Way
Through terrestrial darkness
To celestial day.

5. JESU, meek and gentle,
SON of GOD most high,
Pitying, loving SAVIOUR,
Hear Thy children's cry. Amen.

## 190.

"Our light affliction, which is but for a moment, worketh for us a far more exceeding and eternal weight of glory."

1. O LET him, whose sorrow
No relief can find,
Trust in God, and borrow
Ease for heart and mind.

2. Where the mourner weeping
Sheds the secret tear,
God His watch is keeping
Though none else is near.

3. God will never leave thee,
All thy wants He knows,
Feels the pains that grieve thee,
Sees thy cares and woes.

4. Raise thine eyes to heaven
When thy spirits quail,
When, by tempests driven,
Heart and courage fail.

5. When in grief we languish,
He will dry the tear,
Who His children's anguish
Soothes with succour near.

6. All our woe and sadness
In this world below
Balance not the gladness
We in heaven shall know.

7. Jesu, Holy Saviour,
In the realms above
Crown us with Thy favour,
Fill us with Thy love. Amen.

## 191.

"Where I am there shall also My servant be."

1. CHRIST will gather in His own
To the place where He is gone,
Where their heart and treasure lie,
Where our life is hid on high.

2. Day by day the Voice saith, "Come,
Enter thine eternal home;"
Asking not if we can spare
This dear soul it summons there.

3. Had He asked us, well we know
We should cry, Oh spare this blow!
Yes, with streaming tears should pray,
"Lord we love him, let him stay."

4. But the Lord doth naught amiss,
And, since He hath ordered this,
We have naught to do but still
Rest in silence on His will.

5. Many a heart no longer here
Ah! was all too inly dear;
Yet, O Love, 'tis Thou dost call,
Thou wilt be our All in all. Amen.

## 192.

"What I do thou knowest not now; but thou shalt know hereafter."

1. GOD moves in a mysterious way
His wonders to perform;
He plants His footsteps in the sea,
And rides upon the storm.

2. Deep in unfathomable mines
Of never-failing skill
He treasures up His bright designs,
And works His sovereign will.

3. Ye fearful saints, fresh courage take;
The clouds ye so much dread
Are big with mercy, and shall break
In blessings on your head.

4. Judge not the LORD by feeble sense,
But trust Him for His grace:
Behind a frowning providence
He hides a smiling face.

5. Blind unbelief is sure to err,
And scan His work in vain;
GOD is His own interpreter,
And He will make it plain. Amen.

## 193.

"Worthy is the LAMB that was slain to receive power, and riches, and wisdom, and strength, and honour, and glory, and blessing!"

1. FROM highest heaven th' Eternal SON,
With GOD the FATHER ever One,
Came down to suffer, and to die;
For love of sinful man He bore
Our human griefs and troubles sore,
Our load of guilt and misery.

2. Sing out, ye saints of GOD, and praise
The LAMB Who died, His flock to raise
From sin and everlasting woe;
With angels round the throne above
O tell the wonders of His love,
The joys that from His mercy flow.

3. In darkest shades of night we lay
Without a beam to guide our way,
Or hope of aught beyond the grave;
But He hath brought us life and light,
And opened heaven to our sight,
And lives for ever strong to save.

4. Rejoice, ye saints of GOD, rejoice;
Sing out, and praise with cheerful voice
The LAMB Whom heaven and earth adore.
To Him Who gave His Only SON,
To GOD the SPIRIT with Them One,
Be praise and glory evermore. Amen.

## 194.

"Sing unto the LORD, and praise His Name."

1\. LET every heart exulting beat
With joy at JESU'S Name of bliss;
With every pure delight replete
And passing sweet its music is.

2\. JESUS the comfortless consoles,
JESUS each sinful fever quells,
JESUS the power of hell controls,
JESUS each deadly foe repels.

3\. O speak His glorious Name abroad!
JESUS let every tongue confess;
Let every heart and voice accord
The Healer of our souls to bless.

4\. JESU, the sinner's Friend, abide
With us, and hearken to our prayer;
Thy frail and erring wanderers guide,
In mercy our transgressions spare.

5\. All might, all glory be to Thee
Refulgent with this Name Divine;
All honour, worship, majesty,
JESU, for evermore be Thine. Amen.

## 195.

"The everlasting Father, the Prince of peace.

TO CHRIST the Prince of peace
And SON of GOD most high,
The Father of the world to come,
We lift our joyful cry.

2. Deep in His Heart for us
The wound of love He bore,
That love which still He kindles in
The hearts that Him adore.

3. O Jesu, Victim blest,
What else but love divine
Could Thee constrain to open thus
That sacred Heart of Thine?

4. O Fount of endless life,
O Spring of water clear;
O flame celestial, cleansing all
Who unto Thee draw near!

5. Hide me in Thy dear Heart,
For thither do I fly;
There seek thy grace through life, in death
Thine immortality. Amen.

## 196.

"The kingdoms of this world are become the kingdoms of our Lord and of His Christ; and He shall reign for ever and ever."

1. JESUS shall reign where'er the sun
Doth his successive journeys run:
His kingdom stretch from shore to shore,
Till moons shall wax and wane no more.

2. People and realms of every tongue
Dwell on His love with sweetest song,
And infant voices shall proclaim
Their early blessings on His Name.

3. Blessings abound where'er He reigns;
The prisoner leaps to loose his chains;
The weary find eternal rest,
And all the sons of want are blest.

4. Let every creature rise and bring
Peculiar honours to our King;
Angels descend with songs again,
And earth repeat the loud Amen. Amen.

## 197.

"LORD, Thou hast been our Refuge from one generation to another."

1. O GOD, our help in ages past,
Our hope for years to come,
Our shelter from the stormy blast,
And our eternal home!

2. Beneath the shadow of Thy Throne
Thy saints have dwelt secure;
Sufficient is Thine arm alone,
And our defence is sure.

3. Before the hills in order stood,
Or earth received her frame,
From everlasting Thou art GOD,
To endless years the same.

4. A thousand ages in Thy sight
Are like an evening gone;
Short as the watch that ends the night
Before the rising sun.

5. Time, like an ever-rolling stream,
   Bears all its sons away;
They fly forgotten, as a dream
   Dies at the opening day.

6. O God, our help in ages past,
   Our hope for years to come;
Be Thou our guard while troubles last,
   And our eternal home. Amen.

## 198.

"Praise the Lord, O my soul; and all that is within me praise His Holy Name."

1. PRAISE, my soul, the King of Heaven
   To His feet thy tribute bring,
Ransomed, healed, restored, forgiven,
   Evermore His praises sing,
     Alleluia! Alleluia!
   Praise the everlasting King.

2. Praise Him for His grace and favour
   To our fathers in distress;
Praise Him still the same as ever,
   Slow to chide, and swift to bless:
     Alleluia! Alleluia!
   Glorious in His faithfulness.

3. Father-like, He tends and spares us,
   Well our feeble frame He knows;
In His hands He gently bears us,
   Rescues us from all our foes;
     Alleluia! Alleluia!
   Widely yet His mercy flows.

4. Angels in the height adore Him!
Ye behold Him face to face;
Saints triumphant bow before Him!
Gathered in from every race.
Alleluia! Alleluia!
Praise with us the God of grace. Amen.

## 199.

"Mary hath chosen the good part, which shall not be taken away from her."

1. O LOVE divine, how sweet thou art!
When shall I find my willing heart
All taken up by thee?
I thirst, I faint, I die to prove
The greatness of redeeming love,
The love of CHRIST to me!

2. Stronger His love than death or hell;
Its riches are unsearchable;
The first-born sons of light
Desire in vain its depths to see;
They cannot reach the mystery,
The length and breadth and height.

3. GOD only knows the love of GOD;
O that it now were shed abroad
In this poor stony heart!
For love I sigh, for love I pine:
This only portion, LORD, be mine,
Be mine this better part.

4. For ever would I take my seat
With Mary at the MASTER's feet;
Be this my happy choice;
My only care, delight, and bliss,
My joy, my heaven on earth, be this,
To hear the Bridegroom's voice. Amen.

## 200.

"Whom have I in heaven but Thee, and there is none upon earth that I desire in comparison of Thee."

1. NEARER, my GOD, to Thee,
Nearer to Thee;
E'en though it be a cross
That raiseth me,
Still all my song shall be,
Nearer, my GOD, to Thee,
Nearer to Thee!

2. Though, like a wanderer,
The sun gone down,
Darkness comes over me,
My rest a stone;
Yet in my dreams I'd be
Nearer, my GOD, to Thee,
Nearer to Thee!

3. There let my way appear
Steps unto heaven;
All that Thou sendest me
In mercy given;
Angels to beckon me
Nearer, my GOD, to Thee,
Nearer to Thee!

4. Then, with my waking thoughts
Bright with Thy praise,
Out of my stony griefs
Bethel I'll raise;
So by my woes to be
Nearer, my GOD, to Thee,
Nearer to thee! Amen.

## 201.

"Thy Word is a lantern unto my feet, and a light unto my paths."

1. LORD, Thy Word abideth,
And our footsteps guideth;
Who its truth believeth
Light and joy receiveth.

2. When our foes are near us,
Then Thy Word doth cheer us,
Word of consolation,
Message of salvation.

3. When the storms are o'er us,
And dark clouds before us,
Then its light directeth
And our way protecteth.

4. Who can tell the pleasure,
Who recount the treasure,
By Thy Word imparted
To the simple-hearted?

5. Word of mercy, giving
Succour to the living;
Word of life, supplying
Comfort to the dying!

6. Oh, that we discerning
Its most holy learning,
LORD, may love and fear Thee,
Evermore be near Thee! Amen.

## 202.

"JESUS was transfigured before them."

1. O WONDROUS type, O vision fair,
Of glory that the Church shall share,
Which CHRIST upon the mountain shows,
Where brighter than the sun He glows!

2. From age to age the tale declare,
How with the three disciples there,
Where Moses and Elias meet,
The LORD holds converse high and sweet.

3. The Law and Prophets there have place,
Two chosen witnesses of grace;
The FATHER's voice from out the cloud
Proclaims His Only SON aloud.

4. With shining Face and bright array,
CHRIST deigns to manifest to-day
What glory shall be theirs above,
Who joy in GOD with perfect love.

5. And faithful hearts are raised on high
By this great vision's mystery,
For which in joyful strains we raise
The voice of prayer, the hymn of praise.

6. O Father, with the Eternal Son
And Holy Spirit ever One,
Vouchsafe to bring us by Thy grace
To see Thy glory face to face. Amen.

## 203.

### Holy Communion.

"The cup of blessing which we bless, is it not the communion of the Blood of Christ? The bread which we break, is it not the communion of the Body of Christ?"

1. NOW, my tongue, the mystery telling
Of the glorious Body sing,
And the Blood, all price excelling,
Which the Gentiles' Lord and King,
In a Virgin's womb once dwelling,
Shed for this world's ransoming.

2. Given for us, and condescending
To be born for us below,
He with men in converse blending
Dwelt the seed of truth to sow,
Till He closed with wondrous ending
His most patient life of woe.

3. That last night at supper lying,
'Mid the Twelve, His chosen band,
Jesus, with the law complying,
Keeps the feast its rites demand;
Then, more precious Food supplying,
Gives Himself with His own Hand.

4. Word-made-Flesh true bread He maketh
By His word His Flesh to be;
Wine, His Blood; which whoso taketh
Must from carnal thoughts be free;
Faith alone, though sight forsaketh,
Shows true hearts the mystery.

5. Therefore we, before Him bending,
This great Sacrament revere;
Types and shadows have their ending,
For the newer rite is here;
Faith, our outward sense befriending,
Makes our inward vision clear.

6. Glory let us give and blessing
To the Father and the Son,
Honour, might, and praise addressing,
While eternal ages run;
Ever too, His love confessing,
Who from Both with Both is One.
Amen.

## 204.

"Come, for all things are now ready."

1\. MY GOD, and is Thy table spread,
And doth Thy cup with love o'erflow!
Thither be all Thy children led,
And let them all Thy sweetness know.

2\. Hail, sacred Feast, which JESUS makes,
Rich banquet of His Flesh and Blood!
Thrice happy he who here partakes
That sacred stream, that heavenly food.

3\. Why are its dainties all in vain
Before unwilling hearts displayed?
Was not for them the Victim slain?
Are they forbid the children's bread?

4\. O let Thy table honoured be,
And furnished well with joyful guests;
And may each soul salvation see
That here its sacred pledges tastes.

5\. To FATHER, SON, and HOLY GHOST,
The GOD Whom heaven and earth adore,
From men and from the angel-host
Be praise and glory evermore. Amen.

## 205.

"This do in remembrance of Me."

1. BREAD of heaven, on Thee we feed,
For Thy Flesh is meat indeed;
Ever may our souls be fed
With this true and living Bread;
Day by day with strength supplied,
Through the life of Him Who died.

2. Vine of heaven, Thy Blood supplies
This blest cup of sacrifice;
LORD, Thy Wounds our healing give,
To Thy Cross we look and live:
JESUS, may we ever be
Grafted, rooted, built in Thee. Amen.

## 206.

"JESUS said unto them, I am the Bread of Life."

1. THEE we adore, O hidden SAVIOUR, Thee,
Who in Thy Sacrament dost deign to be;
Both flesh and spirit at Thy presence fail,
Yet here Thy presence we devoutly hail.

2. O blest Memorial of our dying LORD,
Who living Bread to men doth here afford!
O may our souls for ever feed on Thee,
And Thou, O CHRIST, for ever precious be.

3. Fountain of Goodness, Jesu, Lord and God,
Cleanse us, unclean, with Thy most cleansing
Blood;
Increase our faith and love, that we may know
The hope and peace which from Thy presence
flow.

4. O Christ, Whom now beneath a veil we see,
May what we thirst for soon our portion be
To gaze on Thee, and see with unveiled face
The vision of Thy glory and Thy grace.
Amen.

## 207.

"My Flesh is meat indeed, and My Blood is drink indeed."

1. O GOD, unseen yet ever near,
Thy presence may we feel;
And, thus inspired with holy fear,
Before Thine Altar kneel.

2. Here may Thy faithful people know
The blessings of Thy love,
The streams that through the desert flow,
The manna from above.

3. We come, obedient to Thy word,
To feast on heavenly Food;
Our meat, the Body of the Lord,
Our drink, His precious Blood.

4. Thus may we all Thy words obey,
For we, O God, are Thine;
And go rejoicing on our way,
Renewed with strength divine.

5. To Father, Son, and Holy Ghost,
The God Whom we adore,
Be glory, as it was, is now,
And shall be evermore. Amen.

## 208.

### Baptism.

"Ask, and it shall be given you; seek, and ye shall find; knock, and it shall be opened unto you."

1. O FATHER, Thou Who hast created all
In wisest love, we pray,
Look on this babe, who at Thy gracious call
Is entering on life's way,
Bend o'er it now with blessing fraught,
And make Thou something out of naught.
O Father, hear!

2. O Son of God, Who diedst for us, behold
We bring our child to Thee,
Thou tender Shepherd take it to Thy fold,
Thine own for aye to be;
Defend it through this earthly strife,
And lead it on the path of life,
O Son of God!

3. O Holy Ghost, Who broodedst o'er the wave,
Descend upon this child;
Give it undying life, its spirit lave
With waters undefiled;
Grant it while yet a babe to be
A child of God, a home for Thee,
O Holy Ghost!

4. O Triune God, what Thou command'st is done,
We speak, but Thine the might;
This child hath scarce yet seen our earthly sun,
Yet pour on it Thy light,
In faith and hope, in joy and love,
Thou Sun of all below, above,
O Triune God! Amen.

## 209.

"The washing of regeneration."

1. 'TIS done; that new and heavenly birth
Which re-creates the sons of earth,
And cleanses from the guilt of sin
The souls whom Jesus died to win.

2. 'Tis done; the Cross upon the brow
Is marked for weal or sorrow now;
To shine with heavenly lustre bright,
Or burn in everlasting night.

3. O ye who brought that babe to-day
Within a Saviour's arms to lay,
Watch well and guard with careful eye
The heir of immortality.

4. Teach it to know a FATHER's love,
And seek for happiness above,
To CHRIST its heart and treasure give,
And in the SPIRIT ever live.

5. That so before the judgment-seat
In joy and triumph ye may meet;
The battle fought, the struggle o'er,
The kingdom yours for evermore.

6. Praise GOD from Whom all blessings flow,
Praise Him, all creatures here below;
Praise Him above, angelic host;
Praise FATHER, SON, and HOLY GHOST.
Amen.

## 210.

"Buried with Him in Baptism."

1. WITH CHRIST we share a mystic grave,
With CHRIST we buried lie;
But 'tis not in the darksome cave
By mournful Calvary.

2. The pure and bright baptismal flood
Entombs our nature's stain;
New creatures from the cleansing wave
With CHRIST we rise again.

3. Thrice blest, if through this world of sin,
And lust, and selfish care,
Our resurrection-mantle white
And undefiled we wear.

4. Thrice blest, if, through the gate of death,
   Glorious at last and free,
We to our joyful rising pass,
   O Risen LORD, with Thee. Amen.

## 211.

### Confirmation.

"The Comforter which is the HOLY GHOST."

1. COME, HOLY GHOST, Creator blest,
Vouchsafe within our souls to rest;
Come with Thy grace and heavenly aid,
And fill the hearts which Thou hast made.

2. O Comforter, to Thee we cry;
Thou Heavenly gift of GOD most high:
Thou Fount of life, and Fire of love,
And sweet Anointing from above.

3. O Finger of the Hand divine,
The sevenfold gifts of grace are Thine;
The promise of the Father Thou,
Who dost the tongue with power endow.

4. Thy light to every sense impart,
And shed Thy love in every heart;
The weakness of our flesh supply
With strength and courage from on high.

5. Drive far away our ghostly foe,
And peace for evermore bestow;
If Thou be our preventing Guide,
No evil can our steps betide.

6. O Holy Ghost, through Thee alone
We know the Father and the Son;
Be this our never-changing creed,
That Thou dost from Them Both proceed.

7. Praise we the Father and the Son,
And Holy Spirit with them One:
And may the Son on us bestow
The gifts that from the Spirit flow. Amen.

(*The Hymns Nos.* 127, 181, *and* 142, *may also be used.*)

# 212.

## Holy Matrimony.

"A threefold cord is not quickly broken."

1. THE voice that breathed o'er Eden,
That earliest wedding day,
The primal marriage blessing,
It hath not passed away:

2. Still in the pure espousal
Of Christian man and maid
The Holy Three are with us,
The threefold grace is said.

3. For dower of blessèd children,
For love and faith's sweet sake,
For high mysterious union
Which naught on earth may break,

4. Be present, awful FATHER,
To give away this bride,
As Eve Thou gavest to Adam
Out of his own pierced side;

5. Be present, SON of Mary,
To join their loving hands,
As Thou didst bind two natures
In Thine eternal bands;

6. Be present, Holiest SPIRIT,
To bless them as they kneel,
As Thou for CHRIST, the Bridegroom,
The heavenly spouse dost seal.

7. O spread Thy pure wing o'er them,
Let no ill power find place,
When onward to Thine Altar
The hallowed path they trace,

8. To cast their crowns before Thee
In perfect sacrifice,
Till to the home of gladness
With CHRIST'S own Bride they rise.
Amen.

## 213.

"Both JESUS was called, and His disciples, to the marriage."

1. HOW welcome was the call,
And sweet the festal lay,
When JESUS deigned in Cana's hall
To bless the marriage day.

2. And happy was the Bride,
   And glad the Bridegroom's heart,
For He Who tarried at their side
   Bade grief and ill depart.

3. His gracious power divine
   The water vessels knew;
And plenteous was the mystic wine
   The wondering servants drew.

4. O LORD of life and love,
   Come Thou again to-day;
And bring a blessing from above
   That ne'er shall pass away.

5. Oh, bless, as erst of old,
   The Bridegroom and the Bride;
Bless with the holier stream that flowed
   Forth from Thy piercèd Side.

6. Before Thine Altar-throne
   This mercy we implore;
As Thou dost knit them, LORD, in one.
   So bless them evermore. Amen.

## 214.

### Ember Days.

My FATHER hath sent Me, even so send I you."

CHRIST is gone up; yet ere He passed
   From earth, in heaven to reign,
He formed one holy Church to last
   Till He should come again.

2. His twelve Apostles first He made
His ministers of grace;
And they their hands on others laid,
To fill in turn their place.

3. So age by age, and year by year,
His grace was handed on;
And still the holy Church is here,
Although her LORD is gone.

4. Let those find pardon, LORD, from Thee,
Whose love to her is cold;
Bring wanderers in, and let there be
One Shepherd and one fold. Amen.

## 215.

"Let Thy priests be clothed with righteousness."

1. LORD, pour Thy SPIRIT from on high,
And Thine ordainèd servants bless;
Graces and gifts to each supply,
And clothe Thy priests with righteousness.

2. Within Thy temple when they stand,
To teach the truth as taught by Thee,
SAVIOUR, like stars in Thy right hand
Let all Thy Church's pastors be.

3. Wisdom, and zeal, and love impart,
Firmness and meekness from above,
To bear Thy people in their heart,
And love the souls whom Thou dost love:

4. To love, and pray, and never faint,
By day and night their guard to keep,
To warn the sinner, form the saint,
To feed Thy lambs, and tend Thy sheep.

5. So, when their work is finished here,
They may in hope their charge resign;
So, when their Master shall appear,
They may with crowns of glory shine.
Amen.

## 216.

"Unto every one of us is given grace according to the measure of the gift of CHRIST."

1. O GUARDIAN of the Church Divine,
The sevenfold gifts of grace are Thine,
And kindled by Thy hidden fires
The soul to highest aims aspires.

2. Thy Priests with wisdom, LORD, endue,
Their hearts with love and zeal renew;
Turn all their weakness into might,
O Thou the source of life and light.

3. SPIRIT of truth, on us bestow
The faith in all its powers to know;
That with the saints of ages gone,
And those to come, we may be one.

4. Protect Thy Church from every foe,
And peace, the fruit of love, bestow;
Convert the world, make all confess
The glories of Thy righteousness.

5. All praise to God the Father be,
All praise, Eternal Son, to Thee,
Whom with the Spirit we adore
For ever and for evermore. Amen.

## 217.

### Missions.

"Come over. . . .and help us."

1. FROM Greenland's icy mountains,
From India's coral strand,
Where Afric's sunny fountains
Roll down their golden sand,
From many an ancient river,
From many a palmy plain,
They call us to deliver
Their land from error's chain.

2. What though the spicy breezes
Blow soft o'er Ceylon's isle,
Though every prospect pleases,
And only man is vile;
In vain with lavish kindness
The gifts of God are strown,
The heathen in his blindness
Bows down to wood and stone.

3. Can we whose souls are lighted
With wisdom from on high,
Can we to men benighted
The lamp of life deny?
Salvation! oh, Salvation!
The joyful sound proclaim,
Till each remotest nation
Has learnt Messiah's Name.

4. Waft, waft, ye winds, His story,
And you, ye waters, roll,
Till like a sea of glory
It spreads from pole to pole;
Till o'er our ransomed nature
The Lamb for sinners slain,
Redeemer, King, Creator,
In bliss returns to reign. Amen.

## 218.

"The harvest truly is plenteous, but the labourers are few."

1. THE earth, O Lord, is one wide field
Of all Thy chosen seed;
The crop prepared its fruit to yield;
The labourers few indeed.

2. Therefore we come before Thee now
With words of humble prayer,
Beseeching of Thy love that Thou
Wouldst send more labourers there.

3. Not for our land alone we pray,
Though that above the rest,
The realms and islands far away,
O let them all be blest.

4. Endue the Bishops of Thy flock
With wisdom and with grace,
Against false doctrine, like a rock,
To set the heart and face.

5. To all Thy Priests Thy truth reveal,
And make Thy judgments clear;
Make Thou Thy Deacons full of zeal,
And humble and sincere.

6. Give to their flocks a lowly mind
To hear and to obey;
That each and all may mercy find
At Thine appearing day. Amen.

(*This Hymn may also be used on Ember-days.*)

## 219.

"That Thy way may be known upon earth, Thy saving health among all nations."

1. GOD of grace, O let Thy light
Bless our dim and blinded sight;
Like the day-spring on the night
Bid Thy grace to shine.

2. To the nations led astray
Thine eternal love display;
Let Thy Truth direct their way
Till the world be Thine.

3. Praise to Thee, the faithful LORD;
Let all tongues in glad accord
Learn the good thanksgiving word,
Ever praising Thee.

4. Let them moved to gladness sing,
Owning Thee their Judge and King;
Righteous Truth shall bloom and spring
Where Thy rule shall be.

5. Praise to Thee, all-faithful LORD,
Let all tongues in glad accord
Speak the good thanksgiving word,
Heart-rejoicing praise.

6. So the fruitful earth's incrcase,
Bounty of the GOD of peace,
Never in its course shall cease,
Through the length of days;

7. While His grace our life shall cheer,
Furthest lands shall own His fear,
Brought to Him in worship near,
Taught His mercy's ways.
Amen.

## 220.

And GOD said, Let there be light: and there was light."

1. THOU, Whose almighty Word
Chaos and darkness heard,
And took their flight,
Hear us, we humbly pray,
And where the Gospel-day
Sheds not its glorious ray
Let there be light!

2. Thou, Who didst come to bring
On Thy redeeming wing
Healing and light,
Health to the sick in mind,
Sight to the inly blind,
Oh, now to all mankind
Let there be light!

3. SPIRIT of truth and love,
Life-giving, holy Dove,
Speed forth Thy flight;
Move on the waters' face,
Spreading the beams of grace,
And in earth's darkest place
Let there be light!

2. Blessèd and Holy THREE,
Glorious TRINITY,
Grace, Love, and Might:
Boundless as ocean's tide,
Rolling in fullest pride,
Through the world, far and wide,
Let there be light! Amen.

## 221.

### Burial of the Dead.

the ungodly He shall rain snares, fire, and brim-
:one, storm and tempest....He cometh, He cometh
› judge the earth."

1. DAY of Wrath! O day of mourning!
See fulfilled the prophets' warning!
Heaven and earth in ashes burning!

2. Oh, what fear man's bosom rendeth,
When from heaven the Judge descendeth,
On Whose sentence all dependeth!

3. Wondrous sound the trumpet flingeth,
Through earth's sepulchres it ringeth,
All before the Throne it bringeth.

4. Death is struck, and nature quaking,
All creation is awaking,
To its Judge an answer making.

5. Lo, the Book, exactly worded,
Wherein all hath been recorded!
Thence shall judgment be awarded.

6. When the Judge His seat attaineth,
And each hidden deed arraigneth,
Nothing unavenged remaineth.

7. What shall I, frail man, be pleading,
Who for me be interceding,
When the just are mercy needing?

8. King of Majesty tremendous,
Who dost free salvation send us,
Fount of pity, then befriend us!

9. Think, good Jesu, my salvation
Caused Thy wondrous Incarnation;
Leave me not to reprobation.

10. Faint and weary Thou hast sought me,
On the cross of suffering bought me;
Shall such grace be vainly brought me?

11. Righteous Judge! for sin's pollution
Grant Thy gift of absolution,
Ere that day of retribution.

12. Guilty, now I pour my moaning,
All my shame with anguish owning;
Spare, O God, Thy suppliant groaning.

13. Thou the sinful woman savedst;
Thou the dying thief forgavest;
And to me a hope vouchsafest.

14. Worthless are my prayers and sighing,
Yet, good Lord, in grace complying,
Rescue me from fires undying.

15. With Thy favoured sheep O place me,
Nor among the goats abase me;
But to Thy right hand upraise me.

16. While the wicked are confounded,
Doomed to flames of woe unbounded,
Call me, with Thy saints surrounded.

17. Low I kneel, with heart-submission;
See, like ashes, my contrition;
Help me in my last condition.

18. Ah, that day of tears and mourning!
From the dust of earth returning,
Man for judgment must prepare him;
Spare, O God, in mercy spare him!

19. Lord, all pitying, Jesu blest,
Grant *him* Thine eternal rest. Amen.

(*Also Hymns Nos.* 163, 191, *and* 142.)

# 222.

## For those at Sea.

"These men see the works of the LORD, and His wonders in the deep."

1. ETERNAL FATHER, strong to save,
Whose arm hath bound the restless wave,
Who bid'st the mighty ocean deep
Its own appointed limits keep;
O hear us when we cry to Thee
For those in peril on the sea.

2. O CHRIST, Whose voice the waters heard
And hushed their raging at Thy word,
Who walkedst on the foaming deep,
And calm amidst its rage didst sleep;
O hear us when we cry to Thee
For those in peril on the sea.

3. Most Holy SPIRIT, Who didst brood
Upon the chaos dark and rude,
And bid its angry tumult cease,
And give, for wild confusion, peace;
O hear us when we cry to Thee
For those in peril on the sea.

4. O TRINITY of love and power,
Our brethren shield in danger's hour;
From rock and tempest, fire and foe,
Protect them wheresoe'er they go;
Thus evermore shall rise to Thee
Glad hymns of praise from land and sea.
Amen.

# 223.

## Harvest.

"They joy before Thee, according to the joy of harvest."

1. COME, ye thankful people, come,
Raise the song of Harvest-Home!
All is safely gathered in,
Ere the winter-storms begin;
God, our Maker, doth provide
For our wants to be supplied;
Come to God's own Temple, come;
Raise the song of Harvest-Home!

2. What is earth but God's own field,
Fruit unto His praise to yield?
Wheat and tares therein are sown,
Unto joy or sorrow grown;
Ripening with a wondrous power,
Till the final Harvest-Hour:
Grant, O Lord of Life, that we
Holy grain and pure may be,

3. For we know that Thou wilt come,
And wilt take Thy people home;
From Thy field wilt purge away
All that doth offend, that day;
And Thine Angels charge at last
In the fire the tares to cast,
But the fruitful ears to store
In Thy Garner evermore.

4. Come, then, Lord of Mercy, come,
Bid us sing Thy Harvest-Home!
Let Thy Saints be gathered in,
Free from sorrow, free from sin;
All upon the golden floor
Praising Thee for evermore;
Come, with thousand Angels, come;
Bid us sing Thy Harvest-Home! Amen.

## 224.

"Who giveth food to all flesh; for His mercy endureth for ever."

1. PRAISE, O praise our God and King!
Hymns of adoration sing;
For His mercies still endure,
Ever faithful, ever sure.

2. Praise Him that He made the Sun
Day by day his course to run;
For His mercies still endure,
Ever faithful, ever sure:

3. And the silver Moon by night,
Shining with her gentle light;
For His mercies still endure,
Ever faithful, ever sure.

4. Praise Him that He gave the rain
To mature the swelling grain;
For His mercies still endure,
Ever faithful, ever sure:

5. And hath bid the fruitful field
Crops of precious increase yield;
For His mercies still endure,
Ever faithful, ever sure.

6. Praise Him for our Harvest-store,
He hath filled the Garner-floor;
For His mercies still endure,
Ever faithful, ever sure:

7. And for richer Food than this,
Pledge of everlasting bliss;
For His mercies still endure,
Ever faithful, ever sure.

8. Glory to our Bounteous King!
Glory let creation sing!
Glory to the FATHER, SON,
And Blest SPIRIT, Three in One.
Amen

## 225.

"Thou visitest the earth and blessest it; Thou makest it very plenteous."

1. FATHER of mercies, GOD of love,
Whose gifts all creatures share,
The rolling seasons as they move
Proclaim Thy constant care.

2. When in the bosom of the earth
The sower hid the grain,
Thy goodness marked its secret birth,
And sent the early rain.

3. The spring's sweet influence, LORD, was Thine,
The seasons knew Thy call;
Thou mad'st the summer sun to shine,
The summer dews to fall.

4. Thy gifts of mercy from above
Matured the swelling grain;
And now the harvest crowns Thy love,
And plenty fills the plain.

5. Oh, ne'er may our forgetful hearts
O'erlook Thy bounteous care;
But what our FATHER'S Hand imparts
Still own in praise and prayer.

6. To FATHER, SON, and HOLY GHOST,
The GOD Whom we adore,
Be glory, as it was, is now,
And shall be evermore. Amen.

## 226.

"The harvest is the end of the world, and the reapers are the angels."

1. LORD of the harvest, once again
We thank Thee for the ripened grain;
For crops safe carried, sent to cheer
Thy servants through another year;
For all sweet holy thoughts supplied
By seed-time, and by harvest-tide.

2. The bare dead grain, in autumn sown,
Its robe of vernal green puts on;
Glad from its wintry grave it springs,
Fresh garnished by the KING of Kings:
So, LORD, to those who sleep in Thee
Shall new and glorious bodies be.

3. Nor vainly of Thy Word we ask
A lesson from the reaper's task:
So shall Thine angels issue forth;
The tares be burnt; the just of earth,
To wind and storm exposed no more,
Be gathered to their FATHER's store.

4. Daily, O LORD, our prayers be said,
As Thou hast taught, for daily bread;
But not alone our bodies feed,
Supply our fainting spirits' need:
O Bread of Life, from day to day,
Be Thou their Comfort, Food, and Stay!
Amen.

## 227.

(*To be used when there is a deficiency in the crops.*)

"Although the fields shall yield no meat........yet I will rejoice in the LORD, I will joy in the GOD of my salvation."

1. WHAT our FATHER does is well;
Blessèd truth His children tell!
Though He send, for plenty, want,
Though the harvest-store be scant,
Yet we rest upon His love,
Seeking better things above.

2. What our Father does is well;
Shall the wilful heart rebel?
If a blessing He withhold
In the field, or in the fold,
Is it not Himself to be
All our Store eternally?

3. What our Father does is well;
Though He sadden hill and dell,
Upward yet our praises rise
For the strength His Word supplies;
He has called us sons of God,
Can we murmur at His rod?

4. What our Father does is well;
May the thought within us dwell;
Though nor milk nor honey flow
In our barren Canaan now,
God can save us in our need,
God can bless us, God can feed.

5. Therefore, unto Him we raise
Hymns of glory, songs of praise;
To the Father and the Son,
And the Spirit, Three in One,
Honour, might, and glory be,
Now, and through eternity. Amen.

# 228.

## School Festivals.

"That signs and wonders may be done by the Name of Thy Holy Child Jesus."

1. LORD JESUS, God and Man,
For love of men a Child,
The Very God, yet born on earth
Of Mary undefiled;

2. Lord Jesus, God and Man,
In this our festal day
To Thee for precious gifts of grace
Thy ransomed people pray.

3. We pray for childlike hearts,
For gentle holy love,
For strength to do Thy will below
As Angels do above.

4. We pray for simple faith,
For hope that never faints,
For true communion evermore
With all Thy blessèd Saints.

5. On friends around us here
O let Thy blessing fall;
We pray for grace to love them well,
But Thee beyond them all.

6. O joy to live for Thee!
O joy in Thee to die!
O very joy of joys to see
Thy Face eternally!

7. Lord Jesus, God and Man,
We praise Thee and adore.
Who art with God the Father One
And Spirit evermore. Amen.

## 229.

"Out of the mouth of babes and sucklings Thou hast perfected praise."

GOD eternal, mighty King,
Unto Thee our praise we bring;
All the earth doth worship Thee,
We amid the throng would be.

2. Holy, Holy, Holy! cry
Angels round Thy throne on high:
Lord of all the heavenly powers,
Be the same loud anthem ours.

3. Glorified Apostles raise
Night and day continual praise;
Hast not Thou a mission too
For Thy children here to do?

4. With the Prophets' goodly line
We in mystic bond combine;
For Thou hast to us revealed
Things that to the wise were sealed.

5. Martyrs, in a noble host,
Of the cross are heard to boast;
Oh, that we our cross may bear,
And a crown of glory wear.

6. God eternal, mighty King,
Unto Thee our praise we bring;
To the Father, and the Son,
And the Spirit, Three in One. Amen.

## 230.

"Jesus increased in wisdom and stature, and in favour with God and man."

1. O HOLY LORD, content to dwell
In a poor home, a lowly Child,
With meek obedience noting well
Each bidding of Thy mother mild;

2. Lead every child that bears Thy name
To walk in Thy pure upright way,
To shun the paths of sin and shame,
And humbly, like Thyself, obey.

3. Let not this world's unhallowed glow
The fresh baptismal due efface,
Nor blast of sin too roughly blow,
And quench the trembling flame of grace.

4. Gather Thy lambs within Thine arm,
And gently in Thy bosom bear,
Protect them still from hurt and harm,
And bid them rest for ever there.

5. So shall they, waiting here below,
Like Thee, their LORD, a little span,
In wisdom and in stature grow,
And favour both with GOD and man.
Amen.

## 231.

### Almsgiving.

"Inasmuch as ye have done it unto one of the least of these My brethren, ye have done it unto Me."

1. FOUNTAIN of good, to own Thy love
Our thankful hearts incline;
What can we render, LORD, to Thee,
When all the worlds are Thine?

2. But Thou hast needy brethren here,
Partakers of Thy grace,
Whose names Thou wilt Thyself confess
Before the FATHER's face.

3. And in their accents of distress
Thy pleading voice is heard,
In Them Thou may'st be clothed, and fed,
And visited, and cheered.

4. Thy face with reverence and with love
We in Thy poor would see;
O may we minister to them,
And in them, LORD, to Thee. Amen.

# 232.

## Friendly Societies, &c.

"Bear ye one another's burthens, and so fulfil the law of Christ."

1. O PRAISE our God to-day,
   His constant mercy bless,
Whose love hath helped us on our way,
   And granted us success.

2. His Arm the strength imparts
   Our daily toil to bear;
His grace alone inspires our hearts
   Each other's load to share.

3. O happiest work below,
   Earnest of joy above,
To sweeten many a cup of woe
   By deeds of holy love!

4. Lord, may it be our choice
   This blessèd rule to keep,
"Rejoice with them that do rejoice,
   And weep with them that weep."

5. God of the widow, hear!
   Our work of mercy bless;
God of the fatherless, be near,
   And grant us good success. Amen

*See also Hymn* 188.

# 233.

## In times of Trouble.

"Thou that hearest the prayer; unto Thee shall all flesh come."

1. WHEN in the hour of utmost need
We know not where to look for aid,
When days and nights of anxious thought
Nor help nor counsel yet have brought;

2. Then this our comfort is alone,
That we may meet before Thy throne,
And cry, O faithful God, to Thee
For rescue from our misery:

3. To Thee may raise our hearts and eyes,
Repenting sore, with bitter sighs,
And seek Thy pardon for our sin,
And respite from our griefs within.

4. For Thou hast promised graciously
To hear all those who cry to Thee,
Through Him Whose Name alone is great,
Our Saviour and our Advocate.

5. And thus we come, O God, to-day,
And all our woes before Thee lay,
For tried, afflicted, lo! we stand,
Perils and foes on every hand.

6. Ah, hide not, for our sins, Thy face,
Absolve us through Thy boundless grace,
Be with us in our anguish still,
Free us at last from every ill.

7. That so with all our hearts may we
Once more with joy give thanks to Thee,
And walk obedient to Thy word,
And now and ever praise the LORD. Amen.

## 234.

"GOD is our hope and strength, a very present help in trouble."

1. GOD of our life, to Thee we call,
Afflicted at Thy feet we fall;
When the great water-floods prevail,
Leave not our trembling hearts to fail.

2. Friend of the friendless and the faint,
Where shall we pour our sad complaint?
Where but with Thee, Whose open door
Invites the helpless and the poor?

3. Did ever sinner plead with Thee,
And Thou reject his lowly plea?
Does not Thy word still pledged remain,
That none shall seek Thy face in vain?

4. Then hear, O LORD, our humble cry,
And bend on us Thy pitying eye:
To Thee their prayer Thy people make,
Hear us, for our REDEEMER's sake. Amen.

## 235.

WAR.

"The LORD shall give His people the blessing of peace."

1\. O GOD of love, O King of peace,
Make wars throughout the world to cease;
The wrath of sinful man restrain,
Give peace, O GOD, give peace again.

2\. Remember, LORD, Thy works of old,
The wonders that our fathers told,
Remember not our sin's dark stain,
Give peace, O GOD, give peace again.

3\. Whom shall we trust but Thee, O LORD?
Where rest but on Thy faithful word?
None ever called on Thee in vain,
Give peace, O GOD, give peace again.

4\. Where saints and angels dwell above
All hearts are knit in holy love;
O bind us in that heavenly chain,
Give peace, O GOD, give peace again. Amen.

## 236.

PESTILENCE.

"Thou shalt not be afraid.........for the pestilence that walketh in darkness; nor for the sickness that destroyeth in the noon day."

1\. IN grief and fear to Thee, O LORD,
We now for succour fly,
Thine awful judgments are abroad,
O shield us lest we die.

2. The fell disease on every side
Walks forth with tainted breath;
And Pestilence, with rapid stride,
Bestrews the land with death.

3. O look with pity on the scene
Of sadness and of dread,
And let Thine angel stand between
The living and the dead.

4. With contrite hearts to Thee, our King,
We turn who oft have strayed:
Accept the sacrifice we bring,
And let the plague be stayed. Amen.

*In time of Famine, Hymn 227 may be used, as well as Hymns 233 and 234.*

## 237.

### Thanksgiving.

"O praise the LORD, laud ye the Name of the LORD; praise it, O ye servants of the LORD."

1. REJOICE to-day with one accord,
Sing out with exultation;
Rejoice and praise our mighty LORD,
Whose Arm hath brought salvation;
His works of love proclaim
The greatness of His Name;
For He is GOD alone
Who hath His mercy shewn;
Let all His saints adore Him!

2. When in distress to Him we cried,
He heard our sad complaining;
Oh, trust in Him, whate'er betide,
His love is all-sustaining;
Triumphant songs of praise
To Him our hearts shall raise;
Now every voice shall say,
"O praise our God alway;"
Let all His saints adore Him!

3. Rejoice to-day with one accord,
Sing out with exultation;
Rejoice and praise our mighty Lord,
Whose Arm hath brought salvation;
His works of love proclaim
The greatness of His Name;
For He is God alone
Who hath His mercy shewn;
Let all His Saints adore Him! Amen.

## 238.

"O clap your hands together all ye people; O sing unto God with the voice of melody."

1. NOW thank we all our God,
With heart, and hands, and voices,
Who wondrous things hath done,
In Whom His world rejoices;
Who from our mother's arms
Hath blessed us on our way
With countless gifts of love,
And still is ours to-day.

2. O may this bounteous God
Through all our life be near us,
With ever joyful hearts
And blessèd peace to cheer us;
And keep us in His grace,
And guide us when perplexed,
And free us from all ills
In this world and the next.

3. All praise and thanks to God,
The Father, now be given,
The Son, and Him Who reigns
With Them in highest heaven,
The One eternal God,
Whom earth and heaven adore,
For thus it was, is now,
And shall be evermore. Amen.

## 239.

### New Year's Day.

"So teach us to number our days, that we may apply our hearts unto wisdom."

1. FOR Thy mercy and Thy grace,
Constant through another year,
Hear our song of thankfulness;
Jesu, our Redeemer, hear.

2. In our weakness and distress,
Rock of Strength, be Thou our stay;
In the pathless wilderness
Be our true and living way.

3. Who of us death's awful road
In the coming year shall tread,
With Thy rod and staff, O God,
Comfort Thou his dying bed.

4. Make us faithful, make us pure,
Keep us evermore Thine own,
Help Thy servants to endure,
Fit us for the promised crown.

5. So within Thy palace gate
We shall praise, on golden strings,
Thee the only Potentate,
Lord of lords, and King of kings. Amen.

## 240.

"And now, Lord, what is my hope: truly my hope is even in Thee."

1. THE year is gone beyond recall,
With all its hopes and fears,
With all its bright and gladdening smiles,
With all its mourners' tears;

2. Thy thankful people praise Thee, Lord,
For countless gifts received,
And pray for grace to keep the Faith
Which saints of old believed.

3. To Thee we come, O gracious Lord,
The new-born year to bless;
Defend our land from pestilence,
Give peace and plenteousness;

4. Forgive this nation's many sins,
The growth of vice restrain,
And help us all with sin to strive,
And crowns of life to gain.

5. From evil deeds that stain the past
We now desire to flee;
And pray that future years may all
Be spent, good LORD, for Thee.

6. O FATHER, let Thy watchful Eye
Still look on us in love,
That we may praise Thee, year by year,
As angels do above.

7. All glory to the FATHER be,
All glory to the SON,
All glory, HOLY GHOST, to Thee,
While endless ages run. Amen.

# 241.

## Laying the Foundation Stone of a Church.

"The glory of Lebanon shall come unto thee, the fig tree, the pine tree, and the box together, to beautify the place of My sanctuary."

1. O LORD of Hosts, Whose glory fills
The bounds of the eternal hills,
And yet vouchsafes, in Christian lands,
To dwell in temples made with hands;

2. Grant that all we, who here to-day
Rejoicing this foundation lay,
May be in very deed Thine own,
Built on the precious Corner-stone.

3. Endue the creatures with Thy grace,
That shall adorn Thy dwelling-place;
The beauty of the oak and pine,
The gold and silver, make them Thine.

4. To Thee they all pertain; to Thee
The treasures of the earth and sea;
And when we bring them to Thy throne
We but present Thee with Thine own.

5. The heads that guide endue with skill;
The hands that work preserve from ill;
That we, who these foundations lay,
May raise the topstone in its day.

6. Both now and ever, LORD, protect
The temple of Thine own elect;
Be Thou in them, and they in Thee,
O ever-blessèd TRINITY! Amen.

## 242.

## Feast of the Dedication of a Church.

"This is none other but the House of GOD, and this is the gate of heaven."

1. O WORD of GOD above
Who fillest all in all,
Hallow this house with Thy sure love,
And bless our festival.

2. Here from the Font is poured
   Grace on each guilty child;
The blest anointing of the LORD
   Brightens the once defiled.

3. Here CHRIST to faithful hearts
   His Body gives for food;
The LAMB of GOD Himself imparts
   The Chalice of His Blood.

4. Here guilty souls that pine
   May health and pardon win;
The Judge acquits, and grace divine
   Restores the dead in sin.

5. Yea, GOD enthroned on high
   Here also dwells to bless;
Here trains adoring souls that sigh
   His mansions to possess.

6. Against this holy home
   Rude tempests harmless beat,
And Satan's angels fiercely come
   But to endure defeat.

7. All might, all praise be Thine,
   FATHER, co-equal SON,
And SPIRIT, bond of love divine,
   While endless ages run. Amen.

## 243.

"I saw the holy city, New Jerusalem, coming down from God, out of heaven, prepared as a bride adorned for her husband."

1. BLESSÈD city, heavenly Salem,
 Vision dear of peace and love,
Who of living stones art builded
 In the height of heaven above,
And, with angel hosts encircled,
 As a bride to earth dost move;

2. From celestial realms descending,
 Bridal glory round thee shed,
Meet for Him Whose love espoused thee,
 To thy Lord shalt thou be led;
All thy streets, and all thy bulwarks,
 Of pure gold are fashionèd.

3. Bright thy gates of pearls are shining,
 They are open evermore;
And by virtue of His merits
 Thither faithful souls do soar,
Who for Christ's dear Name in this world
 Pain and tribulation bore.

4. Many a blow and biting sculpture
 Polished well those stones elect,
In their places now compacted
 By the heavenly Architect,
Who therewith hath willed for ever
 That His Palace should be decked.

5. Praise and honour to the Father,
   Praise and honour to the Son,
Praise and honour to the Spirit,
   Ever Three, and ever One,
One in might, and One in glory,
   While eternal ages run. Amen.

## 244.

"Behold I lay in Sion a Chief Corner-stone, elect, precious."

1. CHRIST is made the sure Foundation,
   Christ the Head and Corner-stone,
Chosen of the Lord, and precious,
   Binding all the Church in one,
Holy Sion's help for ever,
   And her confidence alone.

2. All that dedicated City,
   Dearly loved of God on high,
In exultant jubilation
   Pours perpetual melody;
God the One in Three adoring
   In glad hymns eternally.

3. To this Temple, where we call Thee,
   Come, O Lord of Hosts, to-day:
With Thy wonted loving-kindness
   Hear Thy servants, as they pray;
And Thy fullest benediction
   Shed within its walls alway.

4. Here vouchsafe to all Thy servants
   What they ask of Thee to gain,
What they gain from Thee for ever
   With the Blessèd to retain,
And hereafter in Thy glory
   Evermore with Thee to reign.

5. Praise and honour to the FATHER,
   Praise and honour to the SON,
Praise and honour to the SPIRIT,
   Ever THREE, and ever ONE,
One in might, and One in glory,
   While eternal ages run. Amen.

## 245.

### The Conversion of St. Paul.

"The voice of the LORD breaketh the cedar trees; yea, the LORD breaketh the cedars of Libanus."

1. THE Shepherd now was smitten;
   The wolf was ravening near,
The scattered flock he threatened,
   But knew not Whose they were.

2. In zealous fury seeking
   To bind and crucify,
A sudden voice withheld him,
   A loud and startling cry:

3. "Saul! Saul! why blindly daring
To persecute thy LORD?
'Tis JESUS Whom thou hatest,
Rebel not at My word."

4. Then forth in prayer he stretcheth
Those hands prepared to slay;
"What would'st Thou with Thy servant?
My LORD and SAVIOUR, say."

5. CHRIST's foe becomes His soldier,
The wolf destroys no more,
A sheep within the sheepfold
He enters by the door.

6. O voice of GOD Almighty,
What wonders hath it wrought!
It rends the lofty cedars,
It bends the haughty thought.

7. JESU, our Shepherd, cease not
Thy flock from harm to free,
And when Thy sheep are wandering
O lead them back to Thee.

8. To FATHER, SON, and SPIRIT,
All glory, praise, and might,
Who called us out of darkness
To His own glorious light. Amen.

## 246.

"Saul, Saul, why persecutest thou Me?"

1. 'GAINST what foemen art thou rushing?
   Saul, what madness drives thee on?
Innocents in fury crushing,
   Children of the sinless One.
      O, how shortly
   Shall He make His vengeance known!

2. See the LORD, from heaven descending,
   Smites him, blinds him, lays him low;
See the persecutor bending
   Humbly, meekly to the blow:
      See him rising,
   Friend to CHRIST, no longer foe

3. Breathing slaughter, chains preparing,
   O, how fierce his anger burned;
Trembling now, and lost his daring,
   Meek obedience he has learned:
      The destroyer
   Now into a lamb is turned.

4. CHRIST, Thy power is man's salvation,
   Hardest hearts Thou mak'st Thine own;
He who wrought such desolation,
   That Thy Name might be o'erthrown,
      Now converted,
   Thro' the world that Name makes known.

5. Praise the FATHER, GOD of heaven,
   Him Who reigns supreme on high;
Praise the SON for sinners given
   Both to suffer, and to die;
      Praise the SPIRIT
   Guiding us most lovingly. Amen.

# 247.

## Presentation of Christ in the Temple

COMMONLY CALLED

## The Purification of St. Mary the Virgin.

"The LORD, Whom ye seek, shall suddenly come to His temple."

1. O SION, open wide Thy gates,
   Let figures disappear,
A Priest and Victim both in one,
   The Truth Himself, is here.

2. No more the simple flock shall bleed;
   Behold, the FATHER's SON
Himself to His own altar comes,
   For sinners to atone.

3. Conscious of hidden Deity
   The lowly Virgin brings
Her new-born Babe, with two young doves,
   Her tender offerings.

4. The hoary Simeon sees at last
His LORD so long desired,
And hails, with Anna, Israel's Hope,
With sudden rapture fired.

5. But silent knelt the Mother blest
Of the yet silent WORD,
And, pondering all things in her heart,
With speechless praise adored.

6. All glory to the FATHER be,
All glory to the SON,
All glory, HOLY GHOST, to Thee,
While endless ages run. Amen.

## 248.

## Annunciation of the Blessed Virgin Mary.

"Behold, a Virgin shall be with child, and shall bring forth a SON, and they shall call His Name EMMANUEL, which being interpreted is, GOD with us."

1. PRAISE we the LORD this day,
This day so long foretold,
Whose promise shone with cheering ray
On waiting saints of old.

2. The Prophet gave the sign
For faithful men to read;
A Virgin, born of David's line,
Shall bear the promised Seed.

3. Ask not how this should be,
   But worship and adore;
Like her, whom heaven's majesty
   Came down to shadow o'er.

4. Meekly she bowed her head
   To hear the gracious word,
Mary, the pure and lowly maid,
   The favoured of the Lord.

5. Blessèd shall be her name
   In all the Church on earth,
Thro' whom that wondrous mercy came
   The Incarnate Saviour's birth.

6. Jesu, the Virgin's Son,
   We praise Thee and adore,
Who art with God the Father One
   And Spirit evermore. Amen.

## 249.

"Hail, thou that art highly favoured, the Lord is with thee; blessed art thou among women."

1. THE God Whom earth, and sea, and sky
   Adore, and laud, and magnify,
Whose might they own, Whose praise they swell,
In Mary's womb vouchsafed to dwell.

2. The Lord, Whom sun and moon obey,
Whom all things serve from day to day,
Was by the Holy Ghost conceived
Of her who through His grace believed.

3. How blest that Mother, in whose shrine
The world's Creator, LORD divine,
Whose hand contains the earth and sky,
Once deigned, as in His ark, to lie:

4. Blest in the message Gabriel brought,
Blest by the work the SPIRIT wrought,
From whom the great Desire of earth
Took human flesh and human birth.

5. O LORD, the Virgin-born, to Thee
Eternal praise and glory be;
Whom with the FATHER we adore
And HOLY GHOST for evermore. Amen.

*This Hymn may also be used on the Purification, &c.*

## 250.

## Nativity of St. John Baptist.

"Behold I will send my Messenger, and he shall prepare the way before Me."

1. THE great forerunner of the morn,
The herald of the WORD, is born;
And faithful hearts shall never fail
With thanks and praise his light to hail.

2. With heavenly message Gabriel came,
That John should be that herald's name,
And with prophetic utterance told
His actions great and manifold.

3. John, still unborn, yet gave aright
His witness to the coming Light;
And CHRIST, the Sun of all the earth,
Fulfilled that witness at His Birth.

4. Of women-born shall never be
A greater prophet than was he,
Whose mighty deeds exalt his fame
To greater than a prophet's name.

5. But why should mortal accents raise
The hymn of John the Baptist's praise?
Of whom, or ere his course was run,
Thus spake the FATHER to the SON:

6. "Behold My herald, who shall go
Before Thy Face Thy way to show,
And shine, as with the day-star's gleam
Before Thine own eternal beam."

7. All praise to GOD the FATHER be;
All praise, Eternal SON, to Thee;
Whom, with the SPIRIT, we adore
For ever and for evermore. Amen.

## 251.

"Repent ye, for the kingdom of heaven is at hand."

1. LO! from the desert homes,
Where he hath hid so long,
The new Elias comes,
In sternest wisdom strong;
The voice that cries
Of CHRIST from high,
And judgment nigh
From opening skies.

2. Your God e'en now doth stand
 At heaven's opening door,
His fan is in His hand,
 And He will purge His floor;
  The wheat He claims
   And with Him stows,
   The chaff He throws
  To quenchless flames.

3. Ye haughty mountains, bow
 Your sky-aspiring heads;
Ye valleys, hiding low,
 Lift up your gentle meads;
  Make His way plain
   Your King before,
   For evermore
  He comes to reign.

4. May thy dread voice around,
 Thou harbinger of Light,
On our dull ears still sound,
 Lest here we sleep in night,
  Till judgment come,
   And on our path
   Shall burst the wrath,
  And deathless doom.

5. O God, with love's sweet might,
 Who dost anoint and arm
Thy soldiers for the fight
 With grace that shields from harm,

Thrice blessèd THREE,
Heaven's endless days
Shall sing Thy praise
Eternally. Amen.

## 252.

### St. Michael and all Angels.

"There was war in heaven; Michael and his angels fought against the dragon; and the dragon fought and his angels."

1. CHRIST, in highest heaven enthronèd,
Equal of the FATHER'S Might,
By pure spirits, trembling, ownèd
GOD of GOD, and LIGHT of LIGHT,
Thee 'mid Angel hosts we sing,
Thee their Maker, and their King.

2. All who circling round adore Thee,
All who bow before Thy Throne,
Burn with flaming zeal before Thee,
Thy behests to carry down;
To and fro, 'twixt earth and heaven
Speed they each on errands given.

3. First of all those legions glorious
Michael waves his sword of flame,
Who of old in war victorious
Did the Dragon's fierceness tame;
Who with might invincible
Thrust the rebel down to hell.

4. They to aid the sick and dying
   Called from heaven do swiftly fly,
Grace divine and strength supplying
   In their mortal agony:
Souls released from bondage here
They to Paradise do bear.

5. To the FATHER praise be given
   By the unfallen angel-host,
Who in His great war have striven
   With the legions of the lost;
Equal praise in highest heaven
To the SON and HOLY GHOST. Amen.

## 253.

"O praise the LORD all ye His hosts; ye servants of His that do His pleasure."

1. PRAISE to GOD Who reigns above,
   Binding earth and heaven in love;
All the armies of the sky
Worship His dread sovereignty.

2. Seraphim His praises sing,
Cherubim on fourfold wing,
Thrones, Dominions, Princes, Powers,
Ranks of Might that never cowers.

3. Angel hosts His word fulfil,
Ruling nature by His will;
Round His throne Archangels pour
Songs of praise for evermore.

4. Yet on man they joy to wait,
All that bright celestial state,
For true Man their Lord they see,
Christ, the Incarnate Deity.

5. On the throne our Lord Who died
Sits in Manhood glorified,
Where His people faint below
Angels count it joy to go.

6. O the depths of joy divine
Thrilling through those orders nine,
When the lost are found again,
When the banished come to reign.

7. Now in faith, in hope, in love,
We will join the choirs above,
Praising, with the heavenly host,
Father, Son, and Holy Ghost. Amen.

## 254.

"Are they not all ministering spirits sent forth to minister for them who shall be heirs of salvation?"

1. THEY come, God's Messengers of love,
They come from realms of peace above,
From homes of never-fading light,
From blissful mansions ever bright.

2. They come to watch around us here,
To soothe our sorrow, calm our fear:
Ye heavenly guides, speed not away,
God willeth you with us to stay.

3. But chiefly at its journey's end
'Tis yours the spirit to befriend,
And whisper to the willing heart,
"O Christian soul, in peace depart."

4. Blest Jesu, Thou whose groans and tears
Have sanctified frail nature's fears,
To earth in bitter sorrow weighed
Thou didst not scorn Thine Angels' aid.

5. An Angel guard to us supply,
When on the bed of death we lie;
And by Thine own Almighty power
O shield us in the last dread hour.

6. To God the Father, God the Son,
And God the Spirit, Three in One,
From all above, and all below,
Let joyful praise unceasing flow. Amen.

## 255.

### All Saints' Day.

"What are these which are arrayed in white robes? and whence came they?"

1. WHO are these like stars appearing,
These, before God's throne who stand?
Each a golden crown is wearing,
Who are all this glorious band?
Alleluia! hark, they sing,
Praising loud their heavenly King.

2. Who are these in dazzling brightness,
Clothed in God's own righteousness;
These, whose robes of purest whiteness
Shall their lustre still possess,
Still untouched by time's rude hand,
Whence come all this glorious band?

3. These are they who have contended
For their Saviour's honour long,
Wrestling on till life was ended,
Following not the sinful throng;
These, who well the fight sustained,
Triumph by the Lamb have gained.

4. These are they whose hearts were riven
Sore with woe and anguish tried,
Who in prayer full oft have striven
With the God they glorified;
Now, their painful conflict o'er,
God has bid them weep no more.

5. These, the Almighty contemplating,
Did as priests before Him stand,
Soul and body always waiting
Day and night at His command:
Now in God's most holy place
Blest they stand before His face. Amen.

## 256.

"And the city had no need of the sun, neither of the moon, to shine in it; for the glory of God did lighten it, and the Lamb is the Light thereof."

1. O HEAVENLY Jerusalem,
Of everlasting halls,
Thrice blessèd are the people
Thou storest in Thy walls.

2. Thou art the golden mansion,
Where saints for ever sing;
The seat of God's own chosen,
The palace of the King.

3. There God for ever sitteth,
Himself of all the Crown;
The Lamb the Light that shineth
And never goeth down.

4. Naught to this seat approacheth
Their sweet peace to molest;
They sing their God for ever,
Nor day nor night they rest.

5. Sure Hope doth thither lead us;
Our longings thither tend;
May short-lived toil ne'er daunt us
For joys that cannot end.

6. To Christ the Sun that lightens
His Church above, below;
To Father, and to Spirit,
All things created bow. Amen.

*See also Hymns 262 and 263.*

# 257.

## Apostles.

"And the wall of the city had twelve foundations, and on them the names of the twelve Apostles of the Lamb."

1. THE eternal gifts of CHRIST the King,
The Apostles' glory, let us sing;
And all, with hearts of gladness, raise
Due hymns of thankful love and praise.

2. For they the Church's princes are,
Triumphant leaders in the war,
In heavenly courts a warrior band,
True lights to lighten every land.

3. Theirs is the steadfast faith of saints,
And hope that never yields nor faints,
And love of CHRIST in perfect glow
That lays the prince of this world low.

4. In them the FATHER'S glory shone,
In them the will of GOD the SON,
In them exults the HOLY GHOST,
Through them rejoice the heavenly host.

5. To Thee, REDEEMER, now we cry,
That Thou wouldst join to them on high
Thy servants, who this grace implore,
For ever and for evermore. Amen.

# 258.

"Their sound went into all the earth, and their words unto the ends of the world."

1. DISPOSER Supreme,
   And Judge of the earth,
Who choosest for Thine
   The weak and the poor;
To frail earthen vessels
   And things of no worth
Entrusting Thy riches
   Which aye shall endure;

2. Those vessels soon fail,
   Though full of Thy light,
And at Thy decree
   Are broken and gone;
Thence brightly appeareth
   Thy truth in its might,
As through the clouds riven
   The lightnings have shone.

3. Like clouds are they borne
   To do Thy great will,
And swift as the winds
   About the world go;
The WORD with His wisdom
   Their spirits doth fill,
They thunder, they lighten,
   The waters o'erflow.

4. Their sound goeth forth,
"CHRIST JESUS the LORD:"
Then Satan doth fear,
His citadels fall:
As when the dread trumpets
Went forth at Thy word,
And one long blast shattered
The Canaanite's wall.

5. O loud be their trump,
And stirring their sound
To rouse us, O LORD,
From slumber of sin;
The lights Thou hast kindled
In darkness around,
Oh, may they illumine
Our spirits within.

6. All honour, and praise,
Dominion, and might,
To GOD, THREE IN ONE,
Eternally be,
Who round us hath shed
His own marvellous light,
And called us from darkness
His glory to see. Amen.

## 259.

"Ye also shall sit upon twelve thrones, judging the twelve tribes of Israel."

1. CAPTAINS of the saintly band,
Lights who lighten every land,
Princes who with JESUS dwell,
Judges of His Israel;

2. On the nations sunk in night
Ye have shed the Gospel light;
Sin and error flee away,
Truth is shining on our way.

3. Not by warrior's spear and sword,
Not by art of human word,
Preaching but the Cross of shame
Rebel hearts for CHRIST ye tame.

4. Earth, that long in sin and pain
Groaned in Satan's deadly chain,
Now to serve its GOD is free
In the law of liberty.

5. Distant lands with one acclaim
Tell the honour of your name,
Who, wherever man has trod,
Teach the mysteries of GOD.

6. Glory to the THREE IN ONE
While eternal ages run,
Who from deepest shades of night
Called us to His glorious light. Amen.

## 260.

### Evangelists.

"Behold upon the mountains the feet of him that bringeth good tidings, that publisheth peace."

1. BEHOLD the messengers of CHRIST,
Who sow in every place
The unveiled mysteries of GOD,
The Gospel of His grace.

2. The things, thro' mists and shadows dim
By holy prophets seen,
In the full light of day they saw
With not a cloud between.

3. What CHRIST, True Man, divinely wrought,
What GOD in Manhood bore,
They wrote as GOD inspired in words
That live for evermore.

4. Although in space and time apart,
One SPIRIT ruled them all:
And in their sacred pages still
We hear that SPIRIT'S call.

5. To GOD, the Blessèd THREE IN ONE,
Be glory, praise, and might,
Who called us from the shades of death
To His own glorious light. Amen.

## 261.

"And a River went out of Eden to water the garden; and from thence it was parted, and became into four heads."

1. COME pure hearts, in sweetest measures
Sing of those who spread the treasures
In the holy Gospels shrined;
Blessèd tidings of salvation,
Peace on earth, their proclamation,
Love from GOD to lost mankind.

2. See the Rivers four that gladden
With their streams the better Eden
Planted by our LORD most dear;
CHRIST the Fountain, these the waters;
Drink, O Sion's sons and daughters,
Drink and find salvation here.

3. O, that we Thy truth confessing,
And Thy holy word possessing,
JESU, may Thy love adore;
Unto Thee our voices raising,
Thee with all Thy ransomed praising,
Ever and for evermore. Amen.

*The Hymn No. 109, parts 2 and 3, may also be used on the Festivals of Apostles or Evangelists, between Easterday and Trinity Sunday.*

## 262.

### Martyrs, &c.

"These are they which came out of great tribulation, and have washed their robes, and made them white in the Blood of the LAMB."

1. HOW bright those glorious spirits shine!
Whence all their white array?
How came they to the blissful seats
Of everlasting day?

2. Lo, these are they from sufferings great
Who came to realms of light:
And in the Blood of CHRIST have washed
Those robes which shine so bright.

3. Now with triumphal palms they stand
   Before the throne on high,
And serve the God they love amidst
   The glories of the sky.

4. Hunger and thirst are felt no more,
   Nor sun with scorching ray;
God is their Sun, Whose cheering beams
   Diffuse eternal day.

5. The Lamb, Who reigns upon the throne,
   Shall o'er them still preside,
Feed them with nourishment divine,
   And all their footsteps guide.

6. 'Mid pastures green He'll lead His flock
   Where living streams appear;
And God the Lord from every eye
   Shall wipe off every tear.

7. To Father, Son, and Holy Ghost,
   The God Whom we adore
Be glory, as it was, is now,
   And shall be evermore. Amen.

## 263.

"Fight the good fight of faith."

1. THE Son of God goes forth to war,
   A kingly crown to gain,
His blood-red banner streams afar;
   Who follows in His train?

2. Who best can drink his cup of woe,
Triumphant over pain,
Who patient bears his cross below,
He follows in His train.

3. The martyr first, whose eagle eye
Could pierce beyond the grave,
Who saw his Master in the sky,
And called on Him to save.

4. Like Him, with pardon on his tongue,
In midst of mortal pain,
He prayed for them that did the wrong;
Who follows in his train?

5. A glorious band, the chosen few
On whom the SPIRIT came,
Twelve valiant saints, their hope they knew,
And mocked the cross and flame.

6. They met the tyrant's brandished steel,
The lion's gory mane,
They bowed their necks, the death to feel;
Who follows in their train?

7. A noble army, men and boys,
The matron and the maid,
Around the SAVIOUR's throne rejoice,
In robes of light arrayed.

8. They climbed the steep ascent of heaven
Through peril, toil, and pain;
O GOD, to us may grace be given
To follow in their train. Amen.

## 264.

"Blessed is the man that endureth temptation, for when he is tried he shall receive the crown of life."

1. O GOD, Thy soldiers' great Reward,
Their Portion, Crown, and faithful LORD
From all transgressions set us free
Who sing Thy martyr's victory.

2. By wisdom taught he learned to know
The vanity of all below,
The fleeting joys of earth disdained,
And everlasting glory gained.

3. Right manfully his cross he bore,
And ran his race of torments sore;
For Thee he poured his life away,
With Thee he lives in endless day.

4. We therefore pray Thee, LORD of love,
Regard us from Thy throne above;
On this Thy martyr's triumph-day,
Wash every stain of sin away.

5. All praise to GOD the FATHER be;
All praise, Eternal SON, to Thee;
Whom, with the SPIRIT, we adore
For ever and for evermore. Amen.

## 265.

"Be thou faithful unto death, and I will give thee a crown of life."

1. FOR man the SAVIOUR shed
His all-atoning Blood,
And oh, shall ransomed man refuse
To suffer for his GOD?

2. Ashamed who now can be
To own the Crucified?
Nay, rather be our glory this,
To die for Him Who died.

3. So felt Thy martyr, LORD;
By Thy right hand sustained
He waged for Thee the battle's strife,
And threatened death disdained.

4. Upon the golden crown
Gazing, with eager breath,
He fought as one who fain would die,
And, dying, conquer death.

5. Alone he stood unmoved
Amid his cruel foes;
O wondrous was the might that then
Above his torturers rose.

6. LORD, give us grace to bear
Like him our cross of shame,
To do and suffer what Thou wilt,
For love of Thy dear Name.

7. JESU, the King of saints,
We praise Thee and adore,
Who art with GOD the FATHER One
And SPIRIT evermore. Amen.

## 266.

"If a man desire the office of a Bishop, he desireth a good work."

1. O THOU Whose all-redeeming might
Crowns every Chief in faith's true fight,
On this commemoration day
Hear us, good JESU, while we pray.

2. In faithful strife for Thy dear Name
Thy servant earned the saintly fame,
Which pious hearts with praise revere
In constant memory year by year.

3. Earth's fleeting joys he counted naught,
For higher, truer, joys he sought,
And now, with angels round Thy Throne,
Unfading treasures are his own.

4. O grant that we, most gracious GOD,
May follow in the steps he trod;
And, freed from every stain of sin,
As he hath won may also win.

5. To Thee, O CHRIST, our loving King,
All glory, praise, and thanks we bring:
Whom with the FATHER we adore,
And HOLY GHOST, for evermore. Amen.

## 267.

"Whosoever shall confess Me before men, him will I confess before My FATHER which is in heaven."

1. NOT by the martyr's death alone
   The saint his crown in heaven has won;
There is a triumph robe on high
For bloodless fields of victory.

2. What though he was not called to feel
The cross, or flame, or torturing wheel,
Yet daily to the world he died,
His flesh, through grace, he crucified.

3. What though nor chains, nor scourges sore,
Nor cruel beasts his members tore,
Enough if perfect love arise
To CHRIST a grateful sacrifice.

4. LORD, grant us so to Thee to turn,
That we to die through life may learn,
And thus, when life's brief day is o'er,
Rejoice with Thee for evermore.

5. O Fount of sanctity and love,
O perfect Rest of saints above,
All praise, all glory be to Thee,
Both now and through eternity. Amen.

# 268.

"Thy Name is as ointment poured forth, therefore do the virgins love Thee."

1. JESU, the virgins' Crown, do Thou
Accept us as in prayer we bow,
Born of that Virgin whom alone
The Mother and the Maid we own.

2. Amongst the lilies Thou dost feed,
And thither choirs of virgins lead;
Adorning all Thy chosen brides
With glorious gifts Thy love provides.

3. And whither, LORD, Thy footsteps wend,
The virgins still with praise attend;
For Thee they pour their sweetest song,
And after Thee rejoicing throng.

4. O gracious LORD, we Thee implore
Thy grace on every sense to pour;
From all pollution keep us free,
And make us pure in heart for Thee.

5. All praise to GOD the FATHER be;
All praise, Eternal SON, to Thee;
Whom, with the SPIRIT, we adore
For ever and for evermore. Amen.

## 269.

"Who can find a virtuous woman? for her price is above rubies: the heart of her husband doth safely trust in her."

1. HOW blest the matron, who, endued
With holy zeal and fortitude,
Has won through grace a saintly fame,
And owns a dear and honoured name.

2. Such holy love inflamed her breast
She would not seek on earth her rest,
But, strong in faith and patience, trod
The narrow way that leads to GOD.

3. She learned, through fasting, to control
The flesh that weigheth down the soul,
And then by prayer's sweet food sustained
To seek the joys she now has gained.

4. O CHRIST, from Whom all virtue springs,
Who only doest wondrous things,
To Thee, the King of Saints, we pray
Accept and bless Thy flock to-day.

5. All praise to GOD the FATHER be;
All praise, Eternal SON, to Thee;
Whom, with the SPIRIT, we adore
For ever and for evermore. Amen.

# 270.

"I, John, who also am your brother and companion in tribulation, and in the kingdom and patience of Jesus Christ, was in the isle that is called Patmos, for the Word of God and for the testimony of Jesus Christ."

1. AN exile for the Faith
Of his Incarnate Lord,
Beyond the stars, beyond all space,
His soul in vision soared:

2. There saw in glory Him
Who liveth, and was dead;
There Judah's Lion and the Lamb
That for our ransom bled;

3. There of the Kingdom learnt
The mysteries sublime;
How, sown in martyrs' blood, the Faith
Should spread from clime to clime.

4. Lord, give us grace, like him,
In Thee to live and die;
To spurn the fleeting things of earth,
And seek for joys on high.

5. Jesu, our risen Lord,
We praise Thee and adore,
Who art with God the Father One
And Spirit evermore. Amen.

# 271.

"Mary Magdalene, out of whom He had cast seven devils."

1. SON of the Highest, deign to cast
   On us a pitying eye,
Thou Who repentant Magdalene
   Didst call to joys on high.

2. The long-lost coin is stored at length
   In treasure-house divine,
The precious gem from filth is cleansed,
   And doth the stars outshine.

3. Jesu, the balm of every wound,
   The sinner's only stay,
Grant us, like Magdalene, to weep
   In this Thy mercy's day.

4. Absolve us by Thy gracious Word,
   Fulfil us with Thy love,
And guide us through the storms of life
   To perfect rest above.

5. All praise, all glory be to Thee,
   One everlasting Lord,
Whose mercy doth our souls forgive,
   Whose bounty doth reward. Amen.

# 272.

"Of whom the world was not worthy."

1. YE servants of our glorious King,
To Him your thankful praises bring;
And tell the deeds that grace has done,
The triumphs by His martyrs won.

2. Since they were faithful to the last,
Their holy struggles now are past;
The bitterness of death is o'er,
And theirs is bliss for evermore.

3. The flame did scorch, the knife lay bare,
And cruel beasts their members tear;
No powers of earth, no powers of hell
The souls that loved their LORD could quell.

4. For ever broken is the chain
That sought to bind them, but in vain:
O let us strive like them to win
Our freedom from the bonds of sin.

3. O SAVIOUR, may our portion be
With those who gave themselves to Thee,
Through all eternity to sing
All praise to Thee, the martyrs' King.

6. All praise to GOD the FATHER be;
All praise, Eternal SON, to Thee;
Whom, with the SPIRIT, we adore
For ever and for evermore. Amen.

## 273.

"And they glorified God in me."

1. FOR Thy dear saint, O Lord,
Who strove in Thee to live,
Who followed Thee, obeyed, adored,
Our grateful hymn receive.

2. For Thy dear saint, O Lord,
Who strove in Thee to die,
And found in Thee a full reward,
Accept our thankful cry.

3. Thine earthly members fit
To join Thy saints above,
In one communion ever knit,
One fellowship of love.

4. Jesu, Thy Name we bless,
And humbly pray that we
May follow them in holiness,
Who lived and died for Thee.

5. All might, all praise be Thine,
Father, co-equal Son,
And Spirit, Bond of love divine,
While endless ages run. Amen.

# INDEX OF FIRST LINES.

---

[*Many of the hymns in this book are original and copyright, and are inserted by the kind permission of their authors and publishers.*]

# APPENDIX TO

# Hymns

# ANCIENT AND MODERN

FOR USE IN THE

## Services of the Church.

"Young men and maidens, old men and children, praise the name of the LORD."

NEW YORK:
POTT & AMERY, COOPER UNION.
1869.

# CONTENTS.

# APPENDIX.

## 274.

### Evening.

"The LORD shall be thine everlasting Light."

1\. THE radiant morn hath passed away,
And spent too soon her golden store;
The shadows of departing day
Creep on once more.

2\. Our life is but a fading dawn,
Its glorious noon how quickly past;
Lead us, O CHRIST, when all is gone,
Safe home at last.

3\. Oh, by Thy soul-inspiring grace
Uplift our hearts to realms on high;
Help us to look to that bright place
Beyond the sky;

4\. Where light, and love, and joy, and peace
In undivided empire reign,
And thronging angels never cease
Their deathless strain;

5\. Where saints are clothed in spotless white,
And evening shadows never fall,
Where Thou, Eternal Light of Light,
Art LORD of all. Amen.

## 275.

"It is Thou, Lord, only that makest me dwell in safety."

1\. THE day is past and over;
All thanks, O Lord, to Thee;
I pray Thee now that sinless
The hours of dark may be
O Jesu, keep me in Thy sight,
And guard me through the coming night.

2\. The joys of day are over;
I lift my heart to Thee,
And ask Thee that offenceless
The hours of dark may be:
O Jesu, keep me in Thy sight,
And guard me through the coming night.

3\. The toils of day are over;
I raise the hymn to Thee,
And ask that free from peril
The hours of dark may be:
O Jesu, keep me in Thy sight,
And guard me through the coming night.

4\. Lighten mine eyes, O Saviour,
Or sleep in death shall I,
And he, my wakeful tempter,
Triumphantly shall cry
"Against him I have now prevailed;
Rejoice! the child of God has failed."

5. Be Thou my soul's preserver,
For Thou alone dost know
How many are the perils
Through which I have to go:
O loving Jesu, hear my call,
And guard and save me from them all.
Amen.

## 276.

"And at even, when the sun did set, they brought unto Him all that were diseased, and all that were possessed with devils. And all the city was gathered together at the door."

1. AT even ere the sun was set,
The sick, O Lord, around Thee lay;
Oh, in what divers pains they met!
Oh, with what joy they went away!

2. Once more 'tis eventide, and we
Oppressed with various ills draw near:
What if Thy form we cannot see?
We know and feel that Thou art here.

3. O Saviour Christ, our woes dispel;
For some are sick, and some are sad,
And some have never loved Thee well,
And some have lost the love they had;

4. And some have found the world is vain,
Yet from the world they break not free;
And some have friends who give them pain,
Yet have not sought a friend in Thee;

5. And none, O Lord, have perfect rest,
For none are wholly free from sin;
And they, who fain would serve Thee best,
Are conscious most of wrong within.

6. O Saviour Christ, Thou too art Man;
Thou hast been troubled, tempted, tried;
Thy kind but searching glance can scan
The very wounds that shame would hide;

7. Thy touch has still its ancient power;
No word from Thee can fruitless fall;
Hear in this solemn evening hour,
And in Thy mercy heal us all. Amen.

# 277.

"God, even our own God, shall give us His blessing."

1. O FATHER, Who didst all things make
That heaven and earth might do Thy will,
Bless us this night for Jesu's sake,
And for Thy work preserve us still.

2. O Son, Who didst redeem mankind,
And set the captive sinner free,
Keep us this night with peaceful mind,
That we may safe abide in Thee.

3. O Holy Ghost, Who by Thy power
The Church elect dost sanctify,
Seal us this night, and hour by hour
Our hearts and members purify.

4. To FATHER, SON, and HOLY GHOST,
The GOD Whom heaven and earth adore,
From men and from the angel-host
Be praise and glory evermore. Amen.

## 278.

"The True Light."

1. HAIL, gladdening Light, of His pure glory poured
Who is the Immortal FATHER, Heavenly, Blest,
Holiest of Holies, JESU CHRIST, our LORD.

2. Now we are come to the sun's hour of rest,
The lights of evening round us shine,
We hymn the FATHER, SON, and HOLY SPIRIT Divine.

3. Worthiest art Thou at all times to be sung
With undefilèd tongue,
SON of our GOD, Giver of life, Alone;
Therefore in all the world Thy glories, LORD, they own. Amen.

## 279.

AT END OF SERVICE.

"The LORD shall give His people the blessing of peace."

1. SAVIOUR, again to Thy dear Name we raise
With one accord our parting hymn of praise;
We stand to bless Thee ere our worship cease,
Then, lowly kneeling, wait Thy word of peace.

2. Grant us Thy peace upon our homeward way;
With Thee began, with Thee shall end the day;
Guard Thou the lips from sin, the hearts from shame,
That in this house have called upon Thy Name.

3. Grant us Thy peace, Lord, thro' the coming night,
Turn Thou for us its darkness into light;
From harm and danger keep Thy children free,
For dark and light are both alike to Thee.

4. Grant us Thy peace throughout our earthly life,
Our balm in sorrow, and our stay in strife;
Then, when Thy voice shall bid our conflict cease,
Call us, O Lord, to Thine eternal peace.
Amen.

## 280.

AT END OF SERVICE.

"O God, Thou art my God."

1. AND now the wants are told, that brought
Thy children to Thy knee;
Here lingering still, we ask for naught,
But simply worship Thee.

2. The hope of heaven's eternal days
Absorbs not all the heart
That gives Thee glory, love, and praise,
For being what Thou art.

3. For Thou art God, the One, the Same,
O'er all things high and bright;
And round us, when we speak Thy Name,
There spreads a heaven of light.

4. O wondrous peace, in thought to dwell
On excellence divine;
To know that naught in man can tell
How fair Thy beauties shine.

5. O Thou, above all blessing blest,
O'er thanks exalted far,
Thy very greatness is a rest
To weaklings as we are;

6. For when we feel the praise of Thee
A task beyond our powers,
We say, "A perfect God is He,
And He is fully ours."

7. All glory to the Father be,
All glory to the Son,
All glory, Holy Ghost, to Thee,
While endless ages run. Amen.

## 281.

### Sunday.

"I was in the Spirit on the Lord's day."

1. THIS is the day of light:
Let there be light to-day;
O Day-spring, rise upon our night,
And chase its gloom away.

2. This is the day of rest:
Our failing strength renew;
On weary brain and troubled breast
Shed Thou Thy freshening dew.

3. This is the day of peace:
Thy peace our spirits fill;
Bid Thou the blasts of discord cease,
The waves of strife be still.

4. This is the day of prayer:
Let earth to heaven draw near;
Lift up our hearts to seek Thee there;
Come down to meet us here.

5. This is the first of days:
Send forth Thy quickening Breath,
And wake dead souls to love and praise,
O Vanquisher of death! Amen.

## 282.

"Upon the first day of the week, when the disciples came together."

1. O DAY of rest and gladness,
O day of joy and light,
O balm of care and sadness,
Most beautiful, most bright;
On thee the high and lowly
Before th' eternal Throne
Sing Holy, Holy, Holy,
To the great THREE IN ONE.

2. On thee, at the creation,
   The light first had its birth;
On thee for our salvation
   CHRIST rose from depths of earth;
On thee our LORD victorious
   The SPIRIT sent from heaven;
And thus on thee most glorious
   A triple light was given.

3. Thou art a cooling fountain
   In life's dry dreary sand;
From thee, like Pisgah's mountain,
   We view our promised land;
A day of sweet refection,
   A day of holy love,
A day of resurrection
   From earth to things above.

4. To-day on weary nations
   The heavenly Manna falls,
To holy convocations
   The silver trumpet calls,
Where Gospel-light is glowing
   With pure and radiant beams,
And living water flowing
   With soul-refreshing streams.

5. New graces ever gaining
   From this our day of rest,
We reach the Rest remaining
   To spirits of the blest;

To Holy Ghost be praises,
  To Father, and to Son;
The Church her voice upraises
To Thee, blest Three in One. Amen.

## 283.

### St. Stephen's Day.

"He, being full of the Holy Ghost, looked up steadfastly into heaven, and saw the glory of God, and Jesus standing on the right hand of God."

1. YESTERDAY, with exultation,
Joined the world in celebration
  Of her promised Saviour's birth;
Yesterday the angel-nation
Poured the strains of jubilation
  O'er the Monarch born on earth;

2. But to-day o'er death victorious,
By his faith and actions glorious,
  By his miracles renowned,
See the Deacon triumph gaining,
'Midst the faithless faith sustaining,
  First of holy martyrs found.

3. Onward, champion, falter never,
Sure of sure reward for ever,
  Holy Stephen, persevere;
Perjured witnesses confounding,
Satan's synagogue astounding
  By thy doctrine true and clear.

4. Thine own Witness is in heaven,
True and Faithful, to thee given,
Witness of thy blamelessness:
By Thy name a Crown implying,
Meet it is thou shouldst be dying
For the Crown of righteousness.

5. For the Crown that fadeth never
Bear the torturer's brief endeavour;
Victory waits to end the strife:
Death shall be thy life's beginning,
And life's losing be the winning
Of the true and better life.

6. Filled with God's most Holy Spirit
See the heaven thou shalt inherit,
Stephen, gaze into the skies:
There God's glory steadfast viewing,
Thence thy victor-strength renewing,
Pant for thy eternal prize.

7. See, as Jewish foes invade thee,
See how Jesus stands to aid thee,
Stands at God's right hand on high:
Tell how opened heaven is shown thee,
Tell how Jesus waits to own thee,
Tell it with thy latest cry.

8. As the dying Martyr kneeleth,
For his murderers he appealeth,
For their madness grieving sore;
Then in Christ he sleepeth sweetly,
And with Christ he reigneth meetly,
Martyr first-fruits, evermore. Amen.

# 284.

## Epiphany.

"The Son of God was manifested."

1. SONGS of thankfulness and praise,
Jesu, Lord, to Thee we raise,
Manifested by the star
To the sages from afar;
Branch of royal David's stem
In Thy birth at Bethlehem;
Anthems be to Thee addrest,
God in Man made manifest.

2. Manifest at Jordan's stream,
Prophet, Priest, and King supreme;
And at Cana wedding-guest
In Thy Godhead manifest;
Manifest in power Divine,
Changing water into wine;
Anthems be to Thee addrest,
God in Man made manifest.

3. Manifest in making whole
Palsied limbs and fainting soul;
Manifest in valiant fight,
Quelling all the devil's might;
Manifest in gracious will,
Ever bringing good from ill;
Anthems be to Thee addrest,
God in Man made manifest.

4. Sun and moon shall darkened be,
Stars shall fall, the heaven shall flee;
CHRIST will then like lightning shine,
All will see His glorious Sign;
All will then the trumpet hear,
All will see the Judge appear;
Thou by all wilt be confest,
GOD in Man made manifest.

5. Grant us grace to see Thee, LORD,
Mirrored in Thy holy Word;
May we imitate Thee now,
And be pure, as pure art Thou;
That we like to Thee may be
At Thy great Epiphany;
And may praise Thee, ever blest,
GOD in Man made manifest. Amen.

## 285.

### Lent.

"Whom resist, steadfast in the faith."

1. CHRISTIAN, dost thou see them
On the holy ground,
How the troops of Midian
Prowl and prowl around?
Christian, up and smite them,
Counting gain but loss;
Smite them by the merit
Of the holy Cross.

2. Christian, dost thou feel them,
How they work within,
Striving, tempting, luring,
Goading into sin?
Christian, never tremble;
Never be down-cast;
Smite them by the virtue
Of the Lenten fast.

3. Christian, dost thou hear them,
How they speak thee fair?
"Always fast and vigil?
Always watch and prayer?"
Christian, answer boldly,
"While I breathe I pray:"
Peace shall follow battle,
Night shall end in day.

4. "Well I know thy trouble,
O My servant true;
Thou art very weary,
I was weary too;
But that toil shall make thee
Some day all Mine own,
And the end of sorrow
Shall be near My Throne." Amen.

## 286.

"In Whom we have redemption through His Blood, the forgiveness of sins."

1. WEARY of earth and laden with my sin,
I look at heaven and long to enter in,
But there no evil thing may find a home:
And yet I hear a voice that bids me "Come."

2. So vile I am, how dare I hope to stand
In the pure glory of that holy land?
Before the whiteness of that Throne appear?
Yet there are Hands stretched out to draw me near.

3. The while I fain would tread the heavenly way,
Evil is ever with me day by day;
Yet on mine ears the gracious tidings fall,
"Repent, confess, thou shalt be loosed from all."

4. It is the voice of JESUS that I hear,
His are the Hands stretched out to draw me near,
And His the Blood that can for all atone,
And set me faultless there before the Throne.

5. 'Twas He Who found me on the deathly wild,
And made me heir of heaven, the FATHER's child,
And day by day, whereby my soul may live,
Gives me His grace of pardon, and will give.

6. O great Absolver, grant my soul may wear
The lowliest garb of penitence and prayer,
That in the FATHER's courts my glorious dress
May be the garment of Thy righteousness.

7. Yea, Thou wilt answer for me, Righteous Lord:
Thine all the merits, mine the great reward;
Thine the sharp thorns, and mine the golden crown,
Mine the life won, and Thine the life laid down.

8. Naught can I bring, dear Lord, for all I owe,
Yet let my full heart what it can bestow;
Like Mary's gift let my devotion prove,
Forgiven greatly, how I greatly love. Amen.

## 287.

"When he thought thereon, he wept."

1. O JÉSU CHRIST, if aught there be
That, more than all beside,
In ever-painful memory
Must in my heart abide,

2. It is that deep ingratitude
Which I to Thee have shown,
Who didst for me in tears and Blood
Upon the Cross atone.

3. Alas, how with my actions all
Has this defect entwined;
How has it poisoned with its gall
My spirit, heart, and mind!

4. Alas, through this, how many a gem
I've rudely cast away,
That might have formed my diadem
In everlasting day!

5. Yet though the time be past and gone,
   Though little more remains,
Though naught is all that can be done,
   E'en with my utmost pains;

6. Still will I strive, O Saviour mine,
   To do what in me lies;
For never did Thy glance divine
   A contrite heart despise. Amen.

## 288.

"Out of the deep have I called unto Thee, O Lord."

1. OUT of the deep I call
   To Thee, O Lord, to Thee;
Before Thy throne of grace I fall,
   Be merciful to me.

2. Out of the deep I cry,
   The woful deep of sin,
Of evil done in days gone by,
   Of evil now within.

3. Out of the deep of fear,
   And dread of coming shame,
From morning watch till night is near
   I plead the Precious Name.

4. Lord, there is mercy now,
   As ever was, with Thee;
Before Thy throne of grace I bow,
   Be merciful to me. Amen.

# 289.

## Hymns on the Passion.

"The Cross of our LORD JESUS CHRIST."

1. SING, my tongue, the glorious battle,
Sing the last, the dread affray;
O'er the Cross, the Victor's trophy,
Sound the glad triumphal lay,
How, the pains of death enduring,
Earth's Redeemer won the day.

2. He, our Maker, deeply grieving
That the first-made Adam fell,
When he ate the fruit forbidden
Whose reward was death and hell,
Marked e'en then this tree the ruin
Of the first tree to dispel.

3. Thus the work for our salvation
He ordainèd to be done;
To the traitor's art opposing
Art yet deeper than his own;
Thence the remedy procuring
Whence the fatal wound begun.

4. Therefore, when at length the fulness
Of th' appointed time was come,
He was sent, the world's Creator,
From the FATHER's heavenly home,
And was found in human fashion,
Offspring of the Virgin's womb.

5. Lo, He lies an Infant weeping,
Where the narrow manger stands,
While the Mother-Maid His members
Wraps in mean and lowly bands,
And the swaddling clothes is winding
Round His helpless Feet and Hands.

## PART II.

1. NOW the thirty years accomplished
Which on earth He willed to see,
Born for this, He meets His passion,
Gives Himself an offering free;
On the Cross the LAMB is lifted,
There the Sacrifice to be.

2. There the nails and spear He suffers,
Vinegar, and gall, and reed;
From His sacred Body piercèd
Blood and Water both proceed;
Precious flood, which all creation
From the stain of sin hath freed.

3. Faithful Cross, above all other
One and only noble Tree,
None in foliage, none in blossom,
None in fruit thy peer may be;
Sweetest wood, and sweetest iron;
Sweetest weight is hung on thee.

4. Bend, O lofty Tree, thy branches,
Thy too rigid sinews bend;
And awhile the stubborn hardness,
Which thy birth bestowed, suspend;
And the Limbs of heaven's high Monarch
Gently on thine arms extend.

5. Thou alone wast counted worthy
This world's ransom to sustain,
That a shipwrecked race for ever
Might a port of refuge gain,
With the sacred Blood anointed
Of the Lamb for sinners slain.

6. Praise and honour to the Father,
Praise and honour to the Son,
Praise and honour to the Spirit,
Ever Three and ever One,
One in might, and one in glory,
While eternal ages run. Amen.

## 290.

### Easter.

"Jesus met them, saying, 'All Hail.'"

1. THE Day of Resurrection!
Earth, tell it out abroad;
The Passover of gladness,
The Passover of God.
From death to life eternal,
From earth unto the sky,
Our Christ hath brought us over
With hymns of victory.

2. Our hearts be pure from evil,
   That we may see aright
The LORD in rays eternal
   Of resurrection-light;
And, listening to His accents,
   May hear so calm and plain
His own "All hail," and hearing
   May raise the victor strain.

3. Now let the heavens be joyful,
   And earth her song begin,
The round world keep high triumph,
   And all that is therein;
Let all things seen and unseen
   Their notes of gladness blend,
For CHRIST the LORD is risen,
   Our Joy that hath no end. Amen.

## 291.

"Lo, the winter is past."

1. COME, ye faithful, raise the strain
   Of triumphant gladness;
GOD hath brought His Israel
   Into joy from sadness;
Loosed from Pharaoh's bitter yoke
   Jacob's sons and daughters;
Led them with unmoistened foot
   Through the Red Sea waters.

2. 'Tis the spring of souls to-day:
 CHRIST hath burst His prison,
And from three days sleep in death
 As a sun hath risen:
All the winter of our sins,
 Long and dark, is flying
From His Light, to Whom we give
 Laud and praise undying.

3. Now the Queen of seasons, bright
 With the Day of splendour,
With the royal Feast of feasts,
 Comes its joy to render;
Comes to glad Jerusalem,
 Who with true affection
Welcomes in unwearied strains
 JESU'S Resurrection.

4. Alleluia now we cry
 To our King Immortal,
Who triumphant burst the bars
 Of the tomb's dark portal;
Alleluia, with the SON
 GOD the FATHER praising;
Alleluia yet again
 To the SPIRIT raising. Amen.

## 292.

"Now is CHRIST risen from the dead, and become the first-fruits of them that slept."

1. ALLELUIA, Alleluia,
   Hearts to heaven and voices raise;
Sing to GOD a hymn of gladness,
   Sing to GOD a hymn of praise;
He, Who on the Cross a Victim
   For the world's salvation bled.
JESUS CHRIST, the King of Glory,
   Now is risen from the dead.

2. CHRIST is risen, CHRIST the first-fruits
   Of the holy harvest field,
Which will all its full abundance
   At His second coming yield;
Then the golden ears of harvest
   Will their heads before Him wave,
Ripened by His glorious sunshine
   From the furrows of the grave.

3. CHRIST is risen, we are risen;
   Shed upon us heavenly grace,
Rain, and dew, and gleams of glory
   From the brightness of Thy face;
That we, with our hearts in heaven,
   Here on earth may fruitful be,
And by angel-hands be gathered,
   And be ever, LORD, with Thee.

4. Alleluia, Alleluia,
Glory be to God on high;
Alleluia to the Saviour,
Who has gained the victory;
Alleluia to the Spirit,
Fount of love and sanctity;
Alleluia, Alleluia,
To the Triune Majesty. Amen.

## 293.

### Ascensiontide.

"Thou art gone up on high, Thou hast led captivity captive, and received gifts for men."

1. SEE the Conqueror mounts in triumph,
See the King in royal state
Riding on the clouds His chariot
To His heavenly palace gate;
Hark, the choirs of angel voices
Joyful Alleluias sing,
And the portals high are lifted
To receive their Heavenly King.

2. Who is this that comes in glory,
With the trump of jubilee?
Lord of battles, God of armies,
He has gained the victory;
He Who on the cross did suffer,
He Who from the grave arose,
He has vanquished sin and Satan,
He by death has spoiled His foes.

3. While He lifts His hands in blessing,
He is parted from His friends;
While their eager eyes behold Him,
He upon the clouds ascends;
He Who walked with God, and pleased Him,
Preaching truth and doom to come,
He, our Enoch, is translated
To His everlasting home.

4. Now our heavenly Aaron enters,
With His Blood, within the veil;
Joshua now is come to Canaan,
And the kings before Him quail:
Now He plants the tribes of Israel
In their promised resting-place:
Now our great Elijah offers
Double portion of His grace.

5. He has raised our human nature
On the clouds to God's right hand;
There we sit in heavenly places,
There with Him in glory stand:
Jesus reigns, adored by angels;
Man with God is on the throne;
Mighty Lord, in Thine Ascension
We by faith behold our own.

## PART II.

1. HOLY GHOST, Illuminator,
   Shed Thy beams upon our eyes,
Help us to look up with Stephen,
   And to see, beyond the skies,
Where the SON of MAN in glory
   Standing is at GOD's right hand,
Beckoning on His martyr army,
   Succouring His faithful band;

2. See Him, Who is gone before us
   Heavenly mansions to prepare,
See Him, Who is ever pleading
   For us with prevailing prayer,
See Him, Who with sound of trumpet
   And with His angelic train,
Summoning the world to judgment,
   On the clouds will come again.

3. Raise us up from earth to heaven,
   Give us wings of faith and love,
Gales of holy aspirations
   Wafting us to realms above;
That, with hearts and minds uplifted,
   We with CHRIST our LORD may dwell,
Where He sits enthroned in glory
   In His heavenly Citadel.

4. So at last, when He appeareth,
   We from out our graves may spring,
With our youth renewed like eagles,
   Flocking round our Heavenly King,
Caught up on the clouds of heaven,
   And may meet Him in the air,
Rise to realms where He is reigning,
   And may reign for ever there.

*The following Doxology may be sung at the end of either part.*

Glory be to God the Father;
   Glory be to God the Son,
Dying, risen, ascending for us,
   Who the heavenly realm has won;
Glory to the Holy Spirit;
   To One God in Persons Three
Glory both in earth and heaven,
   Glory, endless glory be. Amen.

## 294.

### General Hymns.

"O that men would therefore praise the Lord for His goodness."

1. SING praise to God Who reigns above,
   The God of all creation,
The God of power, the God of love,
   The God of our salvation;
With healing balm my soul He fills,
And every faithless murmur stills;
   To God all praise and glory.

2. The angel-host, O KING of kings,
   Thy praise for ever telling,
In earth and sky all living things
   Beneath Thy shadow dwelling,
Adore the wisdom which could span,
And power which formed creation's plan:
   To GOD all praise and glory.

3. What GOD's Almighty power hath made
   His gracious mercy keepeth;
By morning glow or evening shade
   His watchful eye ne'er sleepeth;
Within the kingdom of His might
Lo! all is just and all is right;
   To GOD all praise and glory.

4. The LORD is never far away;
   But, through all grief distressing,
An ever-present help and stay,
   Our peace and joy and blessing:
As with a mother's tender hand
He leads His own, His chosen band
   To GOD all praise and glory.

5. When every earthly hope has flown
   From sorrow's sons and daughters,
Our FATHER from His heavenly throne
   Beholds the troubled waters;
And at His word the storm is stayed
Which made His children's hearts afraid;
   To GOD all praise and glory.

6. Thus all my toilsome way along
   I sing aloud Thy praises,
That men may hear the grateful song
   My voice unwearied raises:
Be joyful in the LORD, my heart;
Both soul and body bear your part;
   To GOD all praise and glory. Amen.

## 295.

"Who led His people through the wilderness: for His mercy endureth for ever."

1. O PRAISE our great and gracious LORD,
   And call upon His Name;
To strains of joy tune every chord,
   His mighty acts proclaim;
Tell how He led His chosen race
   To Canaan's promised land;
Tell how His covenant of grace
   Unchanged shall ever stand.

2. He gave the shadowing cloud by day,
   The moving fire by night;
To guide His Israel on their way,
   He made their darkness light:
And have not we a sure retreat,
   A SAVIOUR ever nigh,
The same clear light to guide our feet,
   The Day-spring from on high?

3. We too have Manna from above,
The Bread that came from heaven;
To us the same kind hand of love
Has living waters given:
A Rock have we, from whence the spring
In rich abundance flows;
That Rock is CHRIST, our Priest, our King,
Who life and health bestows.

4. O may we prize this blessèd Food,
And trust our heavenly Guide;
So shall we find death's fearful flood
Serene as Jordan's tide,
And safely reach that happy shore,
The land of peace and rest,
Where angels worship and adore
In GOD's own Presence blest. Amen.

## 296.

"Rejoice in the LORD alway, and again I say, rejoice."

1. REJOICE, the LORD is King,
Your LORD and King adore;
Mortals, give thanks and sing,
And triumph evermore:
Lift up your heart, lift up your voice;
Rejoice, again I say, rejoice.

2. Jesus the Saviour reigns,
The God of truth and love:
When He had purged our stains,
He took his seat above:
Lift up your heart, lift up your voice;
Rejoice, again I say, rejoice.

3. His Kingdom cannot fail;
He rules o'er earth and heaven:
The keys of death and hell
Are to our Jesus given:
Lift up your heart, lift up your voice;
Rejoice, again I say, rejoice.

4. He sits at God's right hand
Till all His foes submit,
And bow to His command
And fall beneath His feet:
Lift up your heart, lift up your voice;
Rejoice, again I say, rejoice. Amen.

## 297.

"If any man serve Me, let him follow Me; and where I am, there shall also My servant be."

1. O HAPPY band of pilgrims,
If onward ye will tread
With Jesus as your Fellow
To Jesus as your Head.

2. O happy if ye labour
As Jesus did for men:
O happy if ye hunger
As Jesus hungered then.

3. The Cross that Jesus carried
He carried as your due:
The Crown that Jesus weareth
He weareth it for you.

4. The faith by which ye see Him,
The hope in which ye yearn,
The love that through all troubles
To Him alone will turn,

5. The trials that beset you,
The sorrows ye endure,
The manifold temptations
That death alone can cure,

6. What are they but His jewels
Of right celestial worth?
What are they but the ladder
Set up to heaven on earth?

7. O happy band of pilgrims,
Look upward to the skies
Where such a light affliction
Shall win so great a prize. Amen.

# 298.

"Work your work betimes, and in His time He will give you your reward."

1. THE world is very evil,
  The times are waxing late,
Be sober and keep vigil,
  The Judge is at the gate;
The Judge Who comes in mercy,
  The Judge Who comes with might,
Who comes to end the evil,
  Who comes to crown the right.

2. Arise, arise, good Christian,
  Let right to wrong succeed;
Let penitential sorrow
  To heavenly gladness lead,
To light that has no evening,
  That knows nor moon nor sun,
The light so new and golden,
  The light that is but one.

3. O Home of fadeless splendour,
  Of flowers that fear no thorn,
Where they shall dwell as children
  Who here as exiles mourn;
'Midst power that knows no limit,
  Where wisdom has no bound,
The Beatific Vision
  Shall glad the Saints around.

4. O happy, holy portion,
   Refection for the blest,
 True vision of true beauty,
   True cure of the distrest:
 Strive, man, to win that glory;
   Toil, man, to gain that light;
 Send hope before to grasp it,
   Till hope be lost in sight.

5. O sweet and blessèd country,
   The Home of God's elect!
 O sweet and blessèd country,
   That eager hearts expect!
 Jesu, in mercy bring us
   To that dear land of rest;
 Who art, with God the Father,
   And Spirit, ever blest. Amen.

## 299.

"Come unto Me, all ye that labour and are heavy laden, and I will give you rest."

1. ART thou weary, art thou languid,
   Art thou sore distrest?
 "Come to Me," saith One, "and coming
   Be at rest!"

2. Hath He marks to lead me to Him,
   If He be my guide?
 "In His Feet and Hands are Wound-prints,
   And His Side."

3. Hath He Diadem as Monarch
 That His Brow adorns?
 "Yea, a Crown, in very surety,
 But of thorns."

4. If I find Him, if I follow,
 What His guerdon here?
 "Many a sorrow, many a labour,
 Many a tear."

5. If I still hold closely to Him,
 What hath He at last?
 "Sorrow vanquished, labour ended,
 Jordan past."

5. If I ask Him to receive me,
 Will He say me nay?
 "Not till earth, and not till heaven
 Pass away."

6. Finding, following, keeping, struggling,
 Is He sure to bless?
 "Angels, Martyrs, Prophets, Virgins,
 Answer, Yes!" Amen.

## 300.

"To him that overcometh will I grant to sit with Me in My throne, even as I also overcame and am set down with My FATHER in His throne.

1. THE Head that once was crowned with thorns
 Is crowned with glory now;
A royal diadem adorns
 The mighty Victor's brow.

2. The highest place that heaven affords
Is His, is His by right,
The KING of kings, and LORD of lords,
And heaven's eternal Light.

3. The Joy of all who dwell above,
The Joy of all below,
To whom He manifests His love,
And grants His Name to know.

4. To them the Cross, with all its shame,
With all its grace, is given:
Their name an everlasting name,
Their joy the joy of heaven.

5. They suffer with their LORD below,
They reign with Him above,
Their profit and their joy to know
The mystery of His love.

6. The Cross He bore is life and health,
Though shame and death to Him;
His people's hope, His people's wealth,
Their everlasting theme. Amen.

## 301.

"KING of kings, and LORD of lords."

1. ALL hail the power of JESU's Name;
Let angels prostrate fall;
Bring forth the royal diadem
To crown Him LORD of all.

2. Crown Him, ye morning stars of light,
Who fixed this floating ball;
Now hail the Strength of Israel's might,
And crown Him Lord of all.

3. Crown Him, ye martyrs of your God
Who from His altar call;
Of Jesse's stem extol the Rod,
And crown Him Lord of all.

4. Ye seed of Israel's chosen race,
Ye ransomed of the fall,
Hail Him Who saves you by His grace,
And crown Him Lord of all.

5. Hail Him, ye heirs of David's line,
Whom David Lord did call,
The God Incarnate, Man Divine,
And crown Him Lord of all.

6. Sinners, whose love can ne'er forget
The wormwood and the gall,
Go spread your trophies at His feet,
And crown Him Lord of all.

7. Let every tribe and every tongue
Before Him prostrate fall,
And shout in universal song
The crownèd Lord of all. Amen.

# 302.

"I heard the voice of many angels saying, Worthy is the LAMB that was slain to receive power, and riches, and wisdom, and strength, and honour, and glory, and blessing."

1. COME let us join our cheerful songs
   With angels round the Throne;
Ten thousand thousand are their tongues,
   But all their joys are one.

2. "Worthy the LAMB that died," they cry,
   "To be exalted thus;"
"Worthy the LAMB," our lips reply,
   "For He was slain for us."

3. JESUS is worthy to receive
   Honour and power divine;
And blessings, more than we can give,
   Be, LORD, for ever Thine,

4. Let all creation join in one
   To bless the sacred Name
Of Him that sits upon the Throne,
   And to adore the LAMB. Amen.

# 303.

"These things said Esaias, when he saw His glory."

1. BRIGHT the vision that delighted
   Once the sight of Judah's seer;
Sweet the countless tongues united
   To entrance the prophet's ear.

2. Round the LORD in glory seated
   Cherubim and Seraphim
Filled His temple, and repeated
   Each to each the alternate hymn;

3. "LORD, Thy glory fills the heaven,
   Earth is with its fulness stored;
Unto Thee be glory given,
   Holy, Holy, Holy LORD."

4. Heaven is still with glory ringing,
   Earth takes up the angels' cry,
"Holy, Holy, Holy," singing,
   "LORD of hosts, LORD GOD most High."

5. With His seraph train before Him,
   With His holy Church below,
Thus unite we to adore Him,
   Bid we thus our anthem flow;

6. "LORD, Thy glory fills the heaven,
   Earth is with its fulness stored;
Unto Thee be glory given,
   Holy, Holy, Holy LORD." Amen.

## 304.

"The four beasts and four and twenty elders fell down before the LAMB, having every one of them harps, and golden vials full of odours, which are the prayers of the saints."

1. COME, ye faithful, raise the anthem,
   Cleave the skies with shouts of praise;
Sing to Him Who found the ransom,
   Ancient of eternal days,
God of God, the Word Incarnate,
   Whom the heaven of heaven obeys.

2. Ere He raised the lofty mountains,
   Formed the seas, or built the sky,
Love eternal, free, and boundless,
   Moved the Lord of Life to die,
Fore-ordained the Prince of Princes
   For the throne of Calvary.

3. There for us and our redemption,
   See Him all His life-blood pour!
There He wins our full salvation,
   Dies that we may die no more:
Then, arising, lives for ever,
   Reigning where He was before.

4. High on yon celestial mountains
   Stands His gem-built throne, all bright,
Midst unending Alleluias
   Bursting from the sons of light;
Sion's people tell His praises,
   Victor after hard-won fight.

5. Bring your harps, and bring your odours,
   Sweep the string and pour the lay;
 Let the earth proclaim His wonders,
   King of that celestial day;
 He the Lamb once slain is worthy,
   Who was dead and lives for aye.

6. Laud and honour to the Father,
   Laud and honour to the Son,
 Laud and honour to the Spirit,
   Ever Three and ever One,
 Consubstantial, Co-eternal,
   While unending ages run. Amen.

## 305.

"The second Man is the Lord from heaven."

1. PRAISE to the Holiest in the height,
   And in the depth be praise:
 In all His words most wonderful,
   Most sure in all His ways.

2. O loving wisdom of our God!
   When all was sin and shame,
 A second Adam to the fight
   And to the rescue came.

3. O wisest love! that flesh and blood,
   Which did in Adam fail,
 Should strive afresh against the foe,
   Should strive and should prevail;

4. And that a higher gift than grace
Should flesh and blood refine;
God's Presence and His very Self,
And Essence all-divine.

5. O generous love! that He, Who smote
In man for man the foe,
The double agony in man
For man should undergo;

6. And in the garden secretly,
And on the cross on high,
Should teach His brethren, and inspire
To suffer and to die.

7. Praise to the Holiest in the height,
And in the depth be praise:
In all His words most wonderful,
Most sure in all His ways. Amen.

## 306.

"The Lord said unto him, I have hallowed this house to put My Name there for ever, and Mine Eyes and Mine Heart shall be there perpetually."

1. CHRIST is our corner-stone,
On Him alone we build;
With His true saints above
The courts of heaven are filled:
On His great love
Our hopes we place
Of present grace
And joys above.

2. O then with hymns of praise
These hallowed courts shall ring;
Our voices we will raise
The Three in One to sing;
And thus proclaim
In joyful song,
Both loud and long,
That glorious Name.

3. Here, gracious God, do Thou
For evermore draw nigh;
Accept each faithful vow,
And mark each suppliant sigh;
In copious shower
On all who pray
Each holy day
Thy blessings pour.

4. Here may we gain from heaven
The grace which we implore;
And may that grace, once given,
Be with us evermore,
Until that day
When all the blest
To endless rest
Are called away. Amen.

# 307.

"O how amiable are Thy dwellings, Thou LORD of Hosts."

1. PLEASANT are Thy courts above
In the land of light and love;
Pleasant are Thy courts below
In this land of sin and woe:
O, my spirit longs and faints
For the converse of Thy saints,
For the brightness of Thy Face,
For Thy fulness, GOD of grace.

2. Happy birds that sing and fly
Round Thy Altars, O most High;
Happier souls that find a rest
In a heavenly Father's breast;
Like the wandering dove that found
No repose on earth around,
They can to their ark repair,
And enjoy it ever there.

3. Happy souls, their praises flow
Even in this vale of woe;
Waters in the deserts rise,
Manna feeds them from the skies;
On they go from strength to strength,
Till they reach Thy throne at length,
At Thy feet adoring fall,
Who hast led them safe through all.

4. Lord, be mine this prize to win,
Guide me through a world of sin,
Keep me by Thy saving grace,
Give me at Thy side a place;
Sun and shield alike Thou art,
Guide and guard my erring heart;
Grace and glory flow from Thee;
Shower, O shower them, Lord, on me.
Amen.

## 308.

"And they shall be Mine, saith the Lord of Hosts, in that day when I make up my jewels."

1. THINE for ever! God of love,
Hear us from Thy throne above;
Thine for ever may we be
Here and in eternity.

2. Thine for ever! Lord of life,
Shield us through our earthly strife;
Thou the Life, the Truth, the Way,
Guide us to the realms of day.

3. Thine for ever! oh, how blest
They who find in Thee their rest;
Saviour, Guardian, Heavenly Friend,
O defend us to the end.

4. Thine for ever! Saviour keep
Us Thy frail and trembling sheep;
Safe alone beneath Thy care,
Let us all Thy goodness share.

5. Thine for ever! Thou our guide,
All our wants by Thee supplied,
All our sins by Thee forgiven,
Lead us, Lord, from earth to heaven.
Amen.

## 309.

"And He arose and rebuked the wind, and said unto the sea, Peace, be still."

1. FIERCE raged the tempest o'er the deep,
Watch did Thine anxious servants keep,
But Thou wast wrapped in guileless sleep,
Calm and still.

2. "Save, Lord, we perish," was their cry,
"O save us in our agony!"
Thy word above the storm rose high,
"Peace, be still."

3. The wild winds hushed; the angry deep
Sank, like a little child, to sleep;
The sullen billows ceased to leap
At Thy will.

4. So, when our life is clouded o'er,
And storm-winds drift us from the shore,
Say (lest we sink to rise no more),
"Peace, be still." Amen.

## 310.

"Like as the hart desireth the waterbrooks, so longeth my soul after Thee, O God."

1. AS pants the hart for cooling streams
   When heated in the chase,
So longs my soul, O God, for Thee,
   And Thy refreshing grace.

2. For Thee my God, the living God,
   My thirsty soul doth pine:
O when shall I behold Thy Face,
   Thou Majesty Divine?

3. Why restless, why cast down, my soul?
   Hope still, and thou shalt sing
The praise of Him Who is thy God,
   Thy health's eternal Spring.

4. To Father, Son, and Holy Ghost,
   The God Whom we adore,
Be glory, as it was, is now,
   And shall be evermore. Amen.

## 311.

"Thy kingdom come."

1. THY kingdom come, O God,
   Thy rule, O Christ, begin;
Break with Thine iron rod
The tyrannies of sin.

2. Where is Thy reign of peace,
And purity, and love?
When shall all hatred cease,
As in the realms above?

3. When comes the promised time
That war shall be no more,
Oppression, lust, and crime
Shall flee Thy face before?

4. We pray Thee, LORD, arise,
And come in Thy great might;
Revive our longing eyes,
Which languish for Thy sight.

5. Men scorn Thy sacred Name,
And wolves devour Thy fold;
By many deeds of shame
We learn that love grows cold.

6. O'er heathen lands afar
Thick darkness broodeth yet:
Arise, O morning Star,
Arise, and never set. Amen.

## 312.

"If any man sin, we have an Advocate with the FATHER, JESUS CHRIST the Righteous."

1. WHEN at Thy footstool, LORD, I bend
And plead with Thee for mercy there,
Think of the sinners' dying Friend,
And for His sake receive my prayer.

2. O think not of my shame and guilt,
My thousand stains of deepest dye;
Think of the Blood which JESUS spilt,
And let that Blood my pardon buy.

3. Think, LORD, how I am still Thine own,
The trembling creature of Thy hand;
Think how my heart to sin is prone,
And what temptations round me stand.

4. O think upon Thy holy word,
And every plighted promise there;
How prayer should evermore be heard,
And how Thy glory is to spare.

5. O think not of my doubts and fears,
My strivings with Thy grace divine;
Think upon JESU's woes and tears,
And let His merits stand for mine.

6. Thine eye, Thine ear, they are not dull;
Thine arm can never shortened be;
Behold me here; my heart is full;
Behold, and spare and succour me. Amen.

## 313.

"Men ought always to pray, and not to faint."

1. WHAT various hindrances we meet
In coming to the Mercy-seat;
Yet who, that knows the worth of prayer,
But wishes to be often there?

2. Prayer makes the darkened cloud withdraw,
Prayer climbs the ladder Jacob saw,
Gives exercise to faith and love,
Brings every blessing from above.

3. Restraining prayer we cease to fight;
Prayer makes the Christian's armour bright;
And Satan trembles when he sees
The weakest saint upon his knees.

4. When Moses stood with arms spread wide,
Success was found on Israel's side;
But when through weariness they failed,
That moment Amalek prevailed.

5. Have we no words? ah, think again;
Words flow apace when we complain,
And fill our fellow-creature's ear
With the sad tale of all our care.

6. Were half the breath thus vainly spent
To heaven in supplication sent,
Our cheerful song would oftener be,
"Hear what the Lord hath done for me."

7. O Lord, increase our faith and love,
That we may all Thy goodness prove,
And gain from Thy exhaustless store
The fruits of prayer for evermore. Amen.

## 314.

"In everything give thanks."

1. WHEN morning gilds the skies,
My heart awaking cries
May JESUS CHRIST be praised.
Alike at work and prayer
To JESUS I repair;
May JESUS CHRIST be praised.

2. Whene'er the sweet church bell
Peals over hill and dell,
May JESUS CHRIST be praised,
O hark to what it sings,
As joyously it rings,
May JESUS CHRIST be praised.

3. My tongue shall never tire
Of chanting with the choir
May JESUS CHRIST be praised:
This song of sacred joy,
It never seems to cloy;
May JESUS CHRIST be praised.

4. When sleep her balm denies,
My silent spirit sighs
May JESUS CHRIST be praised:
When evil thoughts molest,
With this I shield my breast,
May JESUS CHRIST be praised.

5. Does sadness fill my mind?
A solace here I find,
May Jesus Christ be praised:
Or fades my earthly bliss?
My comfort still is this,
May Jesus Christ be praised.

6. The night becomes as day,
When from the heart we say
May Jesus Christ be praised:
The powers of darkness fear,
When this sweet chant they hear,
May Jesus Christ be praised.

7. In heaven's eternal bliss
The loveliest strain is this,
May Jesus Christ be praised:
Let earth, and sea, and sky
From depth to height reply
May Jesus Christ be praised.

8. Be this, while life is mine,
My canticle divine,
May Jesus Christ be praised:
Be this the eternal song
Through all the ages on,
May Jesus Christ be praised. Amen.

## 315.

"And now abideth faith, hope, charity, these three: but the greatest of these is charity."

1. GRACIOUS SPIRIT, HOLY GHOST,
Taught by Thee we covet most
Of Thy gifts at Pentecost
Holy, heavenly Love.

2. Love is kind and suffers long,
Love is meek, and thinks no wrong,
Love than death itself more strong;
Therefore, give us Love.

3. Prophecy will fade away,
Melting in the light of day;
Love will ever with us stay;
Therefore, give us Love.

4. Faith will vanish into sight;
Hope be emptied in delight;
Love in heaven will shine more bright;
Therefore, give us Love.

5. Faith and Hope and Love we see
Joining hand in hand agree;
But the greatest of the three,
And the best, is Love.

6. From the overshadowing
Of Thy gold and silver wing,
Shed on us, who to Thee sing,
Holy, heavenly Love. Amen.

## 316.

"To him that overcometh."

1. SOLDIERS, who are CHRIST'S below,
Strong in faith resist the foe;
Boundless is the pledged reward
Unto them who serve the LORD.

2. 'Tis no palm of fading leaves
That the conqueror's hand receives;
Joys are his serene and pure,
Light that ever shall endure.

3. For the souls that overcome
Waits the beauteous heavenly Home,
Where the Blessèd evermore
Tread, on high, the starry floor.

4. Passing soon and little worth
Are the things that tempt on earth;
Heavenward lift thy soul's regard;
GOD Himself is thy Reward.

5. FATHER, Who the crown dost give,
SAVIOUR, by Whose death we live,
SPIRIT, Who our hearts dost raise,
THREE IN ONE, Thy Name we praise.
Amen.

# 317.

"He that cometh to Me shall never hunger, and he that believeth in Me shall never thirst."

1. I HEARD the voice of JESUS say
   "Come unto Me and rest;
Lay down, thou weary one, lay down
   Thy head upon My breast:"
I came to JESUS as I was,
   Weary, and worn, and sad;
I found in Him a resting-place,
   And He has made me glad.

2. I heard the voice of JESUS say
   "Behold I freely give
The living water, thirsty one,
   Stoop down, and drink, and live:"
I came to JESUS, and I drank
   Of that life-giving stream;
My thirst was quenched, my soul revived,
   And now I live in Him.

3. I heard the voice of JESUS say
   "I am this dark world's Light;
Look unto Me, thy morn shall rise,
   And all thy day be bright:"
I looked to JESUS, and I found
   In Him my Star, my Sun;
And in that Light of life I'll walk
   Till travelling days are done. Amen.

## 318.

"And on His Head were many crowns."

1. CROWN Him with many crowns,
The LAMB upon His throne;
Hark, how the heavenly anthem drowns
All music but its own:
Awake, my soul, and sing
Of Him Who died for thee,
And hail Him as thy matchless King
Through all eternity.

2. Crown Him the Virgin's Son,
The GOD Incarnate born,
Whose arm those crimson trophies won
Which now His Brow adorn:
Fruit of the mystic Rose,
As of that Rose the Stem;
The Root whence mercy ever flows,
The Babe of Bethlehem.

3. Crown Him the LORD of Love;
Behold His Hands and Side,
Rich Wounds yet visible above
In beauty glorified:
No angel in the sky
Can fully bear that sight,
But downward bends his burning eye
At mysteries so bright.

4. Crown Him the Lord of Peace:
Whose power a sceptre sways
From pole to pole, that wars may cease,
And all be prayer and praise;
His reign shall know no end,
And round His piercèd Feet
Fair flowers of Paradise extend
Their fragrance ever sweet.

5. Crown Him the Lord of years,
The Potentate of time,
Creator of the rolling spheres,
Ineffably sublime.
All hail, Redeemer, hail!
For Thou hast died for me;
Thy praise shall never, never fail
Throughout eternity. Amen.

## 319.

"In the beginning was the Word, and the Word was with God, and the Word was God. All things were made by Him."

1. JESUS is God: the solid earth,
The ocean broad and bright,
The countless stars, like golden dust,
That strew the skies at night,
The wheeling storm, the dreadful fire,
The pleasant wholesome air,
The summer's sun, the winter's frost,
His own creations were.

2. Jesus is God: the glorious bands
Of golden angels sing
Songs of adoring praise to Him,
Their Maker and their King.
He was true God in Bethlehem's crib,
On Calvary's Cross true God,
He Who in heaven eternal reigned
In time on earth abode.

3. Jesus is God: let sorrow come,
And pain, and every ill,
All are worth while, for all are means
His glory to fulfil;
Worth while a thousand years of woe
To speak one little word,
If by that "I believe" we own
The Godhead of our Lord. Amen.

## 320.

"He is the Head of the Body, the Church."

1. The Church's one foundation
Is Jesus Christ her Lord;
She is His new creation
By water and the Word:
From heaven He came and sought her
To be His holy Bride,
With His own Blood He bought her,
And for her life He died.

2. Elect from every nation,
Yet one o'er all the earth,
Her charter of salvation
One LORD, one Faith, one Birth;
One Holy Name she blesses,
Partakes one Holy Food,
And to one hope she presses
With every grace endued.

3. Though with a scornful wonder
Men see her sore opprest,
By schisms rent asunder,
By heresies distrest.
Yet saints their watch are keeping,
Their cry goes up, "How long?"
And soon the night of weeping
Shall be the morn of song.

4. Mid toil, and tribulation,
And tumult of her war,
She waits the consummation
Of peace for evermore;
Till with the vision glorious
Her longing eyes are blest,
And the great Church victorious
Shall be the Church at rest.

5. Yet she on earth hath union
With GOD the THREE IN ONE,
And mystic sweet communion
With those whose rest is won:
O happy ones and holy!
LORD, give us grace that we
Like them, the meek and lowly,
On high may dwell with Thee. Amen.

## 321.

"When the morning stars sang together, and all the sons of GOD shouted for joy."

1. STARS of the morning, so gloriously bright,
Filled with celestial virtue and light,
These that, where night never followeth day,
Raise the "Trisagion"* ever and aye:

2. These are Thy ministers, these dost Thou own,
LORD GOD of Sabaoth, nearest Thy throne;
These are Thy messengers, these dost Thou send
Help of the helpless ones! man to defend.

3. These keep the guard amidst Salem's dear bowers;
Thrones, Principalities, Virtues, and Powers;
Where with the Living Ones, mystical Four,
Cherubim, Seraphim bow and adore.

---

* This word in the Greek Liturgy means the same as the "Sanctus, Sanctus, Sanctus," in the Latin, and the "Holy, Holy, Holy," in the English.

3. Then, when the earth was first poised in mid space,
Then, when the planets first sped on their race,
Then, when were ended the six days' employ,
Then all the sons of God shouted for joy.

4. Still let them succour us; still let them fight,
Lord of angelic hosts, battling for right;
Till, where their anthems they ceaselessly pour,
We with the Angels may bow and adore.
Amen.

## 322.

"Eye hath not seen nor ear heard, neither have entered into the heart of man the things which God hath prepared for them that love Him. But God hath revealed them unto us by His Spirit."

1. LIGHT'S abode, Celestial Salem,
Vision whence true peace doth spring,
Brighter than the heart can fancy,
Mansion of the Highest King;
O how glorious are the praises
Which of thee the prophets sing!

2. There for ever and for ever
Alleluia is out-poured;
For unending, for unbroken
Is the feast-day of the Lord;
All is pure, and all is holy
That within thy walls is stored.

3. There no cloud nor passing vapour
Dims the brightness of the air:
Endless noon-day, glorious noon-day,
From the Sun of suns is there;
There no night brings rest from labour,
For unknown are toil and care.

4. O how glorious and resplendent,
Fragile body, shalt thou be,
When endued with so much beauty,
Full of health, and strong and free,
Full of vigor, full of pleasure
That shall last eternally!

5. Now with gladness, now with courage
Bear the burden on thee laid,
That hereafter these thy labours
May with endless gifts be paid,
And in everlasting glory
Thou with brightness be arrayed.

6. Laud and honour to the FATHER,
Laud and honour to the SON,
Laud and honour to the SPIRIT,
Ever THREE and ever ONE,
Consubstantial, Co-eternal,
While unending ages run. Amen.

## 323.

"Our conversation is in heaven."

1. JERUSALEM on high
My song and city is,
My home whene'er I die,
The centre of my bliss:
O happy place,
When shall I be,
My God, with Thee,
To see Thy Face?

2. There dwells my Lord, my King,
Judged here unfit to live;
There Angels to Him sing,
And lowly homage give:
O happy place,
When shall I be,
My God, with Thee,
To see Thy Face?

3. The Patriarchs of old
There from their travels cease;
The Prophets there behold
Their longed-for Prince of Peace:
O happy place,
When shall I be,
My God, with Thee,
To see Thy Face?

4. The LAMB's Apostles there
   I might with joy behold,
 The harpers I might hear
   Harping on harps of gold;
     O happy place,
       When shall I be,
       My GOD, with Thee,
     To see Thy Face?

5. The bleeding Martyrs, they
   Within these courts are found,
 Clothèd in pure array,
   Their scars with glory crowned:
     O happy place,
       When shall I be,
       My GOD, with Thee,
     To see Thy Face?

6. Ah me! ah me! that I
   In Kedar's tents here stay
 No place like that on high;
   LORD, thither guide my way:
     O happy place,
       When shall I be,
       My GOD, with Thee,
     To see Thy Face? Amen.

## 324.

"The Paradise of God."

1. O PARADISE, O Paradise,
Who doth not crave for rest?
Who would not seek the happy land
Where they that loved are blest?
Where loyal hearts and true
Stand ever in the light,
All rapture through and through,
In God's most holy sight.

2. O Paradise, O Paradise,
The world is growing old;
Who would not be at rest and free
Where love is never cold?
Where loyal hearts and true
Stand ever in the light,
All rapture through and through,
In God's most holy sight.

3. O Paradise, O Paradise,
'Tis weary waiting here;
I long to be where Jesus is,
To feel, to see Him near;
Where loyal hearts and true
Stand ever in the light,
All rapture through and through,
In God's most holy sight.

4. O Paradise, O Paradise,
I want to sin no more,
I want to be as pure on earth
As on thy spotless shore;
Where loyal hearts and true
Stand ever in the light,
All rapture through and through,
In God's most holy sight.

5. O Paradise, O Paradise,
I greatly long to see
The special place my dearest Lord
In love prepares for me;
Where loyal hearts and true
Stand ever in the light,
All rapture through and through,
In God's most holy sight.

6. Lord Jesu, King of Paradise,
O keep me in Thy love,
And guide me to that happy land
Of perfect rest above;
Where loyal hearts and true
Stand ever in the light,
All rapture through and through,
In God's most holy sight. Amen.

# 325.

"The night is far spent, the day is at hand."

1. HARK! hark! my soul; Angelic songs are swelling
O'er earth's green fields, and ocean's wave-beat shore:
How sweet the truth those blessèd strains are telling
Of that new life when sin shall be no more.
Angels of JESUS, Angels of light,
Singing to welcome the pilgrims of the night.

2. Onward we go, for still we hear them singing,
"Come, weary souls, for JESUS bids you come:"
And, through the dark its echoes sweetly ringing,
The music of the Gospel leads us home.
Angels of JESUS, Angels of light,
Singing to welcome the pilgrims of the night.

3. Far, far away, like bells at evening pealing,
The voice of JESUS sounds o'er land and sea,
And laden souls by thousands meekly stealing,
Kind Shepherd, turn their weary steps to Thee.
Angels of JESUS, Angels of light,
Singing to welcome the pilgrims of the night.

4. Rest comes at length, though life be long and dreary,
The day must dawn, and darksome night be past;
Faith's journey ends in welcome to the weary,
And heaven, the heart's true home, will come at last.
Angels of Jesus, Angels of light,
Singing to welcome the pilgrims of the night.

5. Angels, sing on! your faithful watches keeping;
Sing us sweet fragments of the songs above;
Till morning's joy shall end the night of weeping,
And life's long shadows break in cloudless love.
Angels of Jesus, Angels of light,
Singing to welcome the pilgrims of the night.
Amen.

## 326.

"Watch and pray."

1. "CHRISTIAN! seek not yet repose,"
Hear thy guardian angel say;
Thou art in the midst of foes;
"Watch and pray."

2. Principalities and powers,
Mustering their unseen array,
Wait for thy unguarded hours:
"Watch and pray."

3. Gird thy heavenly armour on,
Wear it ever night and day;
Ambushed lies the evil one;
"Watch and pray."

4. Hear the victors who o'ercame;
Still they mark each warrior's way;
All with one sweet voice exclaim
"Watch and pray."

5. Hear, above all, hear thy LORD,
Him thou lovest to obey;
Hide within thy heart His word,
"Watch and pray."

6. Watch, as if on that alone
Hung the issue of the day;
Pray, that help may be sent down;
"Watch and pray."
Amen.

## 327.

"LORD, to whom shall we go?"

1. WHEN wounded sore the stricken heart
Lies bleeding and unbound,
One only Hand, a piercèd Hand,
Can salve the sinner's wound.

2. When sorrow swells the laden breast,
And tears of anguish flow,
One only Heart, a broken Heart,
Can feel the sinner's woe.

3. When penitential grief has wept
Over some foul dark spot,
One only Stream, a Stream of Blood,
Can wash away the blot.

4. 'Tis Jesus' Blood that washes white,
His Hand that brings relief,
His Heart is touched with all our joys,
And feels for all our grief.

5. Lift up Thy bleeding Hand, O Lord,
Unseal that cleansing tide;
We have no shelter from our sin
But in Thy wounded Side. Amen.

## 328.

"Behold, I stand at the door and knock."

1. O JESU, Thou art standing
Outside the fast-closed door,
In lowly patience waiting
To pass the threshold o'er:
Shame on us, Christian brethren,
His Name and sign who bear,
Oh shame, thrice shame upon us
To keep Him standing there.

2. O Jesu, Thou art knocking:
And lo! that Hand is scarred,
And thorns Thy Brow encircle,
And tears Thy Face have marred:
O love that passeth knowledge
So patiently to wait!
Oh sin that hath no equal
So fast to bar the gate!

3. O Jesu, Thou art pleading
In accents meek and low,
"I died for you, My children,
And will ye treat Me so?"
O Lord, with shame and sorrow
We open now the door:
Dear Saviour, enter, enter,
And leave us never more. Amen.

## 329.

"Help us, O God of our salvation, for the glory of Thy Name."

1. LORD of our life, and God of our salvation,
Star of our night, and Hope of every nation,
Hear and receive Thy Church's supplication,
Lord God Almighty.

2. See round Thine ark the hungry billows curling,
See how Thy foes their banners are unfurling;
Lord, while their darts envenomed they are hurling,
Thou canst preserve us.

3. Lord, Thou canst help when earthly armour faileth,
Lord, Thou canst save when deadly sin assaileth,
Lord, o'er Thy Rock nor death nor hell prevaileth,
Grant us Thy peace, Lord.

4. Grant us Thy help till foes are backward driven,
Grant them Thy truth, that they may be forgiven,
Grant peace on earth, and, after we have striven,
Peace in Thy heaven. Amen.

## 330.

"The Lord is my Shepherd."

1. THE King of love my Shepherd is,
Whose goodness faileth never;
I nothing lack if I am His
And He is mine for ever.

2. Where streams of living water flow
My ransomed soul He leadeth,
And, where the verdant pastures grow,
With food celestial feedeth.

3. Perverse and foolish oft I strayed,
But yet in love He sought me,
And on His Shoulder gently laid,
And home, rejoicing, brought me.

4. In death's dark vale I fear no ill
With Thee, dear Lord, beside me;
Thy rod and staff my comfort still,
Thy Cross before to guide me.

5. Thou spread'st a Table in my sight,
Thy Unction grace bestoweth,
And oh! what transport of delight
From Thy pure Chalice floweth.

6. And so through all the length of days
Thy goodness faileth never;
Good Shepherd, may I sing Thy praise
Within Thy house for ever. Amen.

## 331.

"He saith, surely I come quickly: Amen. Even so, come, Lord Jesus."

1. O QUICKLY come, dread Judge of all;
For, awful though Thine advent be,
All shadows from the truth will fall,
And falsehood die, in sight of Thee:
O quickly come: for doubt and fear
Like clouds dissolve when Thou art near.

2. O quickly come, great King of all;
Reign all around us, and within;
Let sin no more our souls enthrall,
Let pain and sorrow die with sin:
O quickly come: for Thou alone
Canst make Thy scattered people one.

3. O quickly come, true Life of all;
For death is mighty all around;
On every home his shadows fall,
On every heart his mark is found:
O quickly come: for grief and pain,
Can never cloud Thy glorious reign.

4. O quickly come, sure Light of all,
For gloomy night broods o'er our way;
And weakly souls begin to fall
With weary watching for the day:
O quickly come: for round Thy throne
No eye is blind, no night is known. Amen.

## 332.

"The time is short."

1. A FEW more years shall roll,
A few more seasons come,
And we shall be with those that rest
Asleep within the tomb:
Then, O my LORD, prepare
My soul for that great day;
O wash me in Thy precious Blood,
And take my sins away.

2. A few more suns shall set
O'er these dark hills of time,
And we shall be where suns are not,
A far serener clime:
Then, O my LORD, prepare
My soul for that blest day;
O wash me in Thy precious Blood,
And take my sins away.

3. A few more storms shall beat
On this wild rocky shore,
And we shall be where tempests cease,
And surges swell no more:
Then, O my Lord, prepare
My soul for that calm day;
O wash me in Thy precious Blood,
And take my sins away.

4. A few more struggles here,
A few more partings o'er,
A few more toils, a few more tears,
And we shall weep no more:
Then, O my Lord, prepare
My soul for that bright day;
O wash me in Thy precious Blood,
And take my sins away.

5. 'Tis but a little while
And He shall come again,
Who died that we might live, Who lives
That we with Him may reign:
Then, O my Lord, prepare
My soul for that glad day;
O wash me in Thy precious Blood,
And take my sins away. Amen.

## 333.

"And he said, I will not let Thee go, except Thou bless me."

1. SHEPHERD Divine, our wants relieve,
   In this our evil day:
To all Thy tempted follower's give
   The power to watch and pray.

2. Long as our fiery trials last,
   Long as the cross we bear,
O let our souls on Thee be cast
   In never-ceasing prayer.

3. The Spirit of interceding grace
   Give us in faith to claim;
To wrestle till we see Thy Face,
   And know Thy hidden Name.

4. Till Thou Thy perfect love impart,
   Till Thou Thyself bestow,
Be this the cry of every heart,
   "I will not let Thee go:

5. "I will not let Thee go, unless
   Thou tell Thy Name to me;
With all Thy great salvation bless,
   And make me all like Thee.

6. "Then let me on the mountain-top
   Behold Thy open Face;
Where faith in sight is swallowed up,
   And prayer in endless praise." Amen.

# 334.

"O, hold Thou up my goings in Thy paths; that my footsteps slip not."

1. BE Thou my Guardian and my Guide,
 And hear me when I call;
Let not my slippery footsteps slide;
 And hold me lest I fall.

2. The world, the flesh, and Satan dwell
 Around the path I tread;
O, save me from the snares of hell,
 Thou Quickener of the dead.

3. And if I tempted am to sin,
 And outward things are strong,
Do Thou, O LORD, keep watch within,
 And save my soul from wrong.

4. Still let me ever watch and pray,
 And feel that I am frail;
That if the tempter cross my way,
 Yet he may not prevail.

5. To FATHER, SON, and HOLY GHOST,
 The GOD Whom we adore,
Be glory, as it was, is now,
 And shall be evermore. Amen.

## 335.

"Every day will I give thanks unto Thee, and praise Thy Name for ever and ever."

1. SAVIOUR, Blessèd SAVIOUR,
   Listen whilst we sing,
Hearts and voices raising
   Praises to our King.
All we have we offer;
   All we hope to be,
Body, soul, and spirit,
   All we yield to Thee.

2. Nearer, ever nearer,
   CHRIST, we draw to Thee,
Deep in adoration
   Bending low the knee:
Thou for our redemption
   Cam'st on earth to die;
Thou, that we might follow,
   Hast gone up on high.

3. Great and ever greater
   Are Thy mercies here,
True and everlasting
   Are the glories there,
Where no pain, or sorrow,
   Toil, or care, is known,
Where the angel-legions
   Worship round Thy throne.

4. Dark and ever darker
   Was the wintry past,
Now a ray of gladness
   O'er our path is cast;
Every day that passeth,
   Every hour that flies,
Tells of love unfeignèd,
   Love that never dies.

5. Clearer still and clearer
   Dawns the light from heaven,
In our sadness bringing
   News of sin forgiven;
Life has lost its shadows,
   Pure the light within;
Thou has shed Thy radiance
   On a world of sin.

6. Brighter still and brighter
   Glows the western sun,
Shedding all its gladness
   O'er our work that's done;
Time will soon be over,
   Toil and sorrow past,
May we, Blessèd SAVIOUR,
   Find a rest at last.

7. Onward, ever onward,
   Journeying o'er the road
Worn by Saints before us,
   Journeying on to GOD;

Leaving all behind us
May we hasten on,
Backward never looking
Till the prize is won.

8. Bliss, all bliss excelling,
When the ransomed soul
Earthly toils forgetting
Finds its promised goal;
Where in joys unheard of
Saints with angels sing,
Never weary raising.
Praises to their KING. Amen.

## 336.

"And all her streets shall say, 'Alleluia.'"

1. SING Alleluia forth in duteous praise,
O citizens of heaven, and sweetly raise
An endless Alleluia.

2. Ye next, who stand before th' Eternal Light,
In hymning choirs re-echo to the height
An endless Alleluia.

3. The Holy City shall take up your strain,
And with glad songs resounding wake again
An endless Alleluia.

4. In blissful antiphons ye thus rejoice
To render to the LORD with thankful voice
An endless Alleluia.

5. Ye who have gained at length your palms in
bliss,
Victorious ones, your chant shall still be this,
An endless Alleluia.

6. There, in one grand acclaim, for ever ring
The strains which tell the honour of your KING,
An endless Alleluia.

7. This is the rest for weary ones brought back,
This is the food and drink which none shall lack,
An endless Alleluia.

8. While Thee, by Whom were all things made,
we praise
For ever, and tell out in sweetest lays
An endless Alleluia.

9. Almighty CHRIST, to Thee our voices sing
Glory for evermore; to Thee we bring
An endless Alleluia.
Amen.

## 337.

"Thou hast been my succour: leave me not, neither forsake me, O GOD of my salvation."

1. WE know Thee Who Thou art,
LORD JESUS, Mary's Son;
We know the yearnings of Thy Heart
To end Thy work begun.

2. That sacred Fount of grace,
'Mid all the bliss of heaven,
Has joy whene'er we seek Thy face,
And kneel to be forgiven.

3. Brought home from ways perverse,
At peace Thine arms within,
We pray Thee shield us from the curse
Of falling back to sin.

4. We dare not ask to live
Henceforth from trials free;
But oh, when next they tempt us, give
More strength to cling to Thee.

5. We know Thee Who Thou art,
Our own redeeming LORD;
Be Thou by will, and mind, and heart,
Accepted, loved, adored. Amen.

## 338.

"This GOD is our GOD for ever and ever: He shall be our guide unto death."

1. GUIDE me, O Thou Great REDEEMER,
Pilgrim through this barren land;
I am weak, but Thou art mighty,
Hold me with Thy powerful hand;
Bread of Heaven,
Feed me now and evermore.

2. Open now the crystal Fountain,
   Whence the healing streams do flow:
 Let the fiery cloudy pillar
   Lead me all my journey through;
     Strong Deliverer,
   Be Thou still my Strength and Shield.

3. When I tread the verge of Jordan,
   Bid my anxious fears subside:
 Death of death, and hell's Destruction,
   Land me safe on Canaan's side;
     Songs of praises
 I will ever give to Thee. Amen.

## 339.

"We must all appear before the judgment seat of CHRIST."

THOU JUDGE of quick and dead,
   Before Whose bar severe
 With holy joy, or guilty dread,
   We all shall soon appear;

2. Our wakened souls prepare
   For that tremendous Day,
 And fill us now with watchful care,
   And stir us up to pray:

3. To pray, and wait the hour,
   The awful hour unknown,
 When, robed in majesty and power,
   Thou shalt from heaven come down,

4. The immortal SON of Man,
To judge the human race,
With all Thy FATHER's dazzling train,
With all Thy glorious grace.

5. To sober earthly joys,
To quicken holy fears,
For ever let the Archangel's voice
Be sounding in our ears;

6. The solemn midnight cry,
"Ye dead, the Judge is come!
"Arise, and meet Him in the sky,
"And meet your instant doom!"

7. O may we thus be found,
Obedient to His word,
Attentive to the trumpet's sound,
And looking for our LORD.

8. O may we thus insure
Our lot among the blest,
And watch a moment, to secure
An everlasting rest. Amen.

## 340.

"Thou hast been a strength to the poor; a strength to the needy in his distress."

1. I NEED Thee, Precious Jesu,
For I am very poor;
A stranger and a pilgrim,
I have no earthly store;
I need the love of Jesus
To cheer me on my way,
To guide my doubting footsteps,
To be my strength and stay.

2. I need Thee, Precious Jesu,
I need a friend like Thee,
A friend to soothe and pity,
A friend to care for me:
I need the Heart of Jesus
To feel each anxious care,
To tell my every trial,
And all my sorrows share.

3. I need Thee, Precious Jesu,
I need Thee, day by day,
To fill me with Thy fulness,
To lead me on my way;
I need Thy Holy Spirit
To teach me what I am,
To show me more of Jesus,
To point me to the Lamb.

4. I need Thee, Precious Jesu,
And hope to see Thee soon
Encircled with the rainbow,
And seated on Thy throne;
There, with Thy Blood-bought children,
My joy shall ever be
To sing Thy praises, Jesu,
To gaze, my Lord, on Thee. Amen.

## 341.

"Let my supplication come before Thee; deliver me, according to Thy Word."

1. JESUS, Lord of life and glory,
Bend from heaven Thy gracious ear;
While our waiting souls adore Thee,
Friend of helpless sinners hear:
By Thy mercy,
O deliver us, good Lord.

2. From the depths of nature's blindness,
From the hardening power of sin,
From all malice and unkindness,
From the pride that lurks within,
By Thy mercy
O deliver us, good Lord.

3. When temptation sorely presses,
In the day of Satan's power,
In our times of deep distresses
In each dark and trying hour,
By Thy mercy,
O deliver us, good Lord.

4. When the world around is smiling,
   In the time of wealth and ease,
 Earthly joys our hearts beguiling,
   In the day of health and peace,
     By Thy mercy,
   O deliver us, good Lord.

5. In the weary hours of sickness,
   In the times of grief and pain,
 When we feel our mortal weakness,
   When the creature's help is vain,
     By Thy mercy,
   O deliver us, good Lord.

6. In the solemn hour of dying,
   In the awful judgment day,
 May our souls, on Thee relying,
   Find Thee still our Hope and Stay.
     By Thy mercy,
   O deliver us, good Lord. Amen.

## 342.

"In the day time also He led them with a cloud, and all the night through with the light of fire."

1. LEAD, kindly Light, amid the encircling gloom,
     Lead Thou me on;
 The night is dark, and I am far from home,
     Lead Thou me on.
 Keep Thou my feet; I do not ask to see
 The distant scene; one step enough for me.

2. I was not ever thus, nor prayed that Thou
Shouldst lead me on;
I loved to choose and see my path; but now
Lead Thou me on.
I loved the garish day; and, spite of fears,
Pride ruled my will: remember not past years.

3. So long Thy power has blest me, sure it still
Will lead me on
O'er moor and fen, o'er crag and torrent, till
The night is gone,
And with the morn those angel faces smile,
Which I loved long since, and lost awhile.
Amen.

## 343.

"There remaineth a rest to the people of God."

1. *O WHAT the joy and the glory must be,
Those endless sabbaths the blessèd ones see;
Crown for the valiant, to weary ones rest;
God shall be all and in all ever blest.

2. What are the Monarch, His court, and His Thone?
What are the peace, and the joy that they own?
O, that the blest ones, who in it have share,
All that they feel could as fully declare.

* *This Hymn according to Mone is for use on Saturday.*

3. Truly Jerusalem, name we that shore,
Vision of Peace, that brings joy evermore;
Wish and fulfilment can severed be ne'er,
Nor the thing prayed for come short of the prayer.

4. There, where no troubles distraction can bring,
We the sweet anthems of Sion shall sing,
While for Thy grace, LORD, their voices of praise
Thy blessèd people eternally raise.

5. There dawns no Sabbath, no Sabbath is o'er,
Those Sabbath-keepers have one evermore;
One and unending is that triumph-song
Which to the angels and us shall belong.

6. Now in the meanwhile with hearts raised on high,
We for that country must yearn and must sigh;
Seeking Jerusalem, dear native land,
Thro' our long exile on Babylon's strand.

7. Low before Him with our praises we fall,
Of Whom, and in Whom, and thro' Whom are all;
Of Whom, the FATHER; and in Whom, the SON;
Thro' Whom, the SPIRIT with Them ever One.
Amen.

## 344.

### The Transfiguration.

"His Face did shine as the sun, and His raiment was white as the light."

1. IN days of old on Sinai
The Lord Almighty came,
In majesty of terror,
In thunder-cloud and flame:

On Tabor, with the glory
  Of sunniest light for vest,
The excellence of beauty
  In Jesus was expressed.

2. All light created paled there,
  And did Him worship meet;
The sun itself adored Him,
  And bowed before His feet;
While Moses and Elias,
  Upon the Holy Mount,
The co-eternal glory
  Of Christ our God recount.

3. O holy, wondrous vision!
  But what, when, this life past,
The beauty of Mount Tabor
  Shall end in heaven at last?
But what, when all the glory
  Of uncreated light
Shall be the promised guerdon
  Of them that win the fight? Amen.

## 345.

### Holy Communion.

"Jesus said, I am the Bread of Life."

1. THE Heavenly Word proceeding forth,
  Yet leaving not the Father's side,
Accomplishing His work on earth
Had reached at length life's eventide.

2. By false disciple to be given
To foemen for His life athirst,
Himself, the very Bread of Heaven,
He gave to His disciples first.

3. He gave Himself in either kind,
His precious Flesh, His precious Blood:
In love's own fulness thus designed
Of the whole man to be the Food.

4. By Birth their Fellow-man was He;
Their Meat, when sitting at the board;
He died, their Ransomer to be;
He ever reigns, their great Reward.

## PART II.

1. O Saving Victim, opening wide
The gate of heaven to man below,
Our foes press on from every side,
Thine aid supply, Thy strength bestow.

2. All thanks and praise to Thee ascend,
For evermore, Blest One in Three;
O grant us life that shall not end
In our true native land with Thee. Amen.

## 346.

"He that eateth My Flesh and drinketh My Blood dwelleth in Me and I in him."

1. O FOOD that weary pilgrims love,
O Bread of angel hosts above,
O Manna of the saints,
The hungry soul would feed on Thee;
Ne'er may the heart unsolaced be
Which for Thy sweetness faints.

2. O Fount of love, O cleansing Tide,
Which from the SAVIOUR's piercèd Side
And Sacred Heart dost flow,
Be ours to drink of Thy pure rill,
Which only can our spirits fill
And all we need bestow.

3. LORD JESU, Whom, by power divine
Now hidden 'neath the outward sign,
We worship and adore,
Grant, when the veil away is rolled,
With open face we may behold
Thyself for evermore. Amen.

## 347.

"We have an Altar."

1. ONCE, only once, and once for all,
His precious life He gave;
Before the Cross our spirits fall,
And own it strong to save.

2. "One offering, single and complete,"
With lips and heart we say;
But what He never can repeat
He shows forth day by day.

3. For, as the priest of Aaron's line
Within the Holiest stood,
And sprinkled all the mercy-shrine
With sacrificial blood;

4. So He, Who once atonement wrought,
Our Priest of endless power,
Presents Himself for Those He bought
In that dark noontide hour.

5. His Manhood pleads where now It lives
On heaven's eternal throne,
And where in mystic rite He gives
Its Presence to His own.

6. And so we shew Thy death, O Lord,
Till Thou again appear;
And feel, when we approach Thy Board,
We have an Altar here.

7. All glory to the Father be,
All glory to the Son,
All glory, Holy Ghost, to Thee
While endless ages run. Amen.

# 348.

"Wisdom saith, Come eat of my bread, and drink of the wine which I have mingled."

1. DRAW nigh and take the Body of the LORD,
And drink the holy Blood for you outpoured.

2. Saved by that Body and that holy Blood,
With souls refreshed, we render thanks to GOD.

3. Salvation's Giver, CHRIST the Only SON,
By His dear Cross and Blood the victory won.

4. Offered was He for greatest and for least,
Himself the Victim and Himself the Priest.

5. Victims were offered by the law of old
Which in a type this heavenly mystery told.

6. He, Ransomer from death, and Light from shade,
Now gives His holy grace His saints to aid.

7. Approach ye then with faithful hearts sincere,
And take the safeguard of salvation here.

8. He, that in this world rules His saints and shields,
To all believers life eternal yields;

9. With heavenly bread makes them that hunger whole,
Gives living waters to the thirsting soul.

10. Alpha and Omega, to Whom shall bow
All nations at the Doom, is with us now.
Amen.

## 349.

"So man did eat angels' Food."

1. LO! the angels' Food is given
To the pilgrim who hath striven;
See the children's Bread from heaven,
Which on dogs may ne'er be spent:
Truth the ancient types fulfilling,
Isaac bound, a victim willing,
Paschal Lamb its life-blood spilling,
Manna to the fathers sent.

2. Very Bread, Good Shepherd, tend us,
Jesu, of Thy love befriend us;
Thou refresh us, Thou defend us,
Thine eternal goodness send us
In the land of life to see:
Thou Who all things canst and knowest,
Who on earth such Food bestowest,
Grant us with Thy saints, though lowest,
Where the heavenly Feast Thou shewest,
Fellow heirs and guests to be. Amen.

## 350.

"Thou art a Priest for ever."

1. ALLELUIA, sing to Jesus,
His the sceptre, His the throne;
Alleluia, His the triumph,
His the victory alone;

Hark, the songs of peaceful Sion
  Thunder like a mighty flood;
JESUS out of every nation
  Hath redeemed us by His Blood.

2. Alleluia, not as orphans
  We are left in sorrow now;
Alleluia, He is near us,
  Faith believes, nor questions how:
Though the cloud from sight received Him,
  When the forty days were o'er,
Shall our hearts forget His promise,
  "I am with you evermore?"

3. Alleluia, Bread of angels,
  Thou on earth our Food, our Stay,
Alleluia, here the sinful
  Flee to Thee from day to day;
Intercessor, Friend of sinners,
  Earth's Redeemer, plead for me,
Where the songs of all the sinless
  Sweep across the crystal sea.

4. Alleluia, King Eternal,
  Thee the LORD of lords we own;
Alleluia, born of Mary,
  Earth Thy footstool, Heaven Thy thone:
Thou within the veil hast entered,
  Robed in flesh, our Great High Priest;
Thou on earth both Priest and Victim
  In the Eucharistic feast.

5. Alleluia, sing to Jesus,
His the sceptre, His the throne;
Alleluia, His the triumph,
His the victory alone;
Hark, the songs of peaceful Sion
Thunder like a mighty flood;
Jesus out of every nation
Hath redeemed us by His Blood. Amen.

# 351.

## Baptism.

"He took them up in His arms, put His Hands upon them, and blessed them."

1. GLAD sight! The holy Church
Spreads forth her wings of love
To welcome to her breast a child
Begotten from above;

2. Begotten at the font
By God the Spirit's power,
A gentle lamb from Satan snatched
In childhood's helpless hour.

3. E'en now around the font,
Unseen by mortal eye,
Bright ministering angels watch
The wondrous mystery

4. There to receive their charge
   In readiness they stand,
And long to guide its feeble steps
   To their own happy land.

5. And all the host of heaven
   Rejoice before the LORD,
To see a child of fallen man
   A child of GOD restored.

6. All glory LORD to Thee
   Whom heaven and earth adore;
To FATHER, SON, and HOLY GHOST,
   One GOD for evermore. Amen.

## 352.

"Thou therefore endure hardness as a good soldier of JESUS CHRIST."

1. IN token that thou shalt not fear
   CHRIST crucified to own,
We print the Cross upon thee here,
   And stamp Thee His alone.

2. In token that thou shalt not blush
   To glory in His name,
We blazon here upon thy front
   His glory and His shame.

3. In token that thou shalt not flinch
   CHRIST's quarrel to maintain,
But 'neath His banner manfully
   Firm at Thy post remain;

4. In token that thou too shalt tread
   The path He travelled by,
 Endure the Cross, despise the shame,
   And sit thee down on high;

5. Thus outwardly and visibly
   We seal thee for His own;
 And may the brow that wears His Cross
   Hereafter share His Crown. Amen.

## 353.

### Confirmation.

"Then laid they their hands on them, and they received the Holy Ghost."

1. BEHOLD us, LORD, before Thee met
 Whom each bright Angel serves and fears,
 Who on Thy Throne rememberest yet
 Thy spotless Boyhood's quiet years,
 Whose feet the hills of Nazareth trod,
 Who art true Man and perfect GOD.

2. To Thee we look, in Thee confide,
 Our help is in Thine own dear Name;
 For who on JESUS e'er relied
 And found not JESUS still the same?
 Thus far Thy love our souls hath brought,
 O stablish well what Thou hast wrought.

3. From Thee was our baptismal grace;
The holy seed by Thee was sown;
And now before our FATHER'S Face
We make the three great vows our own,
And ask, in thine appointed way,
Confirm us in Thy grace to-day.

4. We need Thee more than tongue can speak,
'Mid foes that well might cast us down;
But thousands, once as young and weak,
Have fought the fight and won the crown;
We ask the help that bore them through,
We trust the Faithful and the True.

5. So bless us with the gift complete
By hands of Thy chief pastors given,
That awful Presence kind and sweet
Which comes in sevenfold might from heaven;
Eternal CHRIST, to Thee we bow:
Give us Thy SPIRIT here and now. Amen.

# 354.

"With my whole heart have I sought Thee; O let me not go wrong out of Thy commandments."

1. MY GOD, accept my heart this day,
And make it always Thine,
That I from Thee no more may stray,
No more from Thee decline.

2. Before the Cross of Him Who died,
   Behold, I prostrate fall;
Let every sin be crucified,
   And CHRIST be all in all.

3. Anoint me with Thy heavenly grace,
   And seal me for Thine own;
That I may see Thy glorious Face,
   And worship near Thy throne.

4. Let every thought, and work, and word,
   To Thee be ever given;
Then life shall be Thy service, LORD,
   And death the gate of heaven.

5. All glory to the FATHER be,
   All glory to the SON,
All glory, HOLY GHOST, to Thee,
   While endless ages run. Amen.

## 355.

### Ember Days.

"He gave some Apostles, and some Pastors and Teachers, for the perfecting of the saints, for the work of the ministry, for the edifying of the Body of CHRIST."

1. O THOU Who makest souls to shine
   With light from lighter worlds above,
And droppest glistning dew divine
On all who seek a SAVIOUR's love;

2. Do Thou Thy benediction give
On all who teach, on all who learn,
That so Thy Church may holier live,
And every lamp more brightly burn.

3. Give those who teach pure hearts and wise,
Faith, hope, and love, all warmed by prayer;
Themselves first training for the skies,
They best will raise their people there.

4. Give those who learn the willing ear,
The spirit meek, the guileless mind;
Such gifts will make the lowliest here
Far better than a kingdom find.

5. O bless the shepherd; bless the sheep;
That guide and guided both be one,
One in the faithful watch they keep,
Until this hurrying life be done.

6. If thus, good LORD, Thy grace be given,
In Thee to live, in Thee to die,
Before we upward pass to heaven
We taste our immortality. Amen.

## 356.

### Missions.

"So shall He sprinkle many nations."

1. SAVIOUR, sprinkle many nations,
Fruitful let Thy sorrows be;
By Thy pains and consolations
Draw the Gentiles unto Thee:

Of Thy Cross the wondrous story,
Be it to the nations told;
Let them see Thee in Thy glory,
And Thy mercy manifold.

2. Far and wide, though all unknowing,
Pants for Thee each mortal breast;
Human tears for Thee are flowing,
Human hearts in Thee would rest;
Thirsting, as for dews of even,
As the new-mown grass for rain,
Thee they seek, as God of Heaven,
Thee, as Man, for sinners slain.

3. Saviour, lo, the isles are waiting,
Stretched the hand, and strained the sight,
For Thy Spirit new creating,
Love's pure flame and wisdom's light;
Give the word, and of the preacher
Speed the foot, and touch the tongue,
Till on earth by every creature
Glory to the Lamb be sung. Amen.

## 357.

"Turn us, O God, our Saviour."

1. ALMIGHTY GOD, Whose only Son
O'er sin and death the triumph won,
And ever lives to intercede
For souls who Thy sweet mercy need;

2. In His dear Name to Thee we pray
For all who err and go astray,
For sinners wheresoe'er they be,
Who do not serve and honour Thee.

3. There are who never yet have heard
The tidings of Thy blessèd Word,
But still in heathen darkness dwell,
Without one thought of heaven or hell;

4. And some within Thy sacred Fold
To holy things are dead and cold,
And waste the precious hours of life
In selfish ease, or toil, or strife;

5. And many a quickened soul within
There lurks the secret love of sin;
A wayward will, or anxious fears,
Or lingering taint of bygone years:

6. O give repentance true and deep
To all Thy lost and wandering sheep,
And kindle in their hearts the fire
Of holy love and pure desire.

7. That so from angel-hosts above
May rise a sweeter song of love,
And we, with all the blest, adore
Thy Name, O God, for evermore. Amen.

# 358.

## Burial of a Child

"They are in peace."

1. TENDER Shepherd, Thou hast stilled
Now Thy little lamb's brief weeping;
Ah, how peaceful, pale, and mild,
In its narrow bed 'tis sleeping,
And no sigh of anguish sore
Heaves that little bosom more.

2. In this world of care and pain,
Lord, Thou wouldst no longer leave it;
To the sunny, heavenly plain
Thou dost now with joy receive it;
Clothed in robes of spotless white
Now it dwells with Thee in light.

3. Ah, Lord Jesu, grant that we
Where it lives may soon be living,
And the lovely pastures see
That its heavenly food are giving;
Then the gain of death we prove,
Tho' Thou take what most we love.
Amen.

# 359.

## Harvest.

"While the earth remaineth, seed time and harvest shall not cease."

1. GOD the FATHER, Whose creation
   Gives to flowers and fruits their birth,
Thou, Whose yearly operation
   Brings the hour of harvest mirth,
Here to Thee we make oblation
   Of the August-gold of earth.

2. GOD the WORD, the sun maturing
   With his blessèd ray the corn,
Spake of Thee, O Sun enduring,
   Thee, O everlasting Morn,
Thee in Whom our woes find curing,
   Thee, That liftest up our horn.

3. GOD the HOLY GHOST, the showers
   That have fattened out the grain,
Types of Thy celestial powers,
   Symbols of Baptismal rain,
Shadowed out the grace that dowers
   All the faithful of Thy train.

4. When the harvest of each nation
   Severs righteousness from sin,
And Archangel proclamation
   Bids to put the sickle in,
And each age and generation
   Sink to woe, or glory win;

5. Grant that we, or young or hoary,
   Lengthened be our span or brief,
 Whatsoe'er the life-long story
   Of our joy or of our grief,
 May be garnered up in glory
   As Thine own elected sheaf.

6. Laud to Him, to Whom Supernal
   Thrones and virtues bend the knee;
 Laud to Him, from Whom infernal
   Powers and dominations flee;
 Consubstantial, Co-Eternal,
   Beatific Trinity. Amen.

## 360.

"The eyes of all wait upon Thee, O Lord, and Thou givest them their meat in due season."

1. WE plough the fields, and scatter
   The good seed on the land,
 But it is fed and watered
   By God's Almighty Hand;
 He sends the snow in winter,
   The warmth to swell the grain,
 The breezes, and the sunshine,
   And soft refreshing rain.
     All good gifts around us
       Are sent from heaven above,
     Then thank the Lord, O thank the Lord,
       For all His love.

2. He only is the Maker
   Of all things near and far;
He paints the wayside flower,
   He lights the evening star;
The winds and waves obey Him,
   By Him the birds are fed;
Much more to us, His children,
   He gives our daily bread.
      All good gifts, &c.

3. We thank Thee, then, O FATHER,
   For all things bright and good;
The seed-time and the harvest,
   Our life, our health, our food.
Accept the gifts we offer,
   For all Thy love imparts,
And, what Thou most desirest,
   Our humble, thankful hearts.
      All good gifts around us
         Are sent from heaven above,
      Then thank the LORD, O thank the LORD,
         For all His love. Amen.

## 361.

### For the Young.

"The CHILD JESUS."

1. ONCE in royal David's City
   Stood a lowly cattle shed,
Where a mother laid her Baby
   In a manger for His bed:
Mary was that mother mild,
JESUS CHRIST her little child.

2. He came down to earth from heaven
Who is God and Lord of all,
And His shelter was a stable,
And His cradle was a stall;
With the poor, and mean, and lowly,
Lived on earth our Saviour Holy.

3. And, through all His wondrous childhood,
He would honour and obey,
Love and watch the lowly maiden
In whose gentle arms He lay:
Christian children all must be
Mild, obedient, good as He.

4. For He is our childhood's Pattern,
Day by day like us He grew,
He was little, weak, and helpless,
Tears and smiles like us He knew;
And He feeleth for our sadness,
And He shareth in our gladness.

5. And our eyes at last shall see Him
Through His Own redeeming love,
For that Child so dear and gentle
Is our Lord in Heaven above;
And He leads His children on
To the place where He is gone.

6. Not in that poor lowly stable,
With the oxen standing by,
We shall see Him; but in heaven,
Set at God's right hand on high;
When like stars His children crowned
All in white shall wait around. Amen.

## 362.

"While we were yet sinners, CHRIST died for us."

1. THERE is a green hill far away,
Without a city wall,
Where the dear LORD was crucified
Who died to save us all.

2. We may not know, we cannot tell
What pains he had to bear,
But we believe it was for us
He hung and suffered there.

3. He died that we might be forgiven,
He died to make us good,
That we might go at last to heaven,
Saved by His precious Blood.

4. There was no other good enough
To pay the price of sin,
He only could unlock the gate
Of heaven, and let us in.

5. O, dearly, dearly has He loved,
And we must love Him too,
And trust in His redeeming Blood,
And try His works to do. Amen.

## 363.

"If thou hast little, do thy diligence gladly to give of that little."

1. WE are but little children weak,
Nor born in any high estate;
What can we do for JESU'S sake
Who is so high and good and great?

2. We know the Holy Innocents
Laid down for Him their infant life,
And martyrs brave, and patient saints
Have stood for Him in fire and strife.

3. We wear the cross they wore of old,
Our lips have learned like vows to make;
We need not die; we cannot fight;
What may we do for JESU'S sake?

4. O, day by day each Christian child
Has much to do, without, within;
A death to die for JESU'S sake,
A weary war to wage with sin.

5. When deep within our swelling hearts,
The thoughts of pride and anger rise,
When bitter words are on our tongues
And tears of passion in our eyes;

6. Then we may stay the angry blow,
Then we may check the hasty word,
Give gentle answers back again,
And fight a battle for our LORD.

7. With smiles of peace and looks of love,
Light in our dwellings we may make,
Bid kind good humor brighten there,
And do all still for Jesu's sake.

8. There's not a child so small and weak
But has his little cross to take,
His little work of love and praise
That he may do for Jesu's sake. Amen.

## 364.

"Be ye followers of God, as dear children."

1. HEAVENLY FATHER, send Thy blessing
On Thy children gathered here,
May they all, Thy Name confessing,
Be to Thee for ever dear:
May they be, like Joseph, loving,
Dutiful, and chaste, and pure;
And their faith, like David, proving,
Steadfast unto death endure.

2. Holy Saviour, Who in meekness
Didst vouchsafe a Child to be,
Guide their steps and help their weakness,
Bless and make them like to Thee;
Bear Thy lambs when they are weary
In Thine arms and at Thy breast,
Through life's desert dry and dreary
Bring them to Thy heavenly rest.

3. Spread Thy golden pinions o'er them,
   Holy Spirit, from above,
Guide them, lead them, go before them,
   Give them peace, and joy, and love:
Thy true temples, Holy Spirit,
   May they with Thy glory shine,
And immortal bliss inherit,
   And for evermore be Thine. Amen.

## 365.

"He shall feed His flock like a Shepherd: He shall gather the lambs with His arm, and carry them in His bosom."

1. GRACIOUS SAVIOUR, gentle Shepherd,
   Little ones are dear to Thee;
Gathered with Thine arms, and carried
   In Thy bosom may we be;
Sweetly, fondly, safely tended,
   From all want and danger free.

2. Tender Shepherd, never leave us
   From Thy fold to go astray;
By Thy look of love directed,
   May we walk the narrow way;
Thus direct us, and protect us,
   Lest we fall an easy prey.

3. Cleanse our hearts from sinful folly
In the stream Thy love supplied,
Mingled stream of Blood and Water
Flowing from Thy wounded Side:
And to heavenly pastures lead us
Where Thine own still waters glide.

4. Let Thy holy Word instruct us;
Fill our minds with heavenly light;
Let Thy love and grace constrain us
To approve whate'er is right,
Take Thine easy yoke, and wear it,
And to prove Thy burden light.

5. Taught to lisp the holy praises
Which on earth Thy children sing,
Both with lips and hearts unfeignèd
May we our thank-offerings bring;
Then with all the saints in glory
Join to praise our LORD and King. Amen.

## 366.

"My song shall be alway of the loving kindness of the LORD."

1. COME, sing with holy gladness,
High Alleluias sing,
Uplift your loud Hosannas
To JESUS LORD and King;

Sing, boys, in joyful chorus
  Your hymn of praise to-day,
And sing, ye gentle maidens,
  Your sweet responsive lay.

2. 'Tis good for boys and maidens
  Sweet hymns to CHRIST to sing,
'Tis meet that children's voices
  Should praise the children's King;
For JESUS is salvation,
  And glory, grace, and rest;
To babe, and boy, and maiden
  The one REDEEMER blest.

3. O boys be strong in JESUS,
  To toil for Him is gain,
And JESUS wrought with Joseph,
  With chisel, saw, and plane;
O maidens live for JESUS,
  Who was a maiden's Son;
Be patient, pure and gentle,
  And perfect grace begun.

4. Soon in the golden City
  The boys and girls shall play,
And through the dazzling mansions
  Rejoice in endless day;
O CHRIST, prepare Thy children
  With that triumphant throng
To pass the burnished portals,
  And sing th' eternal song. Amen.

## 367.

"Be not thou ashamed of the testimony of our Lord."

1. THY Cross, O Lord, the holy sign
That we, thereafter, should be Thine,
Was traced upon our infant brow,
And shall we fear to own it now?

2. O God, forbid; before the vain,
The proud, the scoffing, the profane,
We will, through grace, our Lord confess,
His faint but faithful witnesses.

3. His strength in weakness He displays,
From youthful lips He perfects praise,
And we, His little soldiers, stand
Strong in the might of His right hand.

4. Smile on us, Lord, and we will fear
Nor scorn, nor shame, whilst Thou art near;
Reproach is glory, suffering rest,
If borne for Thee, if by Thee blest.

5. Great Judge of all, in that dread day,
When heaven and earth shall flee away,
Before the universe confess
Thy faint but faithful witnesses. Amen.

# 368.

EVENING.

"When thou liest down thou shalt not be afraid: yea, thou shalt lie down and thy sleep shall be sweet."

1. NOW the day is over,
   Night is drawing nigh,
Shadows of the evening
   Steal across the sky.

2. Now the darkness gathers,
   Stars begin to peep,
Birds, and beasts, and flowers
   Soon will be asleep.

3. Jesu, give the weary
   Calm and sweet repose,
With Thy tenderest blessing
   May our eyelids close.

4. Grant to little children
   Visions bright of Thee,
Guard the sailors tossing
   On the deep blue sea.

5. Comfort every sufferer
   Watching late in pain,
Those who plan some evil
   From their sin restrain.

6. Through the long night watches
   May Thine Angels spread
   Their white wings above me,
   Watching round my bed.

7. When the morning wakens,
   Then may I arise
   Pure and fresh and sinless
   In Thy Holy Eyes.

8. Glory to the FATHER,
   Glory to the SON,
   And to Thee, Blest SPIRIT,
   Whilst all ages run. Amen.

## 369.

"In Him was Life, and the Life was the Light of Men."

1. O LIGHT, Whose beams illumine all
   From twilight dawn to perfect day,
   Shine Thou before the shadows fall
   That lead our wandering feet astray;
   At morn and eve Thy radiance pour,
   That youth may love and age adore.

2. O Way, through Whom our souls draw near
   To yon eternal Home of Peace,
   Where perfect love shall cast out fear,
   And earth's vain toil and wandering cease;
   In strength or weakness may we see
   Our heavenward path, O LORD, through Thee.

3. O Truth, before Whose shrine we bow,
Thou priceless pearl for all who seek,
To Thee our earliest strength we vow,
Thy love will bless the pure and meek;
When dreams or mists beguile our sight,
Turn Thou our darkness into light.

4. O Life, the well that ever flows
To slake the thirst of those that faint,
Thy power to bless what seraph knows?
Thy joy supreme what words can paint?
In earth's last hour of fleeting breath
Be Thou our Conqueror over death.

5. O Light, O Way, O Truth, O Life,
O Jesu, born mankind to save,
Give Thou Thy peace in deadliest strife,
Shed Thou Thy calm on stormiest wave;
Be Thou our hope, our joy, our dread,
Lord of the living and the dead. Amen.

# 370.

## Almsgiving.

"Freely ye have received, freely give."

1. O LORD of heaven, and earth, and sea,
To Thee all praise and glory be;
How shall we show our love to Thee,
Who givest all?

2. The golden sunshine, vernal air,
Sweet flowers and fruit Thy love declare;
When harvests ripen, Thou art there,
Who givest all.

3. For peaceful homes, and healthful days,
For all the blessings earth displays,
We owe Thee thankfulness and praise,
Who givest all.

4. For souls redeemed, for sins forgiven,
For means of grace and hopes of heaven,
What can to Thee, O Lord, be given,
Who givest all?

5. We lose what on ourselves we spend,
We have as treasure without end
Whatever, Lord, to Thee we lend,
Who givest all.

6. Whatever, Lord, we lend to Thee,
Repaid a thousandfold will be;
Then gladly will we give to Thee,
Who givest all;

7. To Thee, from Whom we all derive
Our life, our gifts, our power to give;
O may we ever with Thee live,
Who givest all. Amen.

# 371.

"Whoso hath this world's good, and seeth his brother have need, and shutteth up his bowels of compassion from him, how dwelleth the love of God in him?"

1. WE give Thee but Thine own,
Whate'er the gift may be:
All that we have is Thine alone,
A trust, O Lord, from Thee.

2. Oh! hearts are bruised and dead,
And homes are bare and cold,
And lambs, for whom the Shepherd bled,
Are straying from the fold.

3. To comfort and to bless,
To find a balm for woe,
To tend the lone and fatherless
Is angel's work below.

4. The captive to release,
To God the lost to bring,
To teach the way of life and peace,
It is a Christ-like thing.

5. And we believe Thy word,
Tho' dim our faith may be;
Whate'er for Thine we do, O Lord,
We do it unto Thee.

6. All might, all praise be Thine,
Father, Co-equal Son,
And Spirit, Bond of love divine,
While endless ages run. Amen.

## 372.

"Ye ought to remember the words of the LORD JESUS, how He said, It is more blessed to give than to receive."

1. LORD of glory, Who hast bought us
   With Thy life-blood as the price,
Never grudging for the lost ones
   That tremendous sacrifice,
And with that hast freely given
   Blessings countless as the sand
To the unthankful and the evil,
   With Thine own unsparing hand;

2. Grant us hearts, dear LORD, to yield Thee
   Gladly, freely of Thine own;
With the sunshine of Thy goodness
   Melt our thankless hearts of stone;
Till our cold and selfish natures,
   Warmed by Thee, at length believe
That more happy and more blessèd
   'Tis to give than to receive.

3. Wondrous honour hast Thou given
   To our humblest charity,
In Thine own mysterious sentence
   "Ye have done it unto Me."
Can it be, O gracious Master,
   Thou dost deign for alms to sue,
Saying by Thy poor and needy
   "Give as I have given to you?"

4. Yes: the sorrow and the suffering,
   Which on every hand we see,
Channels are for tithes and offerings
   Due by solemn right to Thee;
Right of which we may not rob Thee,
   Debt we may not choose but pay,
Lest that Face of love and pity
   Turn from us another day.

5. Lord of glory, Who hast bought us
   With Thy life-blood as the price,
Never grudging for the lost ones
   That tremendous sacrifice,
Give us Faith, to trust Thee boldly,
   Hope, to stay our souls on Thee;
But oh! best of all Thy graces
   Give us Thine own Charity. Amen.

# 373.

## For Hospitals.

"They brought unto Him all that were diseased, and besought Him that they might only touch the hem of His garment; and as many as were touched were made perfectly whole."

1. THINE arm, O Lord, in days of old
   Was strong to heal and save;
It triumphed o'er disease and death,
   O'er darkness and the grave;

To Thee they went, the blind, the dumb,
The palsied and the lame,
The leper with his tainted life
The sick with fevered frame.

2. And lo, Thy touch brought life and health,
Gave speech, and strength, and sight;
And youth renewed and frenzy calmed
Owned Thee, the LORD of Light;
And now, O LORD, be near to bless
Almighty as of yore,
In crowded street, by restless couch,
As by Gennesareth's shore.

3. Be Thou our great Deliverer still,
Thou LORD of life and death;
Restore and quicken, soothe and bless
With Thine almighty breath;
To hands that work and eyes that see
Give wisdom's heavenly lore,
That whole and sick, and weak and strong,
May praise Thee evermore. Amen.

## 374.

### In time of Cattle Plague.

"Thou, LORD, shalt save both man and beast."

1. ALL creation groans and travails;
Thou, O GOD, shalt hear its groan;
For of man and all creation
Thou alike art LORD alone.

2. Pity then Thy guiltless creatures,
   Who, not less, man's sufferings share:
 For our sins it is they perish;
   Let them profit by our prayer.

3. Cast Thine eye of love and mercy
   On the misery of the land:
 Say to the destroying Angel,
   "'Tis enough: stay now Thine hand."

4. In our homesteads, in our valleys,
   Through our pasture-lands give peace:
 Through the Goshen of Thine Israel
   Bid the grievous murrain cease.

5. But with deeper, tenderer pity,
   Call to mind, O Son of God,
 Those in Thine own Image fashioned:
   Ransomed with Thy precious blood:

6. Hear and grant the supplications,
   Like a cloud of incense, borne
 Up toward Thy Seat of Mercy,
   From Thy people's hearts forlorn:

7. For the widow, for the orphan,
   For the helpless, hopeless poor:
 Helpless, hopeless, if Thou spare not
   Of their basket and their store.

8. So—while these her earnest accents
   Day by day Thy Church repeats,—
 That our sheep may bring forth thousands
   And ten thousands in our streets;

9. That our oxen, strong to labour,
   May not know nor fear decay;
That there be no more complaining,
   And the plague have passed away.

10. And, at last, to all Thy servants,
   When earth's troubles shall be o'er,
Threefold Godhead, give a portion
   With Thyself for evermore. Amen.

# 375.

## New Year's Eve.

"So soon passeth it away, and we are gone."

1. DAYS and moments quickly flying
   Blend the living with the dead;
Soon will you and I be lying
   Each within our narrow bed.

2. Soon our souls to God Who gave them
   Will have sped their rapid flight;
Able now by grace to save them,
   O, that while we can we might!

3. JESU, infinite REDEEMER,
   Maker of this mighty frame,
Teach, O teach us to remember
   What we are and whence we came;

4. Whence we came, and whither wending;
Soon we must through darkness go,
To inherit bliss unending,
Or eternity of woe.

5. As the tree falls, so must it lie;
As the man lives, so will he die;
As the man dies, such must he be,
All through the days of eternity. Amen.

*This Hymn may also be sung at Burial of the Dead, and in Lent, &c.*

## 376.

## The Annunciation of the Blessed Virgin Mary.

"Mary, the Mother of Jesus."

1. SHALL we not love thee, Mother dear,
Whom Jesus loves so well?
And in His Temple, year by year,
Thy joy and glory tell?

2. Bound with the curse of sin and shame
We helpless sinners lay,
Until in tender love He came
To bear the curse away.

3. And thee He chose from whom to take
True flesh His Flesh to be;
In It to suffer for our sake,
By It to make us free.

4. Thy Babe He lay upon thy breast,
   To thee He cried for food;
Thy gentle nursing soothed to rest
   Th' Incarnate SON of GOD.

5. O wondrous depth of grace Divine
   That He should bend so low;
And, Mary, O what joy was thine
   In His dear love to know:

6. Joy to be Mother of the LORD;
   And thine the truer bliss,
In every thought, and deed, and word,
   To be for ever His.

7. And as He loves thee, Mother dear,
   We too will love thee well;
And in His Temple, year by year,
   Thy joy and glory tell.

8. JESU, the Virgin's Holy SON,
   We praise Thee and adore,
WHO art with GOD the FATHER One
   And SPIRIT evermore. Amen.

*This Hymn may also be used, as Hymn 249, on other Festivals of St. Mary.*

# 377.

## Martyrs, &c.

"They are before the throne of GOD, and serve Him day and night in His temple."

1. LO, round the Throne, a glorious band,
The saints in countless myriads stand,
Of every tongue redeemed to GOD,
Arrayed in garments washed in Blood.

2. Through tribulation great they came;
They bore the cross, despised the shame;
From all their labours now they rest,
In GOD's eternal glory blest.

3. They see their SAVIOUR face to face,
And sing the triumphs of His grace;
Him day and night they ceaseless praise;
To Him the loud thanksgiving raise:

4. "Worthy the LAMB, for sinners slain,
Through endless years to live and reign;
Thou hast redeemed us by Thy Blood,
And made us kings and priests to GOD."

5. O may we tread the sacred road
That holy saints and martyrs trod;
Wage to the end the glorious strife,
And win, like them, a crown of life. Amen.

## 378.

"After this I beheld, and lo, a great multitude, which no man could number, of all nations and kindred and people and tongues, stood before the throne and before the LAMB, clothed with white robes, and palms in their hands."

1. HARK! the sound of holy voices
   Chanting, at the crystal sea,
Alleluia, Alleluia,
   Alleluia, LORD to Thee:
Multitude, which none can number,
   Like the stars in glory stands,
Clothed in white apparel, holding
   Palms of victory in their hands.

2. Patriarch, and holy Prophet,
   Who prepared the way of CHRIST,
King, Apostle, Saint, Confessor,
   Martyr, and Evangelist,
Saintly Maiden, godly Matron,
   Widows who have watched to prayer,
Joined in holy concert, singing
   To the LORD of all are there.

3. They have come from tribulation,
   And have washed their robes in blood,
Washed them in the Blood of JESUS;
   Tried they were and firm they stood;

Mocked, imprisoned, stoned, tormented,
Sawn asunder, slain with sword,
They have conquered death and Satan
By the might of CHRIST the LORD.

4. Marching with Thy cross their banner,
They have triumphed following
Thee, the Captain of salvation,
Thee their SAVIOUR, and their King;
Gladly, LORD, with Thee they suffered;
Gladly, LORD, with Thee they died;
And by death to life immortal
They were born and glorified.

5. Now they reign in heavenly glory,
Now they walk in golden light,
Now they drink, as from a river,
Holy bliss and infinite:
Love and peace they taste for ever,
And all truth and knowledge see
In the Beatific Vision
Of the Blessèd Trinity.

6. GOD of GOD, the One-begotten,
Light of Light, EMMANUEL,
In Whose Body joined together
All the saints for ever dwell,
Pour upon us of Thy fulness,
That we may for evermore
GOD the FATHER, GOD the SON, and
GOD the HOLY GHOST adore. Amen.

## 379.

"They were stoned, they were sawn asunder, were tempted, were slain with the sword; being destitute, afflicted, tormented; of whom the world was not worthy."

1. BLESSED feasts of blessèd martyrs,
Holy days of holy men,
With affection's recollections
Greet we your return again.

2. Worthy deeds they wrought and wonders,
Worthy of the Name they bore;
We with meetest praise and sweetest,
Honour them for evermore.

3. Faith prevailing, hope unfailing,
Jesus loved with single heart—
Thus they glorious and victorious
Bravely bore the Martyr's part.

4. Racked with torture, haled to slaughter,
Fire, and axe, and murderous sword,
Chains and prison, foes' derision
They endured for Christ the Lord.

5. So they passed through pain and sorrow,
Till they sank in death to rest;
Earth's rejected, God's elected,
Gained a portion with the blest.

6. By contempt of worldly pleasures,
And by deeds of valour done,
They have reached the land of Angels,
And with them are knit in one.

7. Made co-heirs with CHRIST in glory
His celestial bliss they share:
May they now before Him bending
Help us onward by their prayer;

8. That, this weary life completed,
And its fleeting trials past,
We may win eternal glory
In our Father's home at last. Amen.

## 380.

"Blessed are they which are persecuted for righteousness' sake: for theirs is the kingdom of heaven."

1. LET our Choir new anthems raise;
Wake the song of gladness;
GOD Himself to joy and praise
Turns the martyrs' sadness:
Bright the day that won their crown,
Opened heaven's bright portal,
As they laid the mortal down
To put on th' immortal.

2. Never flinched they from the flame,
From the torture never;
Vain the foeman's sharpest aim,
Satan's best endeavour:
For by faith they saw the land
Decked in all its glory,
Where triumphant now they stand
With the victor's story.

3. Up and follow, Christian men!
   Press through toil and sorrow;
Spurn the night of fear, and then,
   Oh, the glorious morrow!
Who will venture on the strife?
   Blest who first begin it;
Who will grasp the Land of Life?
   Warriors, up and win it! Amen.

## 381.

"He gave some....Pastors and Teachers."

1. JESU, for the beacon-light
   By Thy holy Doctors given,
When the mists of error's night
Gathered o'er the path to heaven,
For the witness that they bare
To the truth they learned of Thee,
For the glory that they share,
Let our praise accepted be.

2. In Jerusalem below
They were workmen at Thy call,
Each with one hand met the foe,
With the other built the wall;
Watchmen on the mountain set,
Scribes instructed in Thy Word,
Fishers with the Gospel net
Drawing souls to Thee their LORD.

3. Like Thy learnèd sons of yore,
Jesu, may Thy Pastors still
Know and teach Thy sacred lore
With brave heart and patient skill;
In these latter days of strife
Keep, O keep them true to Thee,
Till beside the well of life
Light in Thine own Light they see.
Amen.

## 382.

"The memory of the just is blessed."

1. O SHEPHERD of the sheep,
High Priest of things to come,
Who didst in grace Thy servant keep,
And take him sweetly home;

2. Accept our song of praise
For all his holy care,
His zeal unquenched, through length of days,
The trials that he bare.

3. His heart was Thine alone,
From selfish longings free;
Thy throne the Cross, a cross his throne,
His life was hid in Thee.

4. Chief of Thy faithful band,
He held himself the least;
Though Thy dread keys were in his hand,
O everlasting Priest.

5. So, trusting in Thy might,
He won a fair renown;
So, waxing valiant in the fight,
He trod the lion down:

6. Then rendered up to Thee
The charge Thy love had given;
And passed away Thy Face to see
Revealed in highest heaven.

7. On all our Bishops pour
The Spirit of Thy grace;
That as he won the palm of yore,
So they may run their race;

8. That, when this life is done,
They may with him adore
The ever Blessèd Three in One,
In bliss for evermore. Amen.

## 383.

"My Beloved is mine, and I am His."

1. O LAMB of God, Whose love divine
Draws virgin-souls to follow Thee,
And bids them earthly joys resign
If so they may Thy beauty see;

2. The saint of whom we sing to-day
Was faithful to Thy loving call,
And, casting other hopes away,
Took Thee to be her God, her All.

3. To Thee she yielded up her will,
Her heart was drawn to Thine above;
Content if Thou would'st deign to fill
Thine handmaid with Thy perfect love.

4. Beneath Thy Cross she loved to stand,
Like Mary in Thy dying hour,
That blessings from Thy piercèd Hand
Might clothe her with undying power;

5. With power to win the Crown of light
For virgin-martyrs stored on high,
And ready keep her lamp at night
To hail the Bridegroom drawing nigh.

6. And surely Thou at last didst come
To end the sorrows of Thy bride,
And bear her to Thy peaceful home
With Thee for ever to abide.

7. All glory, Jesu, for the grace
That drew Thy saint to follow Thee;
Grant us, too, in Thy love a place
Both now and through eternity. Amen.

## 384.

### Processional.

"Behold, I have given Him....for a Leader and Commander to the people."

1. BRIGHTLY gleams our banner
Pointing to the sky,
Waving wanderers onward
To their home on high.

Journeying o'er the desert,
  Gladly thus we pray,
And with hearts united
  Take our heavenward way.
    Brightly gleams our banner
      Pointing to the sky,
    Waving wanderers onwards
      To their home on high.

2. Jesu, Lord and Master,
  At Thy sacred Feet,
Here with hearts rejoicing
  See Thy children meet;
Often have we left Thee,
  Often gone astray,
Keep us, mighty Saviour,
  In the narrow way.
      Brightly gleams, &c.

3. All our days direct us
  In the way we go,
Lead us on victorious
  Over every foe:
Bid Thine angels shield us
  When the storm-clouds lour,
Pardon Thou and save us
  In the last dread hour.
      Brightly gleams, &c.

4. Then with Saints and Angels
  May we join above,
Offering prayers and praises
  At Thy Throne of love;

When the toil is over,
  Then comes rest and peace,
Jesus in His Beauty,
  Songs that never cease.
    Brightly gleams our banner
      Pointing to the sky,
    Waving wanderers onwards
      To their home on high.

## 385.

"Be strong and of a good courage. . . . And the Lord, He it is that doth go before thee."

1. ONWARD, Christian soldiers,
  Marching as to war,
With the Cross of Jesus
  Going on before.
Christ the Royal Master
  Leads against the foe,
Forward into battle,
  See, His banners go.
    Onward, Christian soldiers,
      Marching as to war,
    With the Cross of Jesus
      Going on before.

2. At the sign of triumph
  Satan's host doth flee;
On, then, Christian soldiers,
  On to victory.

Hell's foundations quiver
  At the shout of praise;
Brothers, lift your voices,
  Loud your anthems raise.
        Onward, &c.

3. Like a mighty army
  Moves the Church of GOD;
Brothers, we are treading
  Where the saints have trod;
We are not divided,
  All one body we,
One in hope, and doctrine,
  One in charity.
        Onward, &c.

4. Crowns and thrones may perish,
  Kingdoms rise and wane,
But the Church of JESUS
  Constant will remain;
Gates of hell can never
  'Gainst that Church prevail;
We have CHRIST's own promise,
  And that cannot fail.
        Onward, &c.

5. Onward, then, ye people,
  Join our happy throng,
Blend with ours your voices
  In the triumph song;

Glory, laud, and honour
  Unto CHRIST the King,
This through countless ages
  Men and Angels sing.
    Onward, Christian soldiers,
      Marching as to war,
    With the Cross of JESUS
      Going on before.

## 386.

"Young men and maidens, old men and children, praise the Name of the LORD."

1. REJOICE ye pure in heart,
  Rejoice, give thanks and sing;
Your festal banner wave on high,
  The Cross of CHRIST your King.

2. Bright youth and snow-crowned age,
  Strong men and maidens meek,
Raise high your free exulting song,
  GOD's wondrous praises speak.

3. Yes onward, onward still,
  With hymn, and chant, and song,
Thro' gate, and porch, and columned aisle,
  The hallowed pathways throng.

4. With all the angel choirs,
  With all the saints on earth,
Pour out the strains of joy and bliss,
  True rapture, noblest mirth.

5. Your clear Hosannas raise,
And Alleluias loud;
Whilst answering echoes upward float,
Like wreaths of incense cloud.

6. With voice as full and strong
As ocean's surging praise,
Send forth the hymns our fathers loved,
The psalms of ancient days.

7. Yes on, through life's long path,
Still chanting as ye go,
From youth to age, by night and day,
In gladness and in woe.

8. Still lift your standard high,
Still march in firm array,
As warriors through the darkness toil
Till dawns the golden day.

9. At last the march shall end,
The wearied ones shall rest,
The pilgrims find their Father's House,
Jerusalem the blest.

10. Then on, ye pure in heart,
Rejoice, give thanks, and sing;
Your festal banner wave on high,
The Cross of CHRIST your King.

11. Praise Him Who reigns on high,
The LORD Whom we adore,
The FATHER, SON, and HOLY GHOST,
One GOD for evermore. Amen.

# INDEX OF FIRST LINES.

www.ingramcontent.com/pod-product-compliance
Lightning Source LLC
LaVergne TN
LVHW021130110826
845150LV00005B/989

* 9 7 8 1 4 2 5 5 4 9 9 6 1 *